2014 Saint Paul ALMANAC

2014 Saint Paul ALMANAC

ARCATA
PRESS
SAINT PAUL

Community editors: Yunisa Abdi, Yonis Ali, Nina Hernandez Beithon, Norita Dittberner-Jax, Shaunté "Dr3amCh8sr" Douglas, Elizabeth Ellis, Pamela R. Fletcher, Shaquan Foster, Kevin Hershey, Farha Ibrahim, Kemet Egypt Imhotep, Richard Merlin Johnson Jr., IBé Kaba, Patricia Kirkpatrick, Abe Levine, Gozong Lor, Jamila Mame, Hafsa Mohamud, Kathryn Pulley, Simone Schneider, Lisa Steinmann, Parthenia Swyningan, Muriel Tate, Ka Zoua Vang, and Diego Vázquez Jr.

Book designer and typesetter: Judy Gilats
Copy editor: Sally Heuer
Cover art © Ken Avidor
Cover designer: Nigel Parry
Events editor: Shaquan Foster
History facts researcher: Steve Trimble
Managing editor: Andrea Rud
Photo editor: Nigel Parry
Proofreader: Sherri Hildebrandt
Publisher: Kimberly Nightingale
Saint Paul listings editor: Clarence White
Senior editors: Pamela Fletcher and Patricia Kirkpatrick
Saint Paul city map and Saint Paul downtown map, third editions © 2013 Roberta Avidor

Limericks © 2013 Garrison Keillor. Used with permission. All rights reserved.
From *Fishing for Myth* by Heid E. Erdrich. Copyright © 1997 by Heid E. Erdrich. Used by permission of New Rivers Press.

The following poems were published by *Everyday Poems for City Sidewalk,* a work of art by Marcus Young, City Artist in Residence, as part of a joint program of Public Art Saint Paul and the City of Saint Paul, and used with permission of the authors: "Alone," Caroline Bassett; (untitled), Susan Downing; "Dusk," D. Stephen Elliot; (untitled), Charles Matson Lume; "A Little Rock," Anna Musielewicz; (untitled), Susan Olsson; (untitled), Jennifer Pennington; "Dragonfly," Paige Riehl; "Reflections," Kaya Solheid; "Haircut," Marcy Steinberg; (untitled), Greg Watson.

This activity is made possible in part by a grant provided by the Minnesota State Arts Board through an appropriation by the Minnesota State Legislature from the State's arts and cultural heritage fund with money from the vote of the people of Minnesota on November 4, 2008.

CLEAN WATER LAND & LEGACY AMENDMENT

MINNESOTA STATE ARTS BOARD

ISBN 978-0-9888681-0-6
Printed by Friesens in Canada

Saint Paul Almanac
275 East Fourth St. Suite 701
Saint Paul, MN 55101
www.saintpaulalmanac.org
Saint Paul Almanac is a subsidiary of Arcata Press, a nonprofit publisher.

Dedication

In memory of
BERTHA GIVINS
1931–2012

My mother and I were driving through the Rondo neighborhood, when she shared a vision with me. "Imagine like John Lennon: *No heaven above us and people living only for the day. Imagine the entire world sharing. No need for greed or hunger.* I told her only in her dreams could this be. She spoke in her poetic voice with Lennon's words: *You may say that I'm a dreamer, but I'm not the only one. Someday I hope you will join us, and the world will live as one.* My mother went on to share this vision with the Saint Paul community, and together we have made that vision a reality. Imagine that!

Michael Givins Douglas

"The long, dark days of winter have finally come and gone, and the long, hot days of summer have returned to claim the throne. It's Saturday night in the city, and we are strolling down Rondo Street. Sweet aromas tease our nostrils 'til they make our stomachs leap.

We smell fried chicken, collard greens, ham and black-eyed peas, and the familiar scent of Bar-B-Q coming out of old Mr. Booker T's."

BERTHA GIVINS, "Summertime Down on Rondo,"
2012 *Saint Paul Almanac*

Contents

For information on events listed in the calendar section,
see pages 294—321.

© Bianca Pettis

Next page: Chinese dancers at the Festival of Nations

© Joseph L Schufman

Acknowledgments

If there is one thing we have learned at the Saint Paul Almanac, it's developing a relationship with *you* that makes our work vibrant and meaningful. If you want to learn more about us, check out our website, email us, and find out how you might want to participate in our growing community of engaged residents, writers, artists, and visitors.

We bring *your* stories to *your* place: Saint Paul. The gritty story, the demanding poem, or the difficult conversation simmers next to a beautiful description of the river or a poem about a grandmother. The messiness of being human, our boundless contradictions—truth and fiction, dream and art—collide within each *Saint Paul Almanac.*

It has been a year of change at the Saint Paul Almanac. I transitioned out of managing the editing of the almanac book, and managing editor Andrea Rud, along with senior editors Pamela Fletcher and Patricia Kirkpatrick, took over the helm. Their collaboration has created our strongest book ever. It was thrilling to read the proofs, stories, and poems blossoming on every page.

Community editors Abe Levine, Diego Vázquez Jr., Elizabeth Ellis, Farha Ibrahim, Gozong Lor, Hafsa Mohamud, IBé Kaba, Jamila Mame, K. Simone Schneider, Kathryn Pulley, Ka Zoua Vang, Kemet Egypt Imhotep, Kevin Hershey, Lisa Steinmann, Muriel Tate, Nina Hernandez Beithon, Norita Dittberner-Jax, Pamela Fletcher, Parthenia Swyningan, Patricia Kirkpatrick, Richard Merlin Johnson Jr., Shaquan Foster, Shaunté Douglas, Yonis Ali, and Yunisa Abdi were the guides for the book you are reading today. They sifted through all the stories submitted through a community editor process of discussion and reflection to choose the pieces that are recorded here. Many incredible stories didn't make it to publication. If yours was one of them, please consider reworking your piece and submitting it again.

Diego Vázquez Jr., IBé Kaba, Pamela Fletcher, and Patricia Kirkpatrick were the professional writers who served as community editors, each bringing his or her own brilliance to mentoring the group through the writing and editorial process. Wendy Brown-Báez acted as visiting writer and teacher, guiding the community editors through two writing workshops that focused on their own writing. That intense writing and deep reflection set the tone for the rest of the writing and editing workshops.

If you are interested in becoming a community editor, please send an email to editor@saintpaulalmanac.org. Provide your name, address, email, and phone number, and describe in a paragraph or two why you want to be a community editor. We accept all ages, fifteen and up. We choose the community editor group with a focus on creating an inclusive community of many ages, ethnicities, and abilities.

Our book designer and typesetter, Judy Gilats, used color and pizzazz for her redesign of our 2014 edition. Sally Heuer expertly copyedited the *Almanac*. Sherri Hildebrandt proofread our big book with accuracy and speed. Shaquan Foster, our events editor for the book this year, recorded many cool activities happening in the city in 2014. Steve Trimble, our trusty Saint Paul historian, researched birth dates, facts, quotes, and trivia with his usual aplomb. Steve also helps out on our marketing committee. Each year Teri Dwyer reliably researches health and fitness activities for our listings section. Thank you to Patrick Coleman, acquisitions librarian at the Minnesota Historical Society, for suggesting the *Almanac* include historical writings and for choosing Harriet Bishop's "A Stranger's Opinion of Saint Paul" and Charles Macomb Flandrau's "The Bustle." Special thanks to Amber Michel for assisting with photo editing.

Artist Ken Avidor illustrated the big, beautiful, bold Union Depot for our *2014 Saint Paul Almanac* cover. Ken's wife, artist extraordinaire Roberta Avidor, illustrated the playful *Almanac* map in the back and updated it this year. Ken and Roberta fell in love with Saint Paul while Roberta worked on the initial map two years ago. They moved from across the river and now live in the Union Depot!

Thank you to the people at Springboard and their Irrigate arts project. Five of our community members participated: Lisa Steinmann, Patricia Young, Diego Vázquez Jr., Shaquan Foster, and myself. We were able to secure funding to create a 100-square-foot banner at University and Western Avenues to recognize and honor Kofi Bobby Hickman using a section of his story "The Brawl in Saint Paul" from the 2012 *Saint Paul Almanac*. Shaquan Foster created the banner with assistance from professional designer Michael Waite. We were also able to print snippets of stories and small poems on posters and display them at Golden's Deli. Visit Golden's at 275 East Fourth Street and check them out.

Our Saint Paul Almanac board is actively engaged in our constant improvement. Thank you to Metric Giles, board chair; Ann McKinnon, vice-chair; Lisa Steinmann, secretary; Leon Daisy, treasurer; and directors Carol Connolly, Clarence White, Patricia Kirkpatrick, Say-moukda Duangphouxay Vongsay, Shaquan Foster, Shaunté Douglas, and Stephanie Wright. Board member Kaye Thompson Peters departed this year to teach in India; we wish her well. We would also like to thank our advisory board: Carolyn Holbrook, Cathie Hartnett, Dan Tilsen, Dave Thune, Karen Starr, L. Kelley Lindquist, Mahmoud El-Kati, Mary Beth McCarthy Yarrow, Pam VanderWiel, Perrin Lilly, Sooriya Foster, Steve Horwitz, Susan Herridge, Tim Nolan, and Uri-Biia Si-Asar. Without the leadership of both boards, we would not be growing and deepening our relationships in Saint Paul, the Twin Cities, Minnesota, and around the nation.

The Saint Paul Almanac has moved to a new office with more space for everyone who works with us. Nigel Parry employs his Scottish wit writing our playful Saint Paul Almanac blogs and other publicity. He is also hard at work as our expert photo editor, website manager, and curator of our visual art contest. Clarence White, with his fine writing and organizational abilities, manages our Twitter and Facebook accounts and keeps our online calendar fresh and updated. Clarence also edited our listings section in the *2014 Saint Paul Almanac*, providing new written content to contextualize each section. Bookkeeper Delphine Wallace and accountant James Fisher work hard to keep all of our numbers organized. Book pro David Unowsky dependably keeps our retail outlets stocked and works with our advertising sponsors. Lisa Steinmann is our tireless development manager, working with the Saint Paul Almanac, the Givens Foundation for African American Literature, and Juxtaposition Arts to strengthen community participation in our development learning and practice. Kelly Retka helps us deepen our relationships with our donors. Thank you to Eric Mortenson of the Minnesota Historical Society for finding much-needed historical photos for the *Almanac* each year. And thank you to Mandy Kelso for helping to organize our annual book-release parties.

Each year we publish the winners and honorable mentions of the *Everyday Poems for City Sidewalk*, a work of art by Marcus Young, City Artist in Residence, as part of a joint program of Public Art Saint Paul and the City of Saint Paul. Congratulations to Caroline Bassett, Susan Downing, D. Stephen Elliot, Charles Matson Lume, Anna Musielewicz, Susan Olsson, Jennifer Pennington, Paige Riehl, Kaya Solheid, Marcy Steinberg, and Greg Watson.

The *2014 Saint Paul Almanac* is dedicated to Bertha Givins, who wrote a playful piece titled "Summertime Down on Rondo" for the *2012 Saint Paul Almanac*. Thank you to her son, Michael Douglas, for helping us navigate the process and for his dedication.

A big thank-you to the Black Dog Café for their longtime collaboration with us on our annual book-release parties and Lowertown Reading Jams. AZ Gallery hosts our art show each September, our book-release party, and our community editor workshops. AZ artists and co-op members Todd Peterson and Tom Reynen are always accommodating and helpful. Clouds in Water Zen Center graciously opens their space each year for our book-release party reading. Ben Krywosz of Nautilus Music-Theater kindly lends us chairs for our book release parties. Kevin Brown at Smart Set manages all of our collateral printing with ease and timeliness.

Besides our book, we conduct twelve *Saint Paul Almanac* readings at coffee shops and bookstores; we support a weekly open mic hosted by the glorious Tish Jones—with Hasani Harris often assisting—at Golden Thyme Coffee Shop each Thursday evening from 6 to 8 p.m.; and we organize the Lowertown Reading Jams at the Black Dog Café. Saint Paul Neighborhood Network (SPNN) airs our Jams. We also hold writing workshops for incarcerated women at Ramsey County Correctional Facility. Check out all we do at www.saintpaulalmanac.org.

All of this workload is lightened by partners who help strengthen our projects: Friends of the Saint Paul Public Library, Aurora/St. Anthony Neighborhood Development Corporation, Saint Paul Neighborhood Network (SPNN), Saint Paul Public Schools, the Givens Foundation for African American Literature, and Juxtaposition Arts.

Thank you to my children and stepchildren for being patient with my demanding schedule: Anna Tilsen-Mogeni, Lea Tilsen-Virkus, Drew Tilsen, Sarahfina Moraa, Kai Goellner, and Brie Goellner; and to their loved ones: Mogeni Oyori, Jeff Virkus, Renee Campbell, Steve Ingram, Emily Goellner, and Joe Sheehan. Thank you to my energetic and loving grandchildren: Kyah, Joshua, Everett, Avery, Alexander, and Kalvinn. Most especially, thank you to Daniel Tilsen, the man who makes me feel cherished every day.

Thank you to our supporters: Without you, we wouldn't thrive.

And lastly, thank *you* for reading this book. May you find a piece or two that speak to your life and your place in the world.

KIMBERLY NIGHTINGALE, *Publisher and Executive Director*

More information about the events listed on the calendar pages is available by checking the event listings, pages 294–321. We try to be as accurate as possible with our event dates, but they are subject to change. The Almanac's website—found at www.saintpaulalmanac.org—has a greatly expanded and regularly updated calendar that offers a diverse listing of events, and includes an online version of our City Guide. Sign up on our website for our regular emails. Join us on Facebook at facebook.com/saintpaulalmanac, and on Twitter@stpaulalmanac.

Thank You to All of Our Supporters

Black Dog Café
The City of Saint Paul Cultural STAR Program
Clouds in Water Zen Center
Common Good Books
COMPAS
F. R. Bigelow Foundation
Friends of the Saint Paul Public Library
Golden's Deli
KFAI Radio
Knight Foundation
Lowertown Future Fund of the Saint Paul Foundation
Lowertown Wine and Spirits
The McKnight Foundation
Mardag Foundation
Metropolitan Regional Arts Council
Micawber's Books
Minnesota State Arts Board
Peapods
Saint Paul Foundation
Saint Paul Neighborhood Network (SPNN)
Subtext: A Bookstore
Travelers' Arts and Diversity Grants Committee
Twin Cities Daily Planet
Wet Paint

Roberta Avidor
Aleli Balagtas
G. E. Bengtson
Elizabeth Boyd
Richard Broderick
Barbara Brooks
Ellen Brown
Wendy Brown-Báez
Mary and Steven Budge
Richard J. Byrne
Gary Carlson
Marisa Carr
Sharon Chmielarz
Dianne Clemmer
Carol Connolly
Shelagh Connolly
Marly Cornell
John (Jay) and Page Cowles
John Crawford
Abel Davis
Theresa A. Davis
Mary and Gerry Devaney
Jeannie Dietz
Louis DiSanto
Norita Dittberner-Jax
Dorothy Drake
Melvin and Georgia Duncan
Freda Ellis
Gayla and Chris Ellis
Joanne Englund
Joanne and Philip Fabel
Anne Field
Michael Finley
Kevin FitzPatrick

Pamela R. Fletcher
Denise Fosse
Dyane Garvey
David George and Carolyn Levitt
Judy Gilats
Metric Giles
Rhoda Gilman
Tom Goldstein
Joan and John Haldeman
Nor Hall
Roger and Dana Hall
Kristin Haltinner
Patricia Hampl and Terrence Williams
Janet Hanafin
Patricia Sweney Hart
Cathie Hartnett
Barbara Haselbeck
Margaret Hasse
Shelly Hauge
Mike Hazard and Tressa Sularz
Kalue Her
Robin Hickman
Jennifer Holder
Karen Hollaus
Steven Neil Horwitz and Julie Schaper
Michelle Johnson
Jeannea Jordan
Ibrahima Kaba
Steve Kaplan
Karen Karsten
Matthew Kazinka
Nathaniel Khaliq

Paul Kirkegaard
Patricia Kirkpatrick
Louise Klas
Evelyn Klein
Margaret Kramer
Georgia, Tineka, and
    Duncan Kurth
Thomas Lacy
May Lee-Yang
Gwen Lerner
Perrin Lilly
Jonathan D. Weiss and
    Brenda Marsh
James McKenzie
Ethna McKiernan
Ann McKinnon
DeLano McRaven
Roger Meyer
Paul Mielke
Minnesota Licensed
    Beverage Association
    (MLBA)
Jennifer Monaghan
James Moore
Sonja Moore
Jennifer Roba and Sean
    Morgan
Jonathan Mostrom
Nora Murphy
Mary and Michael
    Murphy
Clem and Elizabeth
    Nagel
Dr. David Ness
Margaret Newman

Denny and Susie
    Nightingale
Edmund and Betts
    Nightingale
Timothy J. Nolan
Jean O'Connell
Christine Oliver
Geri Patterson
Caroline Pearson
Deb Pleasants
Nieeta Presley
Georgia Ray Ray
Catherine Reid Day
Stacy Remke
Kelly Retka
Paige Riehl
Mary Kay Rummel
Michael and Regula
    Russell
Dr. Charles Sawyer and
    Katharine Klein
Barbara J. Schmidt
Kathleen Schuler
Julie Schumacher
Gail See
Anura and Rekhet
    Si-Asar
Ivar and Peggy Siqveland
Mike Stanke
Karen Starr
Lisa and Jack Steinmann
Caroline and Stewart
    Stone
Joyce Sutphen
Lisa Tabor

Janie Tilsen
Josh Tilsen and Faith
    Latimer
Daniel Tilsen and
    Kimberly Nightingale
Jim Tilsen and Deanna
    Wiener
Joci Tilsen and Jim Bour
Ken Tilsen and Connie
    Goldman
James Toscano
Steven Trimble
David Tripp
Cynthia Unowsky and
    Thomas Badow
David Unowsky
Lee S. and Stacy L.
    Unowsky
Pamela L. Vander-Wiel
Kathleen Vellenga
Saymoukda
    Duangphouxay
    Vongsay
Carol Wall
David Weiss
Jonathan Weiss and
    Brenda Marsh
Michelle Wilson
Irv Williams
Mary Beth Yarrow
Patricia A. Young
Ronald Zaine
Hilary Ziols
Sue Zumberge

Introduction

Passion is the foundation that has regenerated each publication of the *Saint Paul Almanac*, from its first release in 2007 to the present release you hold in your hands.

A hearty welcome to all of the first-time readers, and a huge hello to all the returning readers and contributors who have been key to the success of the *Almanac*.

As you read this book and experience the authentic sharing by people about a place, I suspect you will not be able to control your various emotional responses and reactions . . . a desire to smile, run, explore, reflect, and marvel as you leaf through the pages.

Before I get too excited and carried away with my personal feelings, I want to share with you what is offered inside this book.

The *Almanac* is a collection of stories and poems. It's a calendar of events that brings awareness of upcoming activities in Saint Paul, and it is for Saint Paulites and visitors alike. It can be and has been used as a personal appointment book. It provides historical information; a photo journal; and insightful, profound quotes. It has a two-sided map, with one side displaying communities in Saint Paul, with schools, libraries, rec centers, coffee shops, lakes, theaters, and a host of other structures. On the other side are key institutions, establishments, and parks in downtown Saint Paul.

Many readers of the *Almanac* (and I am at the top of this list) have become loyal ambassadors for the book, which has been recognized as the unofficial ambassador of the city of Saint Paul.

There's a constant goal to improve the presentation of the *Almanac*, and it takes many individuals and entities for that to happen. The best way I can explain what goes into the making of the *Saint Paul Almanac* is to compare it with a glass of milk or water.

For instance, most people go to the local grocery store to buy a gallon of milk. Not much thought goes into how it gets to the grocery store; they just buy the milk. Or they go to their faucet and get a glass of water without thinking much about what it takes to get a purified glass of water. In truth, the process and systems are more complex and detailed than we could ever imagine.

Here are some quick details about the *Almanac*: It contains 100-plus poems and stories from people locally, nationally, and abroad who submit their work for review and possible inclusion in the publication. A diverse group of community editors—made up of both professional and nonprofessional writers of all ages from a variety of communities—goes through an educational process that provides them with the skills they need to review and select the content of what will become the 2014 *Almanac*.

Another need that the Saint Paul Almanac's publication and events tries to address is the need to bridge the opportunity gap—referred to by many as the achievement gap—in our schools. Since its first publication, the *Saint Paul Almanac* has been distributed throughout the Saint Paul public school system. It has inspired many students to extend their reading and writing capacity, and has created other opportunities for positive self-expression and sharing. The Saint Paul Almanac organization has developed a curriculum teachers can use in their classrooms that meets educational standards.

I started my introduction by saying passion has been key to the continual inspiration of the *Saint Paul Almanac*. I would like to share a quote about passion with you:

> "There are many things in life that will catch our eye, but only a few will catch our heart . . . pursue those."

The *Saint Paul Almanac* falls into this category. That is what makes the *Almanac* unique: it creates a space and place for people to share their passion. It allows opportunities for placemaking—people sharing from their heart about the great city of Saint Paul.

It is my hope that you too will feel and share in the passion of this 2014 edition.

METRIC GILES, Saint Paul Almanac Board Chair

2014

JANUARY

S	M	T	W	T	F	S
29	30	31	1	2	3	4
5	6	7	8	9	10	11
12	13	14	15	16	17	18
19	20	21	22	23	24	25
26	27	28	29	30	31	

FEBRUARY

S	M	T	W	T	F	S
26	27	28	29	30	31	1
2	3	4	5	6	7	8
9	10	11	12	13	14	15
16	17	18	19	20	21	22
23	24	25	26	27	28	

MARCH

S	M	T	W	T	F	S
23	24	25	26	27	28	1
2	3	4	5	6	7	8
9	10	11	12	13	14	15
16	17	18	19	20	21	22
23	24	25	26	27	28	29
30	31	1	2	3	4	5

APRIL

S	M	T	W	T	F	S
30	31	1	2	3	4	5
6	7	8	9	10	11	12
13	14	15	16	17	18	19
20	21	22	23	24	25	26
27	28	29	30			

MAY

S	M	T	W	T	F	S
27	28	29	30	1	2	3
4	5	6	7	8	9	10
11	12	13	14	15	16	17
18	19	20	21	22	23	24
25	26	27	28	29	30	31

JUNE

S	M	T	W	T	F	S
1	2	3	4	5	6	7
8	9	10	11	12	13	14
15	16	17	18	19	20	21
22	23	24	25	26	27	28
29	30	1	2	3	4	5

JULY

S	M	T	W	T	F	S
29	30	1	2	3	4	5
6	7	8	9	10	11	12
13	14	15	16	17	18	19
20	21	22	23	24	25	26
27	28	29	30	31		

AUGUST

S	M	T	W	T	F	S
27	28	29	30	31	1	2
3	4	5	6	7	8	9
10	11	12	13	14	15	16
17	18	19	20	21	22	23
24	25	26	27	28	29	30
31						

SEPTEMBER

S	M	T	W	T	F	S
31	1	2	3	4	5	6
7	8	9	10	11	12	13
14	15	16	17	18	19	20
21	22	23	24	25	26	27
28	29	30	1	2	3	4

OCTOBER

S	M	T	W	T	F	S
28	29	30	1	2	3	4
5	6	7	8	9	10	11
12	13	14	15	16	17	18
19	20	21	22	23	24	25
26	27	28	29	30	31	

NOVEMBER

S	M	T	W	T	F	S
26	27	28	29	30	31	1
2	3	4	5	6	7	8
9	10	11	12	13	14	15
16	17	18	19	20	21	22
23	24	25	26	27	28	29
30	1	2	3	4	5	6

DECEMBER

S	M	T	W	T	F	S
30	1	2	3	4	5	6
7	8	9	10	11	12	13
14	15	16	17	18	19	20
21	22	23	24	25	26	27
28	29	30	31	1	2	3

Calendar

....

**Plus Saint Paul
Stories,
Facts,
Quotes,
and Poems**

Coyote on Pickerel Lake
© Tony Ernst/gamelaner on Flickr

JANUARY

Cold ● CAROL CONNOLLY

The midnight sky is bright
with the light of new snow.
Rooftops have gone missing.
Evergreens have gone white.

Across the road, chimney
smoke curls, traffic slows,
silence grows. It is winter
and the freeze is upon us.

Drifts rise, beautiful
and deep as my memory
of him, gone this long year,
missed as the silence grows.

JANUARY 2014

S	M	T	W	T	F	S
			1	2	3	4
5	6	7	8	9	10	11
12	13	14	15	16	17	18
19	20	21	22	23	24	25
26	27	28	29	30	31	

On January 5, 1904, the Saint Paul Board of Aldermen voted to make holding on to a streetcar while on a bicycle or motorcycle a misdemeanor.

MONDAY

DECEMBER

30

TUESDAY

DECEMBER

31

New Year's Eve

WEDNESDAY

1

New Year's Day

Walter Greaza, movie and television actor, was born today in 1897.

THURSDAY

2

Richard M. Schulze, founder of Best Buy and philanthropist, was born today in 1941.

FRIDAY

3

SATURDAY

4

SUNDAY

5

This Week's Events

Monday
Holiday Flower Show
Winter Break K—12

Tuesday
Holiday Flower Show
Winter Break K—12

Wednesday
Holiday Flower Show
Winter Break K—12

Thursday
Holiday Flower Show

Friday
Holiday Flower Show
Land O' Lakes Kennel Club
Dog Show
Broadway Songbook:
George Gershwin

Saturday
Holiday Flower Show
Downtown Saint Paul
Winter Farmers' Market
Land O' Lakes Kennel Club
Dog Show
Broadway Songbook:
George Gershwin

Sunday
Holiday Flower Show
Land O' Lakes Kennel Club
Dog Show
Broadway Songbook:
George Gershwin
Minnesota Boychoir
Concert
Music Under Glass

Untitled

It is not carelessness
　　　　　　to leave a poem
　　lying around

Susan Downing

© Paul Winger/paulwinger.zenfolio.com

Windswept Trees in Como Park

Photograph ● AMY CLARK

The photo had sat on the windowsill for the last twenty years. It had borne the sun's ultraviolet tentacles until they sucked the ink from each pore. The image was that of the first child, a promise of greatness and potential to be cultivated.

The child was born by emergency C-section at St. Joe's Hospital. A choice had to be made: save the life of the mother or the child. My father chose my mother. I think he was more afraid of losing someone he knew than someone who was only an idea to him. The baby was a dream, a thought that was in the future. His wife was cut open and losing blood fast. He had to make a decision.

He had wavered on everything in his life so far: college, the army, and every job he came across. He never had finished anything that had the stamp of respectability. The only mature decision he had made was deciding to marry, and that had scared him. He described my mother as "a classy dame with great legs and smarts to boot." Everyone said he couldn't do any better and he'd be a fool to let her walk away. So he asked, and she said yes. In his words, "There were a lot of formal, hoity-toity shin-dings to go to before we even got to the wedding," but he was good about it all. The couple's showers with friends were memorable and wild, with lots of drinks and fun. The big day came, and even the reception was a party. He liked a social event where he could tell a good story, smoke cigarettes, and have a stiff drink. The stroking of egos, the laughter, and the tears streaming down people's faces after he told a joke were seals of their approval for him.

But there were no buddies in the delivery room, just him to make the decision. So he chose my mom. Yet the baby wasn't about to head out to pasture that quickly, and her vitals slowly got stronger. She was a fighter and must have wanted to stay with my mom. I hope she didn't overhear the decision, but maybe that made her fight harder. Imagine hearing that decision after you have just entered a world from a place you didn't want to leave. It would be a difficult start.

Both mother and baby survived. They both had to stay in the hospital a while longer to get stronger, but they healed. Afterward, my dad stopped into the hospital chapel. He thanked the Lord for getting him through all that and asked Him to make him a better man. Then he left to celebrate at O'Gara's with his friends. He was secretly glad the baby was a girl. He was dreading eighteen years of playing catch with a boy.

I think my dad always felt a bit guilty when it was my sister's birthday. It was weird how she was always closest to my mom. To be honest, I think every time he looked at my sister he was surprised she was there.

Photo courtesy Amy Clark

JANUARY 2014

S	M	T	W	T	F	S
			1	2	3	4
5	6	7	8	9	10	11
12	13	14	15	16	17	18
19	20	21	22	23	24	25
26	27	28	29	30	31	

The "Purdue Panel," a college group that spoke against racism, appeared at a banquet at the St. Anthony Park Congregational Church during "Brotherhood Week" on January 11, 1956.

MONDAY

6

Joseph Forepaugh, Saint Paul dry goods pioneer, was born today in 1834.

TUESDAY

7

Joe Soucheray—columnist, author, and radio personality—was born today in 1949.

WEDNESDAY

8

THURSDAY

9

FRIDAY

10

SATURDAY

11

SUNDAY

12

Willis A. Gorman, lawyer and politician, was born today in 1816.

This Week's Events

Thursday

Cocktails with Culture

MN Sportsmen's, Boat, Camping, and Vacation Show

Saint Paul Almanac Soul Sounds Open Mic

Friday

MN Sportsmen's, Boat, Camping, and Vacation Show

Saturday

Downtown Saint Paul Winter Farmers' Market

MN Sportsmen's, Boat, Camping, and Vacation Show

The Saint Paul Chamber Orchestra

Winter Flower Show

Sunday

Music Under Glass

MN Sportsmen's, Boat, Camping, and Vacation Show

Winter Flower Show

> Through my art, I try to connect to younger people to remember the sacrifices elders made, and for elders to know that our young people are really progressing . . . they're in a fight to find their own identity as a Hmong American."
>
> CHILLI LOR
> *Hmong spoken art performer*

© Tom McGregor/mcgregorart.com

Progress

Silverheels ● MARIANNE McNAMARA

It was my mom's first marriage proposal. At eight, she was the older woman. George was only six. After hasty consideration, Mom turned him down. As she explained to her mother, she couldn't marry George. He liked carrots. She didn't.

Mom and George lived across Watson Avenue from each other, at the corner of Edgcumbe Road in the heart of Saint Paul's Highland Park neighborhood. Besides being a very nice boy, George had a pony named Silverheels stabled in a small shed attached to the garage in his family's back yard. The year was 1930, and people in the city were allowed to keep animals on their property. According to George, when Silverheels moved his hooves, all you could see was a shining flash of silver.

George had a little red sleigh with runners, to use in winter. His father taught him to hitch Silverheels to the sleigh. Then George and Mom would drive off, right down the middle of Edgcumbe Road. There was almost never any traffic, and they had the street to themselves. When summer rolled around, George retired the sleigh and brought out a wicker cart with metal-spoked wheels, fancy upholstered seats, and a small side door that opened. George was always careful to drive at a safe, slow pace.

© Chris Emeott/EmeottPhoto.com

My mom lost track of George when his family moved to Illinois. I smile every time I think of those two small children bundled in the sleigh, sedately driving down a city street. Nothing like that would be possible in today's fast-paced world, but what a great memory.

This story was told to me by my mother, Jeanne Villaume Lepsche. ●

A winter marriage proposal in Rice Park

In Praise of Aging ● WENDY BROWN-BÁEZ

In praise of buses rattling through the streets
In praise of passengers jostling for a seat
In praise of a transfer I didn't need to buy
In praise of snow falling from the sky, and my down coat
Bought secondhand but warm

In praise of hips creaking in the wisdom of my years
In praise of sneezing, runny nose, and tears
In praise of vision dimming and yet wide
In praise of knowing what I can't do and why
In praise of unlimited possibilities
With choices made one by one

In praise of the walker I no longer need
In praise of someone rising to give me a seat
In praise of movement each time I must go
In praise of fast and immediate turned to slow
In praise of loving what I have and letting go
Of what is already done

In praise of parties where I left too soon
In praise of dancing beneath the silver moon
In praise of youthful folly when I was dumb
In praise of turmoil; at least I wasn't numb
In praise of a life full of stories, full of snow, full of sun
In praise of feeling I have really just begun

JANUARY 2014

S	M	T	W	T	F	S
			1	2	3	4
5	6	7	8	9	10	11
12	13	14	15	16	17	18
19	20	21	22	23	24	25
26	27	28	29	30	31	

On January 17, 1946, the City Council agreed to pay for twenty-one structures of temporary housing for WWII veterans on the Belvedere Playground on Saint Paul's West Side.

MONDAY

13

Mawlid Al-Nabi

TUESDAY

14

WEDNESDAY

15

THURSDAY

16

FRIDAY

17

Nancy Anne Parsons, movie and television actor, was born today in 1942.

SATURDAY

18

SUNDAY

19

Bridget Rosemarie Coleman, "New Deal Democrat" and instinctive political strategist, was born today in 1926.

This Week's Events

Monday
Winter Flower Show

Tuesday
Winter Flower Show

Wednesday
Winter Flower Show

Thursday
Winter Flower Show

Saint Paul Almanac Soul Sounds
Open Mic

Friday
Winter Flower Show

The Saint Paul Chamber Orchestra

Saturday
Downtown Saint Paul
Winter Farmers' Market

Winter Flower Show

The Saint Paul Chamber
Orchestra

Sunday
Music Under Glass

Winter Flower Show

Urban Expedition: Spain

> "When I work, I like to have a lot of people around me, a lot of action, sort of keeps the adrenalin going, I get up to a pitch, revved up . . ."
>
> LEROY NEIMAN, *Saint Paul artist*

© Saibal Ghosh/saibalghosh.com

Urban Expedition: Travel the world without leaving Saint Paul! Tibetan dancers during the Landmark Center's 2013 series of country-themed exhibits.

The Drive ● HILAL ISLER

Not wanting to alarm my husband and infant son, in case they've fallen back asleep, I don't call. I don't even text. But I do take a picture with my camera-phone, because I need proof that I've done it, that I'm actually here: sitting in a 2005 Toyota Matrix, outside the Saint Anthony Park Library. This is incredible.

I hold the phone up steady against the window and make sure I get the whole of the building. It's still a little dark outside so the picture's fuzzy. It's six in the morning on a Saturday in January, and I'm just getting started.

I feel encouraged, like I can do more—but how much more? Can I make it to, say, the Target on University Avenue? Maybe. Or no, wait, forget it. The construction. It might be too much for me.

But what about Highland Park? I could drive out there and get my husband some coffee and a Danish from that café on the corner. He loves a good cheese Danish. And if the place isn't open yet, I'll just practice parking. Perhaps even parallel parking.

Yes, Highland Park.

I adjust the seat, tilt the mirror, turn the heat down. I turn the radio on, then off. With my foot on the brake pedal, I shift the car into drive. This makes my stomach fold into itself.

Slowly, I inch away from the curb and toward the stoplight. The light is red, but it turns almost immediately and with it, so do I. Unfortunately, the car on the other side of the intersection turns too. I freeze. I apply the brakes, right there in the middle of the road, and scream simultaneously. The other driver honks and yells something at me. Possibly, she's cursing. I don't understand her but I unhook my hand from the steering wheel and offer a weak, shaky wave.

Sorry, I mouth. I'm so sorry.

You should be, she says. That, I can make out. She presses down on the gas, showing me her anger. It must have been her right of way.

Now Highland Park is definitely off too. And so am I. Going no more than fifteen miles an hour, I instead make the drive home, to our condo on Franklin Avenue in Saint Paul, wondering the whole way what it's going to take. I've been practicing like this for months. How much longer can I do this? I'm in my thirties and I'm too afraid to drive.

At home I find my family awake and in the playroom.

"How'd it go?" my husband asks.

I show him the picture.

"The library! That's great," he says. "Maybe you can take him to story time there this week."

I don't tell him about the lady and the intersection. I don't tell him that I won't be able to take our son anywhere. Not this week. Not just yet.

Most people here learn to drive when they're what, sixteen? At that age, I was living in Saudi Arabia, wearing a face-veil to high school. Driver's ed wasn't on my list of to-dos. It is, in fact, illegal for women to drive there. But I've been here, in America, since college; in the Twin Cities since 2008. I can't still be hiding behind old excuses. My son needs me to be braver than this.

He'll make sure I'm up early tomorrow, before the Sunday church-goers are. That's when I'll head out again. Maybe this time I'll make it to the café at Highland Park.

My husband, after all, really does love a good cheese Danish. ●

JANUARY 2014

S	M	T	W	T	F	S
			1	2	3	4
5	6	7	8	9	10	11
12	13	14	15	16	17	18
19	20	21	22	23	24	25
26	27	28	29	30	31	

Sixteen women applied for membership in the all-male Saint Anthony Park Association on January 25, 1972. They were denied admission on a 47–47 tie vote.

MONDAY

20

Martin Luther King Jr. Day

TUESDAY

21

WEDNESDAY

22

THURSDAY

23

Mahesh Pailoor, award-winning Saint Paul filmmaker, was born today in 1978.

FRIDAY

24

SATURDAY

25

SUNDAY

26

This Week's Events

Monday
Winter Flower Show

Tuesday
Winter Flower Show

Wednesday
Winter Flower Show
Fireside Reading Series
Saint Paul Almanac Lowertown
    Reading Jam

Thursday
Winter Flower Show
Saint Paul Almanac Soul Sounds
    Open Mic
Saint Paul Winter Carnival

Friday
Winter Flower Show
The Saint Paul Chamber Orchestra
Minnesota Division 1 Men's Hockey
    Tournament (MN Cup)
Fourth Friday at the Movies
Saint Paul Winter Carnival

Saturday
Downtown Saint Paul
    Winter Farmers' Market
Winter Flower Show
Minnesota Division 1 Men's
    Hockey Tournament (MN
    Cup)
The Saint Paul Chamber
    Orchestra
Minnesota RollerGirls
Minnesota Opera
Saintly City Cat Show
Orchid Society of Minnesota
    Winter Carnival Orchid
    Show
Saint Paul Winter Carnival

Sunday
Winter Flower Show
The Saint Paul Chamber
    Orchestra
Saintly City Cat Show
Orchid Society of Minnesota
    Winter Carnival Orchid
    Show
Saint Paul Winter Carnival

© Jim Teske

Red Bull Crashed Ice

Five Things to Love about Saint Paul from Someone Who Moved Here from Somewhere Else ● JOHN MOE

1. TRAFFIC

I know this sounds ridiculous: to love the speed by which one can get across town. Big deal, right? *Yes. It is. You have no idea.* Prior to moving to Saint Paul in 2008, I lived in Seattle, a city with an enormous and ever-worsening traffic problem. Zillions of people are constantly moving into Seattle and clogging up the roads in the process. Seattle blew it on transportation by failing to either build enough roads and mass-transit options when it was early enough or, alternately, build enough enormous walls to keep people from moving there. Now it's too late.

But in Saint Paul. O, Saint Paul! I can get from my house to my office downtown in six minutes. Using Google Maps, I can see that someplace is ten minutes away, and I get there in eight. This means I have control over the events of my life and I know what will happen to me in the course of my day.

Please understand that this is not how things work in other major American metropolitan areas. In places like San Francisco, Chicago, Los Angeles, Seattle, or Dallas, people can get in a car to cross a city and have no earthly idea when they'll arrive at their destination.

Still, I hear traffic reports on the radio here about slight congestions on Interstate 94 or the Crosstown Highway, sometimes up to a few minutes. "Ha!" I shout whenever I hear those reports. It's highly cathartic.

2. MEDIUM PACING

Before coming here, I was used to a pretty fast-paced life. I worked in dot-coms in Seattle in the late 1990s. I was in a rock band during the Grunge scare of the early '90s. I know frenetic. So I was nervous to move to the Upper Midwest—what if everything was slow, deliberative, and based on watching crops grow? I didn't even own overalls.

But Saint Paul! O, Saint Paul! In Saint Paul one has time to actually conduct a conversation, but not so much time that the conversation runs aground. One can enjoy the moment but still have another destination to get to *at some point.*

I learned this in a coffee shop soon after moving here, when I realized that the person in front of me had completed her transaction with the barista but had not completed her conversation about snow and whether or not we were about to get more. Because Saint Paul has medium pacing, this meant the chat was not to be rushed along but would conclude eventually. Which it did. Eventually.

3. THINGS HOLD STILL

In Seattle, my house was on a fault line. For real: The fault line ran literally underneath my house. For my wife, this meant constant panic that "The Big One" was about to arrive. For me, a native Northwesterner, it meant the following rationale: I haven't been killed by an earthquake yet; therefore I never will be. Our lives of terror (hers) and stupidity (mine) were inadvisable and, honestly, no way to live.

But in Saint Paul! O, Saint Paul! Everything stays put. And not just seismically. The people stay put too. The tectonic plates of human events don't leave people adrift like human Pangea chunks. "Oh, I'm not from here," said one of my new neighbors when I first moved here, "I grew up in Mendota Heights." What did she do, walk?

I have noticed that plenty of Saint Paul kids do move away for college and a while after but return when it's time to get married, have kids, and settle down. If you'll pardon my Washington state metaphor, they're like salmon: venturing out into the world, returning home to spawn and die.

4. THE OTHERNESS OF NOT BEING MINNEAPOLIS

I'm not interested in the argument about which Twin City is better. I love them both. But Saint Paul is smaller and gets less attention, and is therefore odder and more interesting. Saint Paul is Garfunkel. Saint Paul is Oates. Saint Paul is DJ Jazzy Jeff to Minneapolis's Fresh Prince.

When I knew my family was moving to the Twin Cities, I instantly wanted to live in Saint Paul, even though I knew very little about either city. It just seemed inherently more comedic to live in the smaller place. Especially because it's the capital of The Land of Ten Billion Lakes and the whole city has just six lakes—only two of which I've ever heard of, and I've lived here five years. Come on, that's hilarious.

5. THE INCOMPREHENSIBILITY OF CITY PLANNING

In Seattle, I lived on 45th Avenue. I grew up on 299th Place. In my section of Saint Paul, nothing has a number. Saint Paul is a vast grid of named streets with no discernible logic or order to it. So all you need to do is memorize the order of every street everywhere and you're fine. This frustrates Minneapolitans and out-of-town visitors to no end, thereby lowering the chances that they'll move here and clog up the streets with more traffic. It's the perfect system. •

Empty Promise ● MAYO GARNER

The world is filled with empty promises.
It's like when you tell a person you love them,
and they say it back,
but after that
y'all never speak again.

Sometimes I wake up,
trying to understand,
"is love really real,
or is it just a fairy tale
that everybody wants?"

Because all I see is disaster.
All I see is a child's tear.
All I see is a star without its shine.

I know I left you with an empty promise.
I know I watched your heart shatter,
and I didn't mean to—but don't blame me.

Blame the world.
The world made me crazy.
Waking up, who can I trust
when my close friends are acting shady?

I never thought I would get stabbed,
lie in my own blood.

I know I said I would never lie,
and I did.
I know I said I will never make you cry,
and I did.

I know I said I would protect you,
like God said,
but his words are filled with empty promises.
He abandoned me
in this cold weather.

Chills running through my body.
I'm starving,
looking for a victim.
I'm walking through life,
all alone, standing with these empty promises,
trying to hold on to my last promise.

for what?

Because I made my daughter a promise
that I'll watch her grow up;
that I'll watch her get married;
that I will watch her have a few grandkids.

And I understand that in life,
everybody doesn't get to see that journey.
When your enemies are spying on you.

I'm hoping I don't run into the wrong corner,
and end up like another dead homie.

I think it's time to speak my mind:

Lord,
I know we ain't never seen eye to eye. My Father, that was never
there, and when I need you the most you vanish into thin air. All I
ask you, and nothing more, is to protect my beautiful seed. That's
the least you can do, after all the empty promises. How can you
watch thousands of children be in misery, without feeling any
remorse? Just because some religion says we are part of you? And
I know every human being has some evil conscience, so that means
you must have an evil conscience too. So judge me how you want,
just don't judge my daughter. . . .

It's kind of crazy
that a brother gets arrested
for aiding and abetting,
because he didn't tell the police what he's seen.

If he's guilty
then God's guilty too.
Because all he does is sit
and watch millions of people die.

If he gets five years for that,
then God better not have a release date
for all the murders he's seen.

My thoughts are trouble,
my soul is wicked,
But my daughter,
she still sees innocence in me.

I wonder what she sees in me.

Because my life is filled with empty promises.

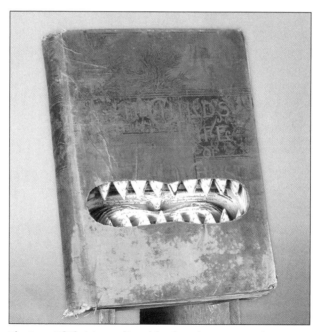

The Jaws Of Christ, *an altered-book sculpture created
by Joshua Hosterman from Hesba Stretton's 1891 tome,*
The Child's Life of Christ.

© Bob Muschewske/370SummitStPaul.com

FEBRUARY

True Myth ● HEID E. ERDRICH

Tell a child she is composed of parts
(her Ojibway quarters, her German half-heart)
she'll find the existence of harpies easy
to swallow. Storybook children never come close
to her mix, but manticores make great uncles,
Sphinx a cousin she'll allow, centaurs better to love
than boys—the horse part, at least, she can ride.
With a bestiary for a family album she's proud.
Her heap of blankets, her garbage grin, prove
she's descended of bears, her totem, it's true.
And that German witch with the candy roof,
that was her ancestor too. If swans can rain
white rape from heaven, then what is a girl to do?
Believe her Indian eyes, her sly French smile,
her breast with its veins skim milk blue—
She is the myth that is true.

FEBRUARY 2014

S	M	T	W	T	F	S
						1
2	3	4	5	6	7	8
9	10	11	12	13	14	15
16	17	18	19	20	21	22
23	24	25	26	27	28	

Marjorie Kohn of 231 Maria was crowned Queen of the Dayton's Bluff Playground on January 30, 1946, by Saint Paul sheriff Tommy Gibbons as part of the Winter Carnival.

MONDAY

JANUARY

27

Howard Y. Williams, Congregational minister and political activist in Saint Paul, was born today in 1889.

TUESDAY

JANUARY

28

WEDNESDAY

JANUARY

29

Father Casimir Kobylinski, longtime priest at St. Casimir Church on Saint Paul's East Side, was born today in 1856.

THURSDAY

JANUARY

30

FRIDAY

JANUARY

31

Chinese New Year

SATURDAY

1

SUNDAY

Groundhog Day

2

This Week's Events

Monday
Winter Flower Show
Saint Paul Winter Carnival

Tuesday
Winter Flower Show
Minnesota Opera

Wednesday
Winter Flower Show
Fireside Reading Series
Saint Paul Winter Carnival

Thursday
Winter Flower Show
Minnesota Opera
Saint Paul Winter Carnival
Saint Paul Almanac Soul Sounds
   Open Mic

Friday
Winter Flower Show
World's Toughest Rodeo
Saint Paul Winter Carnival

Saturday
Winter Flower Show
Minnesota Opera
World's Toughest Rodeo
Saint Paul Winter Carnival
Downtown Saint Paul
   Winter Farmers' Market
The Saint Paul Chamber
   Orchestra

Sunday
Winter Flower Show
Minnesota Opera
Saint Paul Winter Carnival
Music Under Glass

Because of the -32 degree weather, a Saint Paul street-car was frozen onto the tracks on January 30, 1951. It took fifty minutes to chop it free.

© Tom Dunn/TomDunnPhoto.com

Winter Carnival friends

Walks with the Chowhound ● BRITT AAMODT

Selby is a chowhound. An inveterate, unrelenting, willfully indiscriminate gastronome of Saint Paul street food. Naturally he is named after the street where he lives, Selby Avenue, and naturally, when I come to dog sit him, we commence our journeys from that haunt of celebrated eateries, dine-ins, and dessert stops. This poses a problem, as Selby is a beagle, a breed that distinguishes itself by a sniffer so acute it can divine a three-month-old pancake-thin squirrel carcass from a snowbank high as a Himalayan foothill. (Why Saint Paul should have snowbanks of that magnitude is a matter for another story, and of serious inquiry to whichever department is charged with grooming the city's wintertime walks into a Sherpa's mountainside trek.)

So I was speaking of Selby's appetite. Three years ago, when we began our acquaintance, I was under the misapprehension that this sophisticated pooch shared the habits of his rural kindred, that of chasing squirrels, rabbits, and any other bite-size morsel up a tree or down a hole. He would surely attempt these feats, I have no doubt, but for my expert leash-handling skills. In the time I've known Selby, I have salvaged nearly two thousand such creatures from the fate of a take-out lunch.

What I did not anticipate, however, was my charge's adaptability to urban street cuisine. Early on Selby realized what I, a mere suburbanite, have only recently comprehended: that a trek through Saint Paul is like a saunter down the world's longest cafeteria line. I used to trust Selby's instincts when deciding our route, seeing as I was the outsider and he the savvy local. But then it seemed whichever way he turned a half-eaten burger would meet his snout. On Selby Avenue alone, on one early jaunt, he gorged his way past Great Harvest Bread (a slice of honey wheat), Mango Thai (rice noodles), W. A. Frost's (a Korean barbecue chicken wing), and even the hallowed grounds of the Saint Paul Cathedral (a communion wafer, God spare me).

But I too am a skilled adapter, and learned to wend our ways to parts where food did not drop out of diners' hands like manna from dog heaven. I am speaking of the residential areas, blocks of fine houses, which are a feast for the eyes but a poor harvest for the grumbling tummy. Yet even as I appreciated an arched gable, Selby would wolf a discarded apple core, a sticky candy, a wadded napkin.

I adapted again. I grew more vigilant, while the leash grew shorter. We excluded our walks to Summit Avenue, where we encountered nothing but houses and joggers—and the occasional tourist laden with treats purchased from nearby Grand Avenue, wide-eyed and guileless, until set upon by a hungry beagle. Well, Summit could do with a few less tourists, right?

At a guess I would say that Selby has profited more from our walks than I—except for this once. It was a cold January morning. Selby roused me for an urgent call to nature, so out we went. The morning was darker and more desolate than usual, explained shortly when a bell tolled three. That fiend. Well, since he'd already gotten me up, I allowed him to drag me across the Himalayan sidewalks to the bluffs, where I stood rooted by a sight that must have enthralled many a Saint Paulite over the years. The city spread below, a tapestry of light, here and there exhaling its chilly breath in columns of steam, and huddling the dark river that behind stretched to a remote geologic past and ahead reached toward some future beyond my span of years and my wildest imaginings.

I turned to thank Selby for his unexpected gift, but the chowhound was preoccupied with a sugar cookie just then excavated from the snow. ●

© Serena Mira Asta/AstaArt.com

FEBRUARY 2014

S	M	T	W	T	F	S
						1
2	3	4	5	6	7	8
9	10	11	12	13	14	15
16	17	18	19	20	21	22
23	24	25	26	27	28	

Katharine Hepburn starred in Shakespeare's "As You Like It" at the Saint Paul Auditorium, an event sponsored by the Theatre Guild on February 9, 1951.

MONDAY

3

TUESDAY

4

WEDNESDAY

5

John Bodin, early Swedish druggist in Saint Paul, was born today in 1842.

THURSDAY

6

Gordy Jones—author of children's literature, photographer, and sports columnist—was born today in 1955.

FRIDAY

7

SATURDAY

8

SUNDAY

9

This Week's Events

Monday
Winter Flower Show

Tuesday
Winter Flower Show

Wednesday
Winter Flower Show
Fireside Reading Series

Thursday
Winter Flower Show
Saint Paul Almanac Soul Sounds
Open Mic

Friday
Winter Flower Show
The Saint Paul Chamber Orchestra
Rennie Harris Puremovement

Saturday
Winter Flower Show
Downtown Saint Paul Winter
Farmers' Market

Sunday
Winter Flower Show
Music Under Glass
The Saint Paul Chamber
Orchestra
Urban Expedition: Finland
Ladysmith Black Mambazo

> "I would have started much earlier if I had realized the great satisfaction and pleasure I derive from the writing and the association with this marvelous community of crime fiction writers."
>
> CARL BROOKINS, *mystery writer*

© LightTheUnderground.com

Ice sculpture competition at the Winter Carnival

Photograph of My Grandparents

● KORISSA HOWES

Made in black and white
Frayed upon the edges
Free of wrinkles despite
That they were not then
My father's parents
Looked so in love
At a time in the 1930s
When this was unheard of
A Native man and Swedish girl
Met at a table of cards
He was dark and handsome
With slicked-back hair
That white t-shirt
A clean shaved face
She wore high heels
Her hair pinned back
Sitting on his lap
Beautiful and married
With eleven kids
She loved him to the end
Never regretting moments
Living in unity

Small Comfort ● JOYCE SUTPHEN

I remember hearing Kurt Vonnegut, who
was speaking in Saint Paul, say that when
the aliens arrived on a desolated earth,

we should leave them a message, carved in
the walls of the Grand Canyon, and that
message should say: "We could have saved

ourselves, but we were too damn selfish
and too damn lazy." This was the same night he
told us that we had about as much chance

of becoming a professional
baseball player or a senator as
we had making a living as a writer,

but he'd done it and written one of the
best anti-war books ever written. He'd
taught us to say, "So it goes," and so it does.

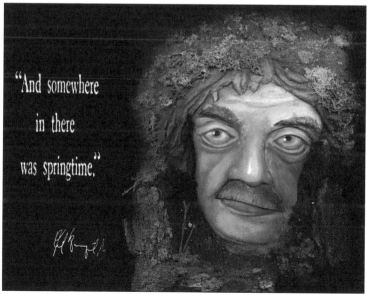

FEBRUARY 2014

S	M	T	W	T	F	S
						1
2	3	4	5	6	7	8
9	10	11	12	13	14	15
16	17	18	19	20	21	22
23	24	25	26	27	28	

Saint Paul firefighters extinguished a chicken-coop blaze near the corner of Greenbrier and Maryland on February 11, 1901.

MONDAY

10

TUESDAY

11

John Allen Wakefield—historian, politician, soldier, physician, and lawyer—was born today in 1797.

WEDNESDAY

12

THURSDAY

13

FRIDAY

14

Valentine's Day

William Bowell, Mississippi riverboat captain, was born today in 1921.

SATURDAY

15

SUNDAY

16

This Week's Events

Monday
Winter Flower Show

Tuesday
Winter Flower Show

Wednesday
Winter Flower Show
Fireside Reading Series

Thursday
Winter Flower Show
Cocktails with Culture
Minnesota Home and Patio Show
Saint Paul Almanac Soul Sounds
Open Mic

Friday
Winter Flower Show
Minnesota Home and Patio Show
The Saint Paul Chamber Orchestra

Saturday
Winter Flower Show
Downtown Saint Paul Winter
Farmers' Market
Minnesota Home and Patio Show
The Saint Paul Chamber Orchestra

Sunday
Winter Flower Show
Music Under Glass
Minnesota Home and Patio
Show
Scottish Ramble

Untitled

Hard candy of love—
what if I bite
down
a
little?

Charles Matson Lume

© Ryan Chernik/RyanChernik.com

Mary Dear ● MARY VIRGINIA WINSTEAD

It snowed that afternoon. Heavy, wet flakes pelted my coat on my walk down the sloping drive toward Cleveland Avenue. By the time I got to the iron gate it was soaked through and smelled of wet lamb's wool.

I looked back. I was an English major at St. Catherine's that snowy day in February 1986. I'd been through a bruising divorce,

Sister Immaculata

and over the past eighteen months Jane Austen had distracted me, my children had caught mud turtles in the Dew Drop, and my professors had listened while I cried. St. Kate's was my refuge.

At the top of the hill, a yellow light shone through the snow from a window on the second floor in Whitby Hall, where I'd been having a cup of tea with my advisor, Jonis.

I'd thought I was all right. But once I started down the snowy hill, the leaden feeling I'd been pushing down all day began to rise up in my throat. By the time I rounded the corner onto Cleveland, the pressure was filling my sinuses. Then I saw her, a tiny woman in a plaid head scarf, overcoat, and galoshes.

Sister Immaculata had taught Shakespeare in the English Department for forty years. I'd done a grammar tutorial with her. She looked up at me, her face shadowed by her woolen scarf, her eyes obscured behind enormous glasses. She was no taller than my shoulder.

"Hello, Mary Dear."

It was how she always greeted me, taking my hands in hers.

With those five gentle syllables my insides broke like glass, and my feelings spilled out in sobs.

"Do you have to be somewhere, Mary Dear?"

That was part of the problem. I had nowhere to go except for my empty apartment on Grand Avenue. My kids were with their dad. This was his wedding day. There had been many other women during our marriage, and today he was marrying one. I didn't say all of this. Instead I choked out, "This." Sob. "Is." Hiccup. "Ex-husband." Sob. "Wedding day."

Sister took me back through the gates and up the hill, past the Dew Drop, under the archway between Derham Hall and the church, across the commons and past O'Shaughnessy to the convent. It all went by in a watery blur.

She led me into a parlor with a sofa. We sat down and she put her arms around me. I easily outweighed her by thirty pounds. And yet I cried in her arms as though I were a baby. Time and the rest of the world were lost to me. When I stopped, head throbbing, the floor covered with wadded-up tissues—where had they come from?—there was her face, as fragile as tissue paper, with guileless eyes that expected nothing but absolute honesty.

"The bathroom is over there, Mary Dear." Inside, I leaned over the sink and splashed water onto my face. I looked like a prizefighter. When I returned, there were cookies and tea. My hands shook, rattling the cup and saucer.

"Sister, I don't know what to say," I said. My voice sounded strange. How long since I'd spoken? "I don't know how to thank you."

"Suffering is a sacred place, Mary Dear," she said. "That is when God draws nearest."

I finished my tea and stood up to go. She took my hands in hers. "Good-bye, Mary Dear."

I stepped into the dark. "Good-bye, Sister." I started my journey back across the campus, and turned around. A soft yellow light was shining in the doorway, and a tiny woman in the middle of it was waving me on. ●

Whitby Hall in the winter snows

FEBRUARY 2014

S	M	T	W	T	F	S
						1
2	3	4	5	6	7	8
9	10	11	12	13	14	15
16	17	18	19	20	21	22
23	24	25	26	27	28	

Our Lady of Guadalupe Church held its first masses in Spanish and English on February 22, 1931.

MONDAY

17

President's Day

Emma Brunson, Saint Paul architect, was born today in 1887.

TUESDAY

18

WEDNESDAY

19

THURSDAY

20

FRIDAY

21

Verna Mikesh, nutrition expert and longtime U of M Extension leader, was born today in 1915.

SATURDAY

22

SUNDAY

23

This Week's Events

Monday
Winter Flower Show

Tuesday
Winter Flower Show

Wednesday
Winter Flower Show
Fireside Reading Series
Maria de Barros
MSHSL Girls Hockey Tournament

Thursday
Winter Flower Show
MSHSL Girls Hockey Tournament
Saint Paul Almanac Soul Sounds
Open Mic

Friday
Winter Flower Show
MSHSL Girls Hockey Tournament
The Saint Paul Chamber Orchestra

Saturday
Winter Flower Show
Downtown Saint Paul
Winter Farmers' Market
MSHSL Girls Hockey
Tournament
The Saint Paul Chamber
Orchestra

Sunday
Winter Flower Show

On February 20, 1901, Saint Paul's Socialist Education Club gave a free lecture, "Young Men in Politics," at 854 Payne Avenue.

© Saibal Ghosh/saibalghosh.com

The Lawson Software building and Saint Paul Hotel (right) above Rice Park in Downtown Saint Paul

What's in a Name? ● YUSEF MGENI

"All over (America), Negro boys and girls are growing into stunted maturity, trying desperately to find a place to stand, and the wonder is not that so many are ruined—but that so many survive!"
    JAMES BALDWIN 1955

Growing up as young Black men in Saint Paul's Rondo neighborhood, we learned a lot from the generation of Black men who preceded us. We, like they before us, were simply known as "the Rondo boys." Rondo was where we learned to survive, to grow and develop—it was where we learned the value of our extended family membership, where we fell in love and got our hearts broken. It was also where we learned what's in a name.

In my lifetime I have been legally classified on official documents as Colored; Negro; Black; Afro-American; African American (with and without a hyphen); and American. As a result, you will have to forgive me if at times I seem somewhat schizophrenic. As evidence of the residue from the negative forces of racism and oppression that surround and shape us, I truly believe that most Black people in America are more or less schizophrenic. I've grown up and interacted throughout my life with Black people who had one personality for dealing with white folks who were strangers, another for dealing with white people who were supervisors, another for dealing with Black folks, one for the police and other authorities, and a few more that sprang up almost without prompting—depending on the circumstance and who the encounter involved. This ability to successfully navigate what author Richard Wright referred to as the "cliff-like margins of many cultures" would serve not only as a survival skill, but truly as one of the wonders of Blackness, through which people of African descent not only survive—but grow and develop.

To be Black in this society and successfully navigate the social, political, cultural, and economic landscape that surrounds us, one needs at times to be a chameleon, recognizing when it is necessary for survival to tell the truth, or to tell folks what they think they want to hear, and knowing when to duck beneath the radar so as not to draw unnecessary attention to one's self. This is not to suggest that one become compliant or assimilate, but rather that one's journey through life and indeed each day can be delayed indefinitely, altered abruptly, ended—or made more bearable—in direct proportion to one's ability to navigate, sense, adapt, prevent, or react to multiple situations concurrently, particularly when they involve whites with power in our society. In terms of navigating racial and cultural minefields, Black people (and people of color in America) are not only the original canaries in the coal mine, but the original multitaskers as well.

The latter of my racial designations ("American") and its juxtaposition is important, because it occurred when I was forty-two years old and traveling on a fellowship across Europe. I was tired after taking a sleepless overnight flight from the Twin Cities to Hamburg, Germany, and then immediately taking the lengthy train ride to Salzburg, Austria. As I passed through customs the next afternoon in Salzburg, I could not help but notice a young Austrian soldier in a wrinkled, oversized uniform. He could not have been more than eighteen, but he appeared more like thirteen and had never shaved, or even smiled, it seemed. His appeared to be a dull and lonely job, standing post all by himself at his national border—in a train station no less. I could not help but wonder if the automatic weapon he carried on his shoulder, though quite deadly, had ever been fired.

As I walked through the train station after leaving customs, I could hear someone shouting and their voice reverberating throughout the enclosed area of the station. "American, halt!" "Stop, American!" the voice kept repeating, with a thick Austrian accent. Like everyone else, I was wondering who in the world they were shouting at and what all the commotion was about. People stopped briefly in their tracks and heads were turning in every direction, including mine. Meanwhile, I had casually walked about seventy-five more yards during the commotion when all of a sudden, I felt someone tap me on the shoulder. I turned, somewhat startled, and noticed the unshaven boy soldier, completely out of breath, and in his outstretched hand, which he gestured toward me, were the sunglasses I had inadvertently left at the customs check point when I presented my passport for inspection.

Having thanked him, accepted the return of my sunglasses, and casually turned to walk away, it dawned on me that the reason I had no idea who he was shouting at was because this was the very first time in my forty-two years on this earth that anyone had ever referred to me as an "American." In the taxi, on the way to the Archbishop's summer palace where I would attend an international seminar on philanthropy and nonprofit organizations I had been invited to, it dawned on me what Richard Wright, James Baldwin, and other Black writers, musicians, and ex-patriots meant when they said that they had to go overseas to fully appreciate what burdens and scars racism had imposed on them in America.

I thought for a brief moment that this would be a good opportunity to reflect and try to internalize my first-in-life "American" experience, but I was both enthralled by the architecture and history of my surroundings, and far too tired from the trip to pursue it at the time. Funny thing, though, is that every time I hear the word "American," I see the young soldier's face and the puzzled look in his eyes because he thought he not only knew who I was—but that he had the God-given right to define me, and here I was, in a foreign country, naively oblivious to that grandest of white privileges—a privilege that Europeans and Americans take for granted. Ironically, having spent an incredible summer in Germany, Austria, Switzerland, and France, the "American" episode in the train station in Salzburg with the boy soldier is the one thing I most remember. At the same time, it was a "real time" reminder of what Richard Wright, Malcolm X, and W. E. B. DuBois so eloquently wrote when they pointed out that as Negroes "We are in America—but not of it," or, "The fact that a cat has kittens in an oven—don't make 'em biscuits."

As DuBois put it, "It is a peculiar sensation, this double-consciousness, this sense of always looking at one's self through the eyes of others, of measuring one's soul by the tape of a world that looks on in amused contempt and pity. One ever feels his twoness,—an American, a Negro; two souls, two thoughts, two unreconciled strivings; two warring ideals in one dark body, whose dogged strength alone keeps it from being torn asunder."

On another occasion, not long after my Austrian experience, I had flown to Canada to participate in a national conference of foundation representatives when a white, female customs officer, while examining my passport, asked me quizzically, "What kind of a name is that [Yusef Mgeni]?" I responded, matter-of-factly, that it was an African name. Looking at my light complexion, seeing my business attire, and hearing my clearly American accent, she stammered in a challenging manner, almost disdainfully, "Why, you're not African!" To which I responded, somewhat irritated, as I snatched my passport back and walked directly past her, "And you're clearly not an anthropologist."

As I walked toward the baggage claim area, one of my traveling companions sought to calm the agent down for fear I would be detained or denied entrance to the country. I could not help but notice the overhead sign as I exited the customs area: "Welcome to Canada." The encounter brought to mind a saying our grandmother used to correct us with, whenever the terms "up North" or "down South" would enter the conversation. "If you're Black," she would tell us, from the throne of her hard-won status as an elder, "everything south of the North Pole is South—and you will do well to remember that!"

As I mentioned earlier, this labeling, this notion of dominant and subordinate, of difference and race would affect us, beginning in early childhood, even before we knew what it was, and would shadow us day in and day out throughout our lives. We were forced to become students and observers of supposed white superiority and white society, primarily because our survival depended on it, immersed in its elitist, capitalist grasp from the time the alarm clock went off in the morning until the sleep timer went off on the radio late at night. I clearly understood that we, as Black people, knew more about white culture than white people did, primarily because we spent every waking moment deflecting and trying to navigate it. At the same time, I found it quite ironic how little white people knew about their own culture—let alone that of any other group—either within or outside the geographic borders of the United States.

Some years later, our nine-year-old son was sprawled out on the living room carpet, watching *Brian's Song*, a movie about Black Chicago Bears halfback Gale Sayers, who scored twenty-two touchdowns in his rookie year in the mid-sixties. Proud that he was enthralled by the rare image of a positive, Black male, adult overachiever (even if in a sport I found little use for), I asked him what he was watching. He told me, somewhat irritated that I was interrupting his viewing, and then I asked him with a hint of pride—hoping he would proclaim "the Black guy"—which one was Gale Sayers? Our son looked at me with incredulity and, frowning, said, "Dad, don't you know who Gale Sayers is? He's number 40!" He immediately turned his attention back to the television, hoping that the unnecessary interlude had not caused him to miss anything important.

Yusef Mgeni
Courtesy Metropolitan State University

This would be another teachable, reflective moment—one that went against much of my upbringing and experience. I had to silently drink it in and admire my own awe, inspired by an innocent Black man-child. While I saw a Black man who had achieved incredible accomplishments in his brief football career—despite the odds and the impressive opposition focused against him every single week—our son, in his impressionable young mind, saw a man who was identified most by a mere number on his jersey. At that moment in time, to his generation the number 40 was a more important characteristic than his race. I couldn't help but wonder at the awesome responsibility that had been placed on the shoulders of our generation of "Rondo boys," and of how serious the challenge and commitment was—to guide and help develop the next generation of young Black men that we had inherited.

Perhaps there was hope yet for the "courageous community" that Dr. King challenged us to build. To cast away forever, the little clouds of inferiority that inhabited our children's mental skies. I hoped with all my heart that this authentic vision of a Black child's world would become more than an exception to all that was happening in our country, in our lives, and in the race-obsessed world we, and he, had inherited. ●

March ● LOUIS JENKINS

It hadn't occurred to me until someone at work brought it to my attention that this winter has been going on for eleven years. I said, "That can't be. Surely not." But then I got thinking about it. It was eleven years ago November we moved into this house. You remember, snow was just beginning and we had so much trouble getting the refrigerator down the driveway and through the door. Danny was eight and we got him a sled for Christmas. It's amazing how one gets concerned with other things and the time just goes by. Here it is March and now that I've noticed it, the snow has begun to melt a little. During the day there's water running in the street. It's like a bird singing in a tree that flies just as you become aware of it. When you think about it, the world, cold and hard as it is, begins to fall apart.

(From Tin Flag: New and Selected Prose Poems, *Will o' the Wisp Books, copyright © 2013 by Louis Jenkins)*

MARCH 2014

S	M	T	W	T	F	S
						1
2	3	4	5	6	7	8
9	10	11	12	13	14	15
16	17	18	19	20	21	22
23	24	25	26	27	28	29
30	31					

Saint Paul City Park Commission was created on February 25, 1887.

MONDAY

FEBRUARY

24

TUESDAY

FEBRUARY

25

WEDNESDAY

FEBRUARY

26

THURSDAY

FEBRUARY

27

FRIDAY

FEBRUARY

28

Mary Ly, Hmong American actor, was born today in 1986.

SATURDAY

1

A. J. Hoban, early Saint Paul contractor, was born today in 1857.

SUNDAY

2

This Week's Events

Monday
Winter Flower Show

Tuesday
Winter Flower Show

Wednesday
Winter Flower Show
Fireside Reading Series
Saint Paul Almanac Lowertown
Reading Jam

Thursday
Winter Flower Show
MSHSL Wrestling Tournament

Friday
Winter Flower Show
MSHSL Wrestling Tournament
Fourth Friday at the Movies

Saturday
Winter Flower Show
MSHSL Wrestling Tournament
Downtown Saint Paul Winter
Farmers' Market
Minnesota Opera
The Saint Paul Chamber Orchestra

Sunday
Winter Flower Show
Urban Expedition: Cambodia

skeleton of a nation

jagged rocks dusted red
bleed rose water from ancient
springs
who was baptized here
saved and sustained by sacrificial
land

skyscrapers and cars
the skeleton of a nation comes
from this belly
but the immigrant forge
and children formed in heat and
cold
are forgotten

the heritage of a nation
is traced upon rails, highway and
shipping lanes
as a vein leads to the heart
back to this place

Carter Norman

© Frank J. Brown

The Big Race, *clay sculpture*

Calling Gadahlski ● JANE HOLLIS

Gadahlski refers to the garage door of the house I grew up in. The house was a modern rambler sitting on a hill in the pristine, well-educated community of St. Anthony Park. My parents, my sister, and I did whatever we could to fit into the mold of "the Park." The house expressed this desire for perfection with its regularly mowed lawn, clipped hedges, and fresh paint. Even the flower and vegetable gardens were neat and orderly.

Gadahlski did not fit the mold. After living in the Park for five years, my father mixed up the most hideous concoction of green and yellow paint imaginable and proceeded to paint the garage door. The color resembled the "pea soup" the actress, Linda Blair, spit at the priest in *The Exorcist*. At ages eight and eleven, my sister and I protested, but my father had the final say. Months went by, and we got used to it. Then he decided to paint the trim on the house with the same color. What was happening to this perfect house, and what would the neighbors think?

In the 1950s garage doors were usually operated manually, meaning someone had to get out of the car and open it. There was always some unpleasant, but barely audible, bickering about who would get out of the car to heave open the heavy door. Barely audible because we couldn't have the neighbors think we didn't always get along.

One morning after church when we arrived home, complete with prayer books and white gloves, my father announced he had purchased a garage door opener. Maybe going to church had created a miracle, since my thrifty father had spent money on a luxury item.

He instructed us that the garage door could only be opened by calling "Gadahlski!" loud enough so that whatever device was hooked up to it would "hear" it and it would open. This led to several months of all four of us opening the car windows and yelling "Gadahlski!" On some occasions, Gadahlski's receptor signals weren't working as well so we'd have to yell as loud as we could, all in unison. If my sister and I had friends in the car, they'd have to join in as well. All the voice power was needed.

As time went on, I noticed my mother wasn't really putting much energy into yelling Gadahlski. Then I saw it, the mechanical device my father used inside the car to open the garage door. We'd been had! We'd been sticking our heads out the window and yelling Gadahlski so loud all the neighbors could hear.

Over the years, my father always kept a ready supply of that green paint on hand. When my daughter was three, she and her grandfather made two birdhouses together; one they painted a Gadahlski green and one a soft bluebird color. For some reason, the birds preferred the Gadahlski green house and it helped raise many families over the years. It was worn and battered from use while the blue house remained almost perfectly intact.

Maybe, like my dad, the birds wanted to have a little fun with raising a family and not have to care, at least sometimes, about what others thought. I didn't bother to keep the blue birdhouse, but I still have the old green one in a storage locker. I like it; it reminds me of calling Gadahlski! ●

© William Birawer/WilliamBirawer.com

MARCH 2014

S	M	T	W	T	F	S
						1
2	3	4	5	6	7	8
9	10	11	12	13	14	15
16	17	18	19	20	21	22
23	24	25	26	27	28	29
30	31					

Charles Rauch opened the Apollo Hall in 1852. It was Saint Paul's first restaurant and was located on Third Street near Wabasha.

MONDAY

3

TUESDAY

4

Mardi Gras

WEDNESDAY

5

Ash Wednesday

Houston Branch, prolific screenwriter, was born today in 1899.

THURSDAY

6

Marion A. Carpenter—first woman national press photographer to cover Washington, D.C., and the White House—was born today in 1920.

FRIDAY

7

SATURDAY

8

International Women's Day

SUNDAY

9

Daylight Saving Time Begins

This Week's Events

Monday
Winter Flower Show

Tuesday
Winter Flower Show
Minnesota Opera

Wednesday
Winter Flower Show
MSHSL Boys Hockey Tournament

Thursday
Winter Flower Show
Minnesota Opera
MSHSL Boys Hockey Tournament
Saint Paul Almanac Soul Sounds
Open Mic

Friday
Winter Flower Show
MSHSL Boys Hockey Tournament
Let's Play Hockey Expo

Saturday
Winter Flower Show
Downtown Saint Paul Winter
Farmers' Market

Minnesota Opera
MSHSL Boys Hockey
Tournament
Let's Play Hockey Expo
Minnesota RollerGirls
The Saint Paul Chamber
Orchestra

Sunday
Winter Flower Show
Minnesota Opera

▶ "Peace is the burden of
the prayer with which every
service in the synagogue
concludes. . . . The Jew
who is true to himself will
labor with special energy
in the cause of peace."

W. GUNTHER PLAUT,
Saint Paul rabbi and writer

© Joseph L Schufman

Booker Taliaferro Washington and Me ● PATRICIA YOUNG

As founder and president of Tuskegee Normal and Industrial Institute (now Tuskegee University), Booker T. Washington valued education and instilled in his students of African heritage values of hard work, creativity, and entrepreneurship. These values have touched my family members and me throughout our family's history.

Booker Taliaferro Washington, born in approximately 1856, was enslaved in Virginia on a plantation. The young Booker yearned to learn to read and to serve. After slavery was abolished, Washington went to school and became an educator. In 1881, as the principal of Tuskegee Normal and Industrial Institute in Alabama, he transformed the campus from a rundown building to an educational institution offering thirty-eight trades. His first book, *Up From Slavery*, tells his story and is highly acknowledged today. Washington also authored thirteen other books.

In addition to being an author and educator, Washington founded the National Negro Business League. He contended that through hard work and owning businesses in agriculture, bricklaying, carpentry, and design, Americans of African heritage would become financially independent and empowered, yielding "indispensable" members of society.

My great-grandfather Harry taught my grandfather George to persevere and to walk in Mr. Washington's footprints. Like Washington, my great-grandfather had been born a slave; he was sold twice. Due to his father's encouragement and expectations, Grandpa George attained a college education and became a teacher of young male students, training them in trades and industry skills. He also built a school and designed homes. I wish I had learned to design his unusual topiaries.

Grandpa George's wife—my grandmother, Ethel—desired to attend Tuskegee and applied. She received a letter of acceptance that Principal Washington had signed. My grandmother Ethel, however, changed her plans and decided to attend a college in Arkansas. After graduation, she became an elementary school teacher.

Grandmother Ethel's daughter—my mother, Lois Anita—graduated from Tuskegee in 1949. Afterward, she moved to Saint Paul, Minnesota, where she married James, my father: They're still married today, fifty-eight years later.

My mom used our family's values and work ethic as a registered nurse, evening supervisor, and director of health education for twenty-five years at the original Children's Hospital of Saint Paul that was located at 311 Pleasant Avenue. She continued her education, after retiring and raising four civically engaged children. In 1973 my mom became the first African American graduate of Metropolitan State University. In addition, she has published articles about healthcare and has founded L'Nita Designs, creating beautiful jewelry.

Our home library always held books of prized authors, many obtained from Tuskegee when Mom was a student. I read the works of Benjamin Franklin, Victor Frankl, Richard Wright, Louisa May Alcott, Lorraine Hansberry, and Booker T. Washington, among others. Reading opened doors to a new world for me.

On April 29, 1969, when I was seventeen years old, I stood in the Oval Office of the White House, with the late President Richard Milhous Nixon. I felt as if I were standing in Mr. Washington's footsteps, because in 1901, President Theodore Roosevelt invited him to the White House. Mr. Washington became the first African American to have this honor. In a similar light, I was the first of two high school seniors to represent Junior Achievement at the White House. As we stood in the Oval Office, President Nixon said to me, "I congratulate you on your good management. Now come on down here and fix up our budget."

© Harris & Ewing/Library of Congress

After graduating high school, I attended a technical college and earned a degree in accounting. Subsequently, I found employment, using my business skills. Booker T. Washington's values were woven into the backbones of my great-grandfather, grandfather, grandmother, and mother, and then passed down to me. ●

Booker T. Washington

MARCH 2014

S	M	T	W	T	F	S
						1
2	3	4	5	6	7	8
9	10	11	12	13	14	15
16	17	18	19	20	21	22
23	24	25	26	27	28	29
30	31					

The Minnesota Conservation and Agriculture Development Congress opened a three-day meeting in Saint Paul on March 16, 1910.

MONDAY

10

TUESDAY

11

Richard Toensing, award-winner in the field of electronic music composition, was born today in 1940.

WEDNESDAY

12

THURSDAY

13

FRIDAY

14

SATURDAY

15

Marion Cuthbert—African American poet, writer, and leadership educator of women—was born today in 1896.

SUNDAY

Purim

16

This Week's Events

Monday
  Winter Flower Show

Tuesday
  Winter Flower Show
  Seniors in Mind

Wednesday
  Winter Flower Show

Thursday
  Winter Flower Show
  The Saint Paul Chamber Orchestra
  Saint Paul Almanac Soul Sounds
    Open Mic

Friday
  Winter Flower Show
  The Saint Paul Chamber Orchestra

Saturday
  Winter Flower Show
  Downtown Saint Paul Winter
    Farmers' Market
  The Saint Paul Chamber Orchestra
  Saint Patrick's Day Parade

Sunday
  Winter Flower Show
  Irish Day Dance

A Little Rock

A rock on the ground,
next to the rock a tree,
on the tree is a bird,
its feathers like the river,
in the river's a fish,
scales that shine like the moon,
after the moon's the sun,
the sun shines down on the
    ground,
and on the ground,
a little rock.

Anna Musielewicz

> "I believe that art can be used as a vehicle for enlightenment and change. I create art to heal the hearts and souls of people by evoking a positive spirit."
>
> **TA-COUMBA AIKEN**
> *African American artist*

© Patrick McCutchan/PatrickMcCutchan.com

Movie night at the restored Union Depot station

Wafers ● KEVIN HERSHEY

My father and I used to go door-to-door delivering wafers in a tiny gold case. I imagined my father gave me this job to make me feel special when all of the older kids went to school. When they disappeared behind the doors of St. Mark's School with their starched uniforms and shiny pencil cases, I felt left out. As a remedy, my father quickly got me started in the business of delivering communion to neighborhood elders.

When we would enter to collect our goods, our church was always completely vacant. It smelled dank and had dim, yellow light. I remember marveling at the flickering rainbow shapes that settled on my hands, superimposed from the sun that shone through the stained glass. Before he opened the golden cabinet where the blessed wafers waited, my father made sure I bowed at the altar—even though nobody was watching. You never would have known he was not a real baptized Catholic. He played the game so well—sitting, standing, kneeling, flawlessly performing the repertoire of religious gymnastics I knew by heart. I didn't even pause to question his faith until I was in college and I realized that a lot of youth had parents who were not Catholic.

Like our cavernous sanctuary, the old people's homes carried the same aroma—ancient, damp, and stale. Most of the elders were bent over so that I could see only a wispy cloud of white hair where I would expect to see a face. Some lifted their heads to smile at me, to offer me a grainy lollipop or a stale piece of chocolate. Others virtually ignored both my father and me, concentrating purely on the wafer in its gold case. Chewing the wafer with calculated intention, each of them closed their eyes and created a silence that was far too loud for my young racing mind. I often felt tempted to pull a face while their eyes were closed, but a reverent fear of the sacred silence left me petrified. Their old homes seemed as delicate as their old bodies—if I made more than a whisper, their teetering stacks of old *National Geographic*s might collapse upon me.

One woman I never saw. Leaving me outside, my father would disappear into her crumbling white bungalow saying, "Trudi's had a hard life." Nothing more. I waited on Trudi's lawn, running my fingers over the points of her wrought-iron fence. My imagination conjured the truly grotesque: her body bloody and beaten like that in the images of the tortured Christ that lined our church. My father always left Trudi's house in a deferential silence, one that told me not to ask questions. He never told me what was wrong with her. He also never told me he wasn't Catholic, but he entered the pew each Sunday with the same deferential silence.

Soon, I no longer needed to be the deliverer of Christ's body to feel special. School pushed the walls of my universe far beyond the deteriorating plaster that made up our church and those old folks' houses. The church became just another old building, the wafer just another flavorless snack, and the time with my father just another chore.

Years later, I came back from college an openly gay man. Then my father's walks around the neighborhood to deliver the Eucharist came to an end. I asked him why. "I cannot be part of a church that doesn't love my son," he responded. More of the same silence—his Trudi silence, his church silence, his father-son silence.

On breaks home from school, I entered the church alone, at odd hours of the day to ensure my solitude. The ancient smell remained, and the windows still cast multicolored patterns onto my hands. I would light a candle and sit for a while in the very back pew, far from the altar where my father and I used to bow. Now, life was full of things to make me feel special, and the church no longer filled that void. I made solitary visits to sit in a place where I felt insignificant. The same deteriorating bricks, the same staring saints—they had not noticed me leave.

© Bianca Pettis

After 52.6% of Minnesota voters rejected a constitutional amendment to ban same-sex marriage in November 2012, the Minnesota Legislature passed a same-sex marriage bill in May 2013, which Governor Mark Dayton signed on May 14. Same-sex marriage became legal in Minnesota on August 1, 2013.

MARCH 2014

S	M	T	W	T	F	S
						1
2	3	4	5	6	7	8
9	10	11	12	13	14	15
16	17	18	19	20	21	22
23	24	25	26	27	28	29
30	31					

The Minnesota Farm Holiday Association marched through Saint Paul and to the Capitol on March 22 of 1933 to protest agricultural conditions in the state.

MONDAY

17

Purim

St. Patrick's Day

TUESDAY

18

William "Bill" B. Lava, musical composer and arranger in the classic era of Warner Brothers, was born today in 1911.

WEDNESDAY

19

THURSDAY

20

Spring Equinox

FRIDAY

21

George Wagner, Saint Paul owner of the Wagner Motorcycle Company in business from 1901 to 1914, was born today in 1865.

SATURDAY

22

SUNDAY

23

This Week's Events

Monday
Irish Celebration/St. Patrick's Day

Tuesday

Wednesday

Thursday
Big Ten Hockey Championship
Saint Paul Almanac Soul Sounds
   Open Mic

Friday
Big Ten Hockey Championship
AXIS Dance Company
The Saint Paul Chamber Orchestra

Saturday
Downtown Saint Paul Winter
   Farmers' Market
Big Ten Hockey Championship
The Saint Paul Chamber Orchestra
Spring Flower Show

Sunday
Spring Flower Show

> "I am interested in class in general and in the things that happen when you approach all kinds of boundaries: class, gender, race, etc. When you mix two usually unmixable things, you're bound to get something interesting."
>
> DAVID HAYNES
> *African American writer and teacher*

© Tom McGregor/mcgregorart.com

Working Late

Bald-headed Men and Sundays ● ETHNA MCKIERNAN

Comments on Saint Paul by my kids at nine and ten years old

My boys viewed their mid-1980s births
in the old Midway Hospital on University
between Porky's and Ax-Man
as an embarrassment, a slight
their Saint Paul mom had designed to punish them
by withholding the polished corridors
of HCMC in their own hometown.

"It's just something when we cross the Lake Street Bridge
that reminds us of church, makes us think of those
bald guys, the old ones. It's not personal, Mom."

Never having lived in that city of noble elms
with doomed shoulders arced over Summit Avenue,
or known the pine magic tang of Crosby Park
at night on cross country skis
or visited their mother's frayed, grand house on Osceola,
they simply lacked fuel for comparison.

Their domain was Minneapolis,
the jazzy skate parks,
glitz of Holidazzle each December,
Sunday forays onto 8th and Hennepin
for Magic cards at Shinder's after church,
that cherry in a giant spoon they longed to climb
in Walker Sculpture Park.

What did they know of meandering streets
named not for numbers but for places
and for people? Of the majesty of that Cathedral,
heady slopes of Ramsey Hill or west side cliffs,
the white tinsel-glitter of the Winter Carnival?
How could they imagine the train yards off of Shepard Road,
where their mother in her youth ditched the railroad cops
to hop a few freights west to California?

When they'd forgotten their Ax-Man treasures,
home to everything you never knew
you couldn't live without,
I quelled the urge
to pull them backward to when
they were young and ignorant
of the rivalry between two cities;
when snow fell deep and their requests each night
were for more words from Peter Rabbit.

© Bianca Pettis

© Tony Ernst/gamelaner on Flickr

*Entering the Ax-Man Surplus store, on the corner of University Avenue and
North Fry Street, after which things do get weirder. Inset: Exhibit A*

MARCH 2014

S	M	T	W	T	F	S
						1
2	3	4	5	6	7	8
9	10	11	12	13	14	15
16	17	18	19	20	21	22
23	24	25	26	27	28	29
30	31					

On March 25, 1888, the Saint Paul *Globe* started publishing a series of articles by Eva McDonald Valesh (aka "Eva Gay") that revealed working women's lives in the Twin Cities.

MONDAY

24

Arnellia Allen—African American owner of Arnellia's Bar, a longtime blues and soul food venue—was born today in 1938.

TUESDAY

25

WEDNESDAY

26

THURSDAY

27

FRIDAY

28

Catherine Piccolo, WAC leader during WWII and Saint Paul school-board member, was born today in 1916.

SATURDAY

29

SUNDAY

30

This Week's Events

Monday
Spring Flower Show

Tuesday
Spring Flower Show
The Gershwins' Porgy and Bess

Wednesday
Spring Flower Show
The Gershwins' Porgy and Bess
Saint Paul Almanac Lowertown
Reading Jam

Thursday
Spring Flower Show
The Gershwins' Porgy and Bess
Saint Paul Almanac Soul Sounds
Open Mic

Friday
Spring Flower Show
The Gershwins' Porgy and Bess
The Saint Paul Chamber Orchestra
Donnie Smith Bike Show
Fourth Friday at the Movies

Saturday
Downtown Saint Paul
Winter Farmers' Market
Spring Flower Show
The Gershwins' Porgy and Bess
Donnie Smith Bike Show
2014 NCAA Men's Ice Hockey
West Regional

Sunday
Spring Flower Show
The Gershwins' Porgy and Bess
The Saint Paul Chamber
Orchestra
Donnie Smith Bike Show
2014 NCAA Men's Ice Hockey
West Regional

The twenty-fifth annual Philippines Day, featuring food and music, was held in Saint Paul's Landmark Center on March 25, 2012.

Light rail construction workers are working to bring us together.

A Stranger's Opinion of St. Paul ● HARRIET E. BISHOP

Harriet E. Bishop is a name familiar to anyone interested in the history of Saint Paul. Born in Vermont, Bishop came to Minnesota in 1847 and here achieved many firsts—Saint Paul's first teacher, founder of the first Sunday school in Minnesota, first leader of the women's suffrage movement, and a driving force behind several social movements. She was well known in the city's literary circles[1] and wrote about Minnesota and Saint Paul, though her writings often include language that today would be considered racist, revealing attitudes toward Native Americans common to the era but whose effects are still felt to this day. In this chapter from *Floral Home; or, First Years of Minnesota* (1857), Bishop quotes letters from visitors to Saint Paul as "witnesses" to the virtues and potential of her beloved city.

* * *

The language of the interested citizens of St. Paul, respecting their young and thriving city, is universally the same, and might be regarded as a "one-sided view." We therefore choose, as far as possible, to allow *disinterested* persons to speak, that in the "mouth of two or three witnesses" the truth may be established in the mind of the reader. We subjoin a letter from a gentleman, making a second visit here, bearing date—

JUNE 28, 1856.
"St. Paul has advanced very considerably for twelve months past, more so, perhaps, than any place I have visited. Not that its population has increased very materially or in a greater ratio than many other cities of the West. Its advance has been one more of wealth, enterprise and energy, than of population. The question, 'Will St. Paul be a large city?' appears to have been solved, and that in the affirmative, since my last visit; and there is little or no croaking regarding the 'crash' that people all around had predicted would overwhelm it sooner or later. The fact is, its position as a great commercial center of Minnesota—as a grand center for the territory, North and West—is now fairly and irrevocably established, and St. Paul cannot fail to become a large and populous city.

---

1. Norma Sommerdorf, "Harriet E. Bishop: A Doer and a Mover," *Minnesota History Magazine*, vol. 55:7 (1997): pp. 320–23. http://collections.mnhs.org/MNHistoryMagazine/articles/55/v55i07p320-323.pdf.

Those whose fortunes are locked up in her 'corner lots,' now feel safe; they talk, act and walk with a firm, don't-care-gait, and rattle the loose change in their pockets as if they 'dined on ducats.' Her merchants also feel satisfied; ask prices with a 'stiff upper lip;' despatch a customer without worshiping him, and drive fast horses after business hours, that will vie with any city in the Union. St. Paul is comparatively an infant city, with a population of probably ten thousand souls; but here, 'every man counts.' Here men are picked, not from the fossilized haunts of old fogyism, but from the swiftest blood of the nation. Every man here, to use a western expression, 'is a steamboat,' and is determined to make his mark in the history of Minnesota.

"One thing is sure to attract the attention of eastern men on their first visit to St. Paul. They come expecting to find a new, unshaped city, with a rude, rough and unrefined people; but they find a much higher degree of elegance, fashion and display, than in any other city of its size in the world. It is decidedly fast in its character. The ladies revel in finest silks and satins; the gents carry gold-headed canes, keep splendid driving establishments, and there is a much larger display of finery and jewelry than is consistent with a modest taste. All this, however, is indicative of success. It requires prosperity to keep up such luxuries; and although extravagance may be indulged in to an extent not commendable, still, as the city settles down, these matters will regulate themselves.

"There are a large number of new buildings in course of erection all over the city; some of a most permanent and costly character. Several large ware-

Engraver: John Chester Buttre, 1860, courtesy Minnesota Historical Society

Harriet E. Bishop

houses are building; some of stone, others of brick, on a scale of magnitude known only in the West.

"The new hotel, one of the largest out of New York, to be kept by Messrs. Long & Brother, well known as the first landlords in the Territory, will be equal to the best in the United States.

"The progress of St. Paul has not been only material. In all that pertains to intellectual and spiritual advancement, there is a healthy action kept up by the people. Schools and churches are well and willingly supported, and societies, both literary and benevolent, are kept up with spirit and zeal.

"A bridge is about to be built across the Mississippi at this point.

"The bluffs all around the city are now being thickly dotted with splendid residences; and if things progress as they have, during the past year, it will not be many years before St. Paul casts in the shade some of the older eastern cities of wealth and importance."

Another writer from the "Great West," thus discourses with an eastern editor:

"It is a strange medley, indeed, that which you meet aboard a Mississippi steamer. An Australian gold-hunter, just returned by way of England, from Melbourne; a merchant on a trip of pleasure; a professor in an eastern University, going out to invest in Minnesota; a St. Croix raftsman, returning from a trip down river, with a small fortune of logs; a New York doctor, with a pocket full of land warrants; an eastern man, who administers electrochemical baths; a South Carolina boy, with one thousand dollars and a knowledge of double-entry; a sturdy frontier man, with a saw mill for the interior; an engineer, who escaped the Panama fever on the Isthmus railroad; a Yankee schoolmaster, who has become a small speculator in oats; and scores of others of doubtful character, who sport heavy moustaches, and keep their mouths shut. Verily, a strange medley do you find aboard a Mississippi steamer!

"Now, half wearied by observation, you sit listlessly in the front gallery of the great steamer, watching the golden clouds piling themselves high towards the zenith, in preparation for a regal sunset. Presently the crowd thickens about you, the knowing ones are on the alert, and all catch the spirit. You turn to your next neighbor and ask him the cause of excitement. He glances at the shore and replies, 'St. Paul's just round the next curve.' The boat presses nobly against the current, and you feel yourself swinging around towards the west. The ladies have come from their cabin to the forward deck, books are laid aside, Fremont and Buchanan are forgotten, conversation flags, and all eyes are strained towards one point. Another turn of the wheel, we shoot from behind the forest, and the miraculous city bursts into view. First, an amphitheater-like basin, benched with ephemeral houses and a huge steam-mill puffing in the mid arena. Then the high bluff, crowded with more substantial tenements of brick or stone, from among which spires and cupolas of churches and public buildings rise with sharp outlines against the orange clouds. Coaches from the different hotels, warned by our whistle, already cluster around the plank. Runners from different establishments show a commendable zeal in skimming the cards of their respective establishments. 'Winslow House!' 'Snelling House!' 'Merchant's!' 'American!' 'Fuller House!' are shouted from the coaches. One by one the vehicles are filled and rolled away; the freight of stoves, groceries, grain and machinery, is being carried ashore, when we press our way through the crowd, and seek a private boarding-house high up the bluff. . . .

"The history of the town is brief, and no where out of the Great West can we find an analogous instance of prosperity. Eight years ago, had we come up the river as we have done to-day, and swept in against the unimproved levee, quite a different scene would have been spread before us. Then high on the bluff a half dozen huts environed the diminutive Catholic Chapel, and had the whole town turned out to meet us we would not have seen over one hundred and fifty people. Even at that time a small irregular town plot had been staked out, but no one, not even the projectors of the village, had yet, in imagination or judgment, penetrated the teeming future of their infant settlement. . . .

"When on the 3d of March, 1849, Congress organized the territory, and by an organic act constituted St. Paul the capital of the inchoate state, then were the people's eyes anointed, then they saw a second Chicago springing up on the forest-covered bluff, and property at a single leap went up two hundred per cent. Addition followed addition, quarter section after quarter section was cut into building lots, until the city plan reached its present limits. Each addition was laid off according to the caprice of the owner, and such was the variety of tastes that the finished plot of St. Paul has much of the irregularity of a European metropolis.

"From the date of the organic act immigrants flocked into the

new capital in great numbers. They came chiefly from the Northern States. Maine has a great many hardy men, reared among the pineries of the Penobscot and Kennebec, and perhaps is the most numerously represented of any of the States." . . .

In 1850 only seven [steam]boats were engaged in the trade, in 1856 there were seventy-nine. . . . The average annual increase of the number of boats for the last 12 years, is thirty-six per cent. An increase for the next four years of only twenty per cent will make the number of arrivals in 1860 nearly 1,600. Think of this, you, who have doubts as to what St. Paul is, and what it will be! ●

The modern-day equivalent: New Orleans's Mississippi Queen *visits Saint Paul.*
© Tom Reynen/tom-reynen.artistwebsites.com

Opposite: Steamboats at Saint Paul Levee, 1880
Photo courtesy Minnesota Historical Society

City Trees, Coffee Shop, Spring ● NORITA DITTBERNER-JAX

Some days trees are all I see.
Today they're getting fringed in leaves
at the crown. Underneath
there's a huge ball of root
that nobody sees except my son
as a five-year-old who drew one
exactly as a botanist might,
side view, x-ray vision.

Nobody talks about trees over cappuccino
outside the coffee shop. Friends
laugh over Friday night's game.
A jogger passes me; a car horn shrieks.
Nothing terrible happens—no stray
bullet, no pedestrian death.

A perfect morning, traffic rolling
toward the freeway, old city trees
dressing up for spring.

Nina's Coffee Café
© Ken Avidor/AvidorStudios.com

			APRIL 2014			
S	M	T	W	T	F	S
		1	2	3	4	5
6	7	8	9	10	11	12
13	14	15	16	17	18	19
20	21	22	23	24	25	26
27	28	29	30			

The statue of Germania was removed from Saint Paul's Germania Insurance Building on April 1, 1918, because of a wave of anti-German feeling during WWI.

MONDAY

MARCH

31

TUESDAY

April Fools' Day

1

WEDNESDAY

2

THURSDAY

3

Lloyd Lewis Brown—novelist, short-fiction writer, journalist, and labor organizer—was born today in 1913.

FRIDAY

4

SATURDAY

5

Dr. Frederic Eugene Basil Foley, a urologist who invented the Foley catheter and other medical devices, was born today in 1891.

SUNDAY

6

This Week's Events

Monday
Spring Flower Show
Spring Break K—12

Tuesday
Spring Flower Show
Spring Break K—12

Wednesday
Spring Flower Show
Spring Break K—12

Thursday
Spring Flower Show
Spring Break K—12
Saint Paul Almanac Soul Sounds
Open Mic
The Saint Paul Chamber Orchestra

Friday
Spring Flower Show
Spring Break K—12
The Saint Paul Chamber Orchestra

Saturday
Spring Flower Show
Downtown Saint Paul Farmers'
Market

The Saint Paul Chamber
Orchestra
Minnesota RollerGirls
27th Minnesota Book
Awards

Sunday
Spring Flower Show
Downtown Saint Paul
Farmers' Market

"Anyone can become an inventor as long as they keep an open and inquiring mind and never overlook the possible significance of an accident or apparent failure."

PATSY SHERMAN
3M chemist, inventor of Scotchgard

© Ken Friberg/RatRaceStudios.com

The Saint Paul Farmers' Market earlier in the season

What Saint Paul Owes to Whiskey

● CYNTHIA SCHREINER SMITH

During an 1883 visit to Saint Paul, the great Mark Twain observed: "How solemn and beautiful is the thought, that the earliest pioneer of civilization, the van-leader of civilization, is never the steamboat, never the railroad, never the newspaper, never the Sabbath-school, never the missionary—but always whiskey! Such is the case."[1]

Mr. Twain was right. Such is the case with Saint Paul, which grew up around a wild and wooly little tavern known as "Pig's Eye Pandemonium." The tavern keeper was Pierre "Pig's Eye" Parrant, a cantankerous old French Canadian fur trader of dubious morals and character whose favorite hobby seemed to be keeping the soldiers at Fort Snelling as drunk as possible. Parrant had one squinty, blind eye surrounded by a pinkish color giving "a piggish expression to his sodden, low features."[2] So they took to calling him Pig's Eye. Parrant and other squatters had been living within Fort Snelling, but the commander, Major Joseph Plympton, got so fed up with this motley bunch that he kicked them out—twice. The second time, Plympton burned their houses down just to demonstrate he was serious. Undeterred, Pig's Eye set up his whiskey still just outside the fort on the banks of the Mississippi in what is now the Lowertown area of Saint Paul.

In 1837 the whiskey bottles were uncorked in Pig's Eye Pandemonium, and the wild little town that would become the city of Saint Paul was accidentally born. Since the town had not actually been planned, no one bothered to name it. But Pierre Parrant was very infamous up and down the mighty Mississippi, and the town soon became known as "Pig's Eye Landing." A few years later, Father Lucien Galtier came to town to build its first church. In his dedication speech, he implored the young city to change its colorful but dubious moniker. And so the town was renamed in honor of a more respectable establishment, Father Galtier's church, Saint Paul the Apostle. James Goodhue, Saint Paul's first newspaper editor, declared: "Pig's Eye, converted thou shalt be like Saul; Arise and

---

1.   Mark Twain, *Life on the Mississippi* (James R. Osgood & Co., 1883).

2.   J. Fletcher Williams, *A History of the City of Saint Paul, and of the County of Ramsey, Minnesota* (The Society, 1876).

henceforth, St. Paul."[3]
Perhaps Mr. Goodhue
was relieved he didn't
have to name his news-
paper the *Pig's Eye Pio-
neer Press.*

As Mr. Twain stated,
Saint Paul was founded
on the power of whiskey,
but its status as political
center was nearly lost
until once again, whis-
key and a wily French-
man came into the pic-
ture. Saint Paul had been
the capital of the terri-
tory, but some wanted

Father Lucien Galtier, circa 1855

it moved elsewhere when Minnesota became a state. Territorial
Governor Willis Gorman especially hated Saint Paul due to political
disagreements and a bit of greed. He was determined to make the
capital St. Peter, where he happened to own a lot of land. Governor
Gorman nearly got his way.

In 1857 the territorial legislature passed a bill making St. Peter
the new capital. But the governor had not counted on Representa-
tive "Jolly" Joe Rolette, another colorful French fur trader who happened to love Saint Paul. And he also happened to be the lawmaker
in charge of bringing that bill to the governor to sign. Instead, Jolly
Joe and the bill disappeared. Legend says Joe snuck into a local hotel
where he partied for days eating fine foods and getting rip-roaring
drunk. By the time he emerged, the legislative session was over and
it was too late for the governor to sign the bill. Not wanting to wait
two more years for the next session, Minnesota accepted statehood
in 1858 and Saint Paul became the capital by default.

So the next time you're in Saint Paul enjoying a fine drink, raise a
toast to two colorful Frenchmen and the power of whiskey. ●

---

3. James Goodhue, "New Year's Eve address," *The Pioneer* (January 1,
1850).

APRIL 2014

S	M	T	W	T	F	S
		1	2	3	4	5
6	7	8	9	10	11	12
13	14	15	16	17	18	19
20	21	22	23	24	25	26
27	28	29	30			

Nine nurses, graduates of Mounds Park Sanitarium in Saint Paul, received their diplomas at the First Swedish Baptist Church at Sims and Payne on April 12, 1912.

MONDAY

7

TUESDAY

8

Lawrence Perlman, Saint Paul attorney and businessman, was born today in 1938.

WEDNESDAY

9

THURSDAY

10

FRIDAY

11

SATURDAY

12

Seong Moy, Chinese American artist who lived in Saint Paul, was born today in 1921.

SUNDAY

13

Palm Sunday

Dr. Cherzong V. Vang (Thajkhu Vaj Txiab), educator and longtime president of the Lao Veterans of America, was born today in 1943.

This Week's Events

Monday
Spring Flower Show

Tuesday
Spring Flower Show

Wednesday
Spring Flower Show

Thursday
Spring Flower Show
Saint Paul Almanac Soul Sounds
Open Mic
Cocktails with Culture

Friday
Spring Flower Show
American Craft Council Saint Paul
Show

Saturday
Spring Flower Show
Downtown Saint Paul Farmers'
Market
American Craft Council Saint Paul
Show
Asian Pacific Heritage Day

The Saint Paul Chamber
Orchestra
Minnesota Opera

Sunday
Spring Flower Show
Downtown Saint Paul
Farmers' Market
American Craft Council
Saint Paul Show
Minnesota Opera
Urban Expedition: Senegal

> "I decided to take a walk into Frogtown. . . . I turned the corner and was struck by the sight of a mélange of families, all on the same block—Asian, black, and white—enjoying the day. . . . It was intoxicating to witness such an exotic mix."
>
> WING YOUNG HUIE, *photographer*

© Stefanie Berres/StefanieBerres.com

The beautiful Mississippi

My Name Is Hmoob:
Call Me Freedom ● JONATHAN SIAB YAWG

My name is not "Exotic . . ."
My name is Freedom
My people are worth more than eye
candy and shallow praise,
My people have no home, no country
We are from stolen territory
We are now sojourners in foreign lands
But we will not fit in the palm of a hand
To be controlled. We live in resistance
And die in resistance
We are offspring of Genocide,
survivors of imposed assimilations

Our legacy is the blood that streams through my veins,
through large arteries
pumping stories of forgotten people,

Hmong*
Kuv lub npe yog Ani Siab Yawg
(My name is Jonathan Shia Yawg)

Kuv Pog hu kuv Ani vim hais tias kuv yoj Vajtswv tu khoom plig
(My Grandma calls me Jonathan, because I am a "Gift from God")

Kuv yah Shia vim hais tias kuv muaj siab, kuv lub siab siab tshaj
(I am Shia** [heart] because I have life, my heart is the highest)

---

*"Hmong" means free
**"Shia/Siab" means heart, tall or high, life

Lawv hais thia kuv paug hlub
(People say that I know how to love)

. . . Kuv lub peb Shia
(My name is Shia)

. . . Kuv lub peb yog kuv tsev neeg
(My name is my family)

. . . Kuv lub peb yog HMOOB
(My name is Hmong)

© Patience Zalanga

APRIL 2014

S	M	T	W	T	F	S
		1	2	3	4	5
6	7	8	9	10	11	12
13	14	15	16	17	18	19
20	21	22	23	24	25	26
27	28	29	30			

The Woman's Loyal Union and John Brown Industrial Club, an African American improvement association, was formed at the home of Mrs. T. H. Lyles on April 20, 1896.

MONDAY

14

TUESDAY

Passover Begins

15

WEDNESDAY

16

Joseph Burger, Civil War Medal of Honor recipient from Saint Paul, was born today in 1848.

THURSDAY

17

FRIDAY

Good Friday

18

SATURDAY

19

SUNDAY

Easter

20

This Week's Events

Monday
Spring Flower Show
American Craft Council Saint Paul
  Show

Tuesday
Spring Flower Show
Minnesota Opera

Wednesday
Spring Flower Show

Thursday
Spring Flower Show
Saint Paul Almanac Soul Sounds
  Open Mic
Minnesota Opera

Friday
Spring Flower Show

Saturday
Spring Flower Show
Downtown Saint Paul Farmers'
  Market
Minnesota Opera
Minnesota RollerGirls

Sunday
Spring Flower Show
Downtown Saint Paul
  Farmers' Market

Untitled

It's spring! DerFrühling! Printemps!
Ring bells! Play the sackbut and
  shawm!
Excel. Rise and shine.
Do something so fine
It will please and astonish your
  mom.

Garrison Keillor

© Mike Hazard/thecie.org

Dylan, Yeepeng, and Mason share a toy at the Saint Paul Farmers' Market.

A 1968 photo of Dorothy Day from the Milwaukee Journal
Courtesy of the Marquette University Archives

Remembering Dorothy Day ● MONTE HANSON

Dorothy Day and I go way back.

Granted, I never met her, but I can't help but feel a connection after volunteering every third Saturday for the past twenty years at the Dorothy Day Center in downtown Saint Paul. I first went there on a lark, something to try once because I had just moved to the Twin Cities and wanted to meet new people. I never got around to stopping.

The Dorothy Day Center is a refuge in the city, a place where people can get hot meals, shelter, mental health services, and medical care. I work with a team from Immanuel Lutheran Church in Saint Paul that prepares the noon meal. Our menu never varies. Every third Saturday, we serve sloppy joes, beans and franks, hard-boiled eggs, cookies, bananas, and milk.

We typically attract 250 to 300 people, mostly men but some women and occasionally even children. Many are unemployed and homeless; others have mental or physical challenges. I've talked with people who live under bridges or camp among clumps of trees along the interstate.

They may be wearing hand-me-downs or pushing their belongings in shopping carts, but they never lose their sense of dignity. They want to be treated with respect and courtesy, just like anybody else. Dorothy Day would have expected no less.

But who exactly was Dorothy Day? Turns out, she doesn't have much to do with Saint Paul and probably never set foot here.

Dorothy Day was a rabble-rouser. Born in Brooklyn in 1897, she was a critic of capitalism and a lifelong pacifist who opposed U.S. involvement in World War II. She cofounded the Catholic Worker Movement, which was committed to nonviolence, prayer, and serving the poor. She believed in civil disobedience and was jailed many times. Critics labeled her an anarchist and socialist; she called herself a "Christian personalist."

Above all, Dorothy Day believed in the teachings of scripture and took a vow of poverty that she believed bound her to the poor, homeless, sick, and desperate.

She was a fierce woman who could be intimidating and stubborn at times. I know a woman who worked with Dorothy Day in New York back in the 1960s and said she was deathly afraid of her. Another volunteer who worked with Day described her as a tall woman who looked as if she had been carved with an axe.

You wouldn't disagree with that description if you saw the giant black-and-white portrait of her that overlooks the lunchroom at the Dorothy Day Center in Saint Paul. She has a stern, no-nonsense look that seems to be saying, "Eat your peas or I'll box your ears." Her face would be right at home on Mount Rushmore.

She made plenty of enemies during her remarkable life, but she accomplished much and never let anyone get in the way of her goals. She was a champion of the poor and wasn't afraid to fight for them. We could use a few more Dorothy Days today. •

APRIL 2014

S	M	T	W	T	F	S
		1	2	3	4	5
6	7	8	9	10	11	12
13	14	15	16	17	18	19
20	21	22	23	24	25	26
27	28	29	30			

On April 25, 2012, the St. Anthony Park Community Band began its thirtieth year of playing in the Saint Paul neighborhood with a spring concert.

MONDAY

21

TUESDAY

22

Earth Day

WEDNESDAY

23

Jimmy "The Kid" Wetch of Humboldt High School, a successful professional pool player, was born today in 1968.

THURSDAY

24

FRIDAY

25

Robert Edward Dill, a Saint Paul member of the U.S. Hockey Hall of Fame, was born today in 1920.

SATURDAY

26

SUNDAY

27

This Week's Events

Monday
Spring Flower Show

Tuesday
Spring Flower Show

Wednesday
Spring Flower Show
Saint Paul Almanac Lowertown
Reading Jam

Thursday
Spring Flower Show
Saint Paul Almanac Soul Sounds
Open Mic
The Saint Paul Chamber Orchestra

Friday
Spring Flower Show
The Saint Paul Chamber Orchestra
Saint Paul Art Crawl
Fourth Friday at the Movies

Saturday
Spring Flower Show
Downtown Saint Paul
Farmers' Market
The Saint Paul Chamber
Orchestra
Saint Paul Art Crawl

Sunday
Spring Flower Show
Downtown Saint Paul
Farmers' Market
Saint Paul Art Crawl
Rose Ensemble Concert

> "Many people consider the things the government does for them to be social progress, but they regard the things government does for others as socialism."
>
> WARREN BURGER
> *U.S. Supreme Court justice*

© Amber Michel/AAphotographyinMN.com

Buskers at the Spring Saint Paul Art Crawl

College Entrance Essay ● JESUS VEGA

During my twenty years of living I have made some really good and really bad choices. The worst choice I made was getting involved in gangs and drugs, which led to my unwilling trip to Mexico and life-changing events. Being in a gang is like playing chess: Only the king and queen survive, while the rest are and always remain pawns.

A gangster life does not suit my personality in any way, shape, or form. I was born in a small town in Mexico, the size of four football fields, so coming to the United States as a child of migrant workers had a lot of influences on me. I was the oldest and alone in a big world. In seventh grade my only friends were my books and my cousin. I became closer and closer to the "Surenos," a well-known Mexican gang also known as "SUR 13." Walking down the hallway shaking hands and throwing gang signs up like fireworks on the Fourth of July made me feel popular, and made me feel protected. I was young and stupid back then, getting into fights for a simple word or the difference between black and blue. Now I realize it wasn't me fighting—it was my so-called friends pushing me to the bathroom, grabbing my arm, and punching their enemies.

The fight—the fight that broke my nose—was when I realized I was in someone else's shoes. It was too late; I was already dancing in the small, crowded, stinky bathroom. As I was pounding his face and busting his lip open I stopped, and everything froze. A voice deep inside my head told me, "What the hell am I doing here?" This was not me. My rival got smart and took advantage of those few seconds, cracking my nose and filling the bathroom floor with blood. Getting home and seeing my mother cry ripped my heart in millions of pieces. She made me see that I was doing wrong, but it was too late. Next thing I know, I'm on flight 412b heading to Mexico.

Sending me to Mexico was the hardest but smartest choice my parents ever made. In those six months I found myself making new friends and forgetting about my old ones in the gang life. I became more confident in myself and away went my mile-long blue belt and with it the old me. Even then when I was over the gang life, my blood still fired up when I saw a rival. I felt the rage of beating him up vibrate under my skin. It's not easy changing lifestyles—you need patience and you need time. After six months I returned to Minnesota and began high school. I was done with the gangster life. The time I spent in Mexico gave me time to think and realize that I had put my family and myself through a lot of pain. Now I'm a new, better, and improved person.

Coming to a new country had blinded me. My new friends and their way of living had closed my windows to the rest of the world, closed the door that led back to my culture. Coming to the U.S.A. knowing barely enough English to ask where the bathroom was, coming from a four-room middle/high school and entering a two-story mile-long middle school, was shocking to me. Having no family member attending school with me, I felt like an ant in the middle of a safari. Adapting was hard for me so I put aside my background, my people, and my poverty. I started hanging out with the other Mexicans in the school, but there was something different in them—something that I did not have. Little did I know it was evolving. They were gangsters, feared and respected in school. My mom always told me not to get involved with those kinds of people. She always reminded me where we had come from and how difficult it was to get here. But I was way past brainwashed; their long blue belts with the shining chrome tip had looped me and dragged me away. You see, that's what gangs do: they go after the new kid in school, the innocent, scared immigrant like me that just arrived. They eat you alive and spit you out into their dangerous world. Going back to Mexico and spending time with my lost loved ones made me truly realize that I did not need to be in a gang to be famous or happy. All I needed was my family and my soul. Spending time in Mexico with my grandma in her small house made of rocks was something special. She was the most important person. She made me realize that I was doing wrong. Even though we're not rich, and we sleep on pillows stuffed with old jeans and tee shirts, people were always visiting her, and she knew everyone in town.

In life you go through challenges, and going through the gangster world was challenging for me. It's not easy to change lifestyles; it takes time and patience. It took me six months to figure out that my weak and fragile side had taken over and sent me down the wrong path. Now when I see a gangster I crack up at their joy of being in a gang. I laugh not because it's funny but because that used to be me, and it's sad to see that more and more kids are joining gangs for any reason they can make up. But as I've gotten older and wiser, I've become a much better person, holding down a job and attending school—getting my life back together. ●

Next page: Illustration © Kirk Anderson/MolotovComics.com

The Day Marvin Gaye Died ● EMMANUEL ORTIZ

Every generation has its historical moments
Of collective grief and disbelief
Moments we forever remember
Exactly where we were when . . .

The deaths of Kennedy, King, Clemente
The space shuttle Challenger explosion
When the planes hit the towers on 9/11

Some of these things I was around for
Some I was not.

But I remember the day Marvin Gaye died
It was the day I saw my father cry.

In 1984
I was halfway to manhood,
Living halfway between Motown
And Michael Jackson's hometown,
I knew nothing of Orwell's Big Brother,
Reaganomics,
Beirut, or the Contras.
My world consisted of playing guns with my brothers
A meager allowance
And the Dallas Cowboys.

I was nine years old—almost 10—
That April Fool's Day.
My father and I seated side by side
On the burgundy brick-patterned couch,
Living room awash
In the electric blue-gray glow of the television
Father and son
Sharing a can of Pepsi
As fathers and sons are wont to do
In the last remnants of a spring Sunday evening
Before it slips away into work and school.

The talking head announces
The shooting of a soul
Singer
By his father in a furious fit
On the day before his forty-fifth birthday.
My own father,
Barely thirty,
Slumps back
As if a bullet has struck him in the chest
Puts his working man's hands
To his music lover's ears
As if by blocking out the messenger's voice
He can make the message come undone.
I watch my father
Watch the newscaster,
Waiting for the whole thing to be called a ruse,
An April Fool's Day prank,
So we can laugh and say
"That was a good one,
They really had us fooled!"

Emmanuel Ortiz performing spoken word at a January 2013 Lowertown Reading Jam

But the punch line never comes
There is no rebuttal.
The newscaster is onto the next story,
And my father's face
Is a Pamplona of tears.

In 1984
Marvin's "Sexual Healing"
May have been my father's soundtrack,
But Michael Jackson's "Thriller" was mine.

More than a decade would pass
Before I'd come to fully understand and appreciate
Marvin's gift for music,
His turbulent life,
Or my father's sense of loss that day
Weeping for a man he never knew
But a soul whose troubles mirrored his own.

So what's a boy to do
When his father cries like a baby
For the crimes of another son's father?

He reaches out his nine-year-old arms
Brushes away the saltwater bulls
Running down his father's face,
Wraps his small arms around his neck
And hugs him until . . .

And should I someday be blessed
With sons of my own
May they never be afraid
To sing like Marvin
Cry like my father
And love
As if eternally nine.

An Interview with Mr. F. Steven Winfield . . . about His Last Baseball Game Played

● KEMET IMHOTEP, "TROUBLED-SOUL19"

I was given a choice . . . at a very early age . . . "GO BY MY RULES . . . OR YOU CAN GET OUT!" I was living with my Aunt Willa Mae Johnson on the "Hill Top" . . . Central and St. Albans in Saint Paul. Mae was born in 1918. I always repeat that because it is so deep in me . . . that I was raised by her . . . and she grew up in that time frame. Wow! She did what she knew . . . and understood . . . to raise me. I drove her crazy. I always had a comeback statement that would usually get me slapped . . . under the table somewhere . . . but I still had to finish the task at hand.

Well, something took over one day, and I was like . . . "I'm out of here." I verbally expressed to Mae that I could no longer go along . . . with the way she conducted . . . her administration toward me. There was no discussion. When Willa Mae yelled . . . that last time, my reply was . . . "When do I start packing?"

As I was packing . . . it felt so good to know I would not have to deal with this _____ anymore! I was entering my junior year of high school, however, . . . all on my own. I was living on the street . . . had used up all my clean undergarments . . . and did not have any money or place to wash. One day I was taking what is called a "sponge bath" in the White Castle on University and Lexington, feeling really low . . . hours passed, 2 p.m. . . . traveled down to the Loft Teen Center and filled up on penny candy, sitting on the corner of Oxford and Carroll Avenue. A grey four-door car pulled up slowly . . . right next to me . . . my head was down, very close to the street gutter entrance . . . I could smell the stench of whatever was down there. I heard a deep, smooth, radio personality voice saying, "What's the matter, man?"

I was like, "What?" I couldn't believe it. "I need some clean draws . . . and socks!" I answered. This voice replied, "Get in." Wow! My angel on Earth. Steve bought me a pack of clean boxers and socks. Then he allowed me to shower at his house so I could go to school . . . clean.

That was my first meeting with Steve Winfield.

Years later I was running errands with Mr. Winfield one day and in bits and pieces, Steve shared with me little . . . tweet versions of what happened on the day he played his last physical baseball game. "What a story!" I said. "Can I share this . . . with the *Saint Paul Almanac*?"

"I don't have a problem with that," he answered.

So here's the conversation that took place. Location: the Golden Thyme Coffee Café, one Thursday lunchtime . . . after eating two very delicious turkey tacos . . . we began.

TROUBLED-SOUL19: Mr. Winfield . . . how did you feel that morning, as soon as you were . . . blessed to open your eyes . . . knowing this was your last day playing the game you always loved?

MR. WINFIELD: Well, it really was not a big deal for me that morning or getting ready for the game. I had already known, or prepared myself for this moment. The year prior, I had made the decision that I would play one more year. Then I would transition to training and instructing.

TROUBLED-SOUL19: I hear you, Steve. However, what force or emotion helped you make the decision to say, "Next year will be my last year playing"?

MR. WINFIELD: It was no emotional situation, nothing like that. My brother and I love and respect the art form called baseball. I feel it should be played at the highest level possible at all times. So I knew it was time for me to transition to the training/instruction side of the art form.

My brother and I grew up on Oxford playground when it was first built in the late '50s, early '60s. We grew up and lived on that playground. I started playing baseball at nine years of age. I always loved the game. David and I were introduced to baseball by our big cousin, Tom Hardy. We used to watch and learn from him. I have played the sport of baseball from the age of nine to my middle fifties at such a high level, never slacking, or taking for granted the people I met, and the wonderful lessons learned, in the time frame. I started coaching at the age of twelve.

TROUBLED-SOUL19: What do you mean, Steve, at the age of twelve . . . weren't you too young to be coaching?

MR. WINFIELD: No! One day our coach didn't show up for whatever reason, I cannot remember, so I just stepped up and got started with practice, and I have been coaching, playing, and instructing since that time.

I feel this baseball skill—love, talent, ability—is a gift God has blessed me with. I can still teach and pass on some good or valuable information that will help anyone who wants to learn to be a better player or coach. I am truly blessed, forty-five years of playing ball, not too many injuries. I can count on one hand how many games I missed. We have good genes (smiling as he spoke).

My last year playing for Liberty-O'Gara's—the bank and bar were longtime sponsors and community institutions—my goal was to get to the State Tournament. And lo and behold, we made it to the State Tournament. What a feeling that gave me, my last season, my last game, I was on cloud nine. However, the team we had to play against was such a good, tough team . . . I like performing at a certain level.

TROUBLED-SOUL19: What do you mean, Steve . . . when you say "certain level"?

MR. WINFIELD: *(Kinda chuckling as he responded . . .)* I was hitting lead-off at fifty-four years old. I hit my last home run at fifty-four years old. I stole my last base at fifty-five years old.

Steve Winfield
Courtesy Steve Winfield

That last game was such a tough team. The last game of my career I got two RBIs. I got a hit. That hit drove in two runs in the championship game. Then it was two outs and I was on deck. One more chance to get back up to hit, knowing that if I was to get back up to bat, I could have drove my teammates into the home plate. Well, it didn't work out that way. The game was over, and we ended up losing that game.

(NOTE TO THE READER: The following moment is what inspired me to do this interview. Before the closing of this not-so-structured interview . . . there was a peaceful silence . . . where words did not have to be shared . . . I'm glad I was able to record this moment . . .)

MR. WINFIELD: After the game, my son and my grandsons were in the stands. My grandsons made their way to the baseball field. They gave me a hug, then they stood by my side.

TROUBLED-SOUL19: Steve, where was your last game played?

MR. WINFIELD: At the Saint Paul Saints stadium.

I expressed to my grandsons, "This was Pa-pa's last game. And I'm leaving this all to you. To play this game at the highest level you can at all times." My grandsons are aspiring baseball-players-to-be. I looked at the tall green wall, the center field number that read "400 feet."

"Grandsons," I told them, "run and touch that wall. I'm leaving that for you to roam. That's your wall now." My grandsons ran and touched the wall and returned to my side. Then we looked at the bases ninety feet apart from one another.

"Grandsons, you see these bases? Start from home plate, and run the bases." They ran the bases, then returned to my side. "Those are your bases now, to maintain, and own. I'm leaving the game as a player. It's up to you both to take the torch and play this game at the highest level you can at all times."

Thank you, Mr. Winfield. However . . . there is more. After his grandsons . . . returned from touching the 400-foot wall . . . and running the bases . . . they all stood there . . . in silence once again. After Steve told me this . . . I was asking myself . . . "What is it I'm feeling . . . or witnessing?"

The passing of the torch . . . from the older generation . . . to the younger . . . generation . . . the way it is . . . to be done. . . . ●

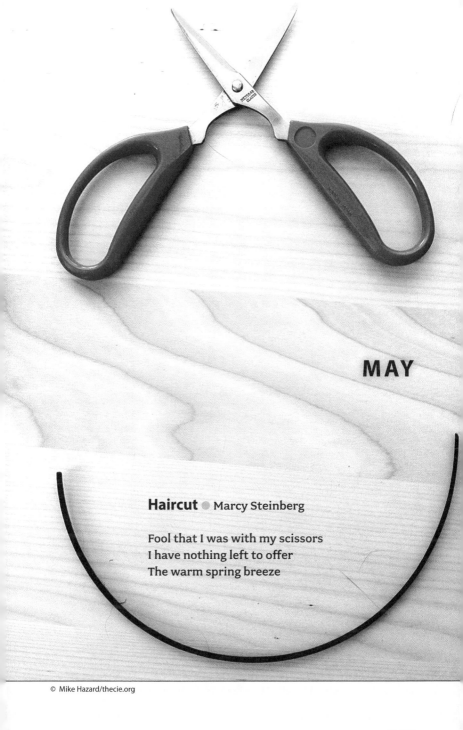

MAY

Haircut ● Marcy Steinberg

Fool that I was with my scissors
I have nothing left to offer
The warm spring breeze

MAY 2014

S	M	T	W	T	F	S
				1	2	3
4	5	6	7	8	9	10
11	12	13	14	15	16	17
18	19	20	21	22	23	24
25	26	27	28	29	30	31

The last passenger train, a west-bound Empire Builder, left Saint Paul's Union Depot on April 30, 1971.

MONDAY

APRIL

28

Pat Donahue—songwriter, champion finger-style guitarist, and Grammy nominee—was born today in 1953.

TUESDAY

APRIL

29

Eleanore Griffin, Oscar-winning screenwriter of the movie *Boy's Town*, was born today in 1904.

WEDNESDAY

APRIL

30

THURSDAY

1

May Day

FRIDAY

2

SATURDAY

3

SUNDAY

4

Theophilus L. Haecker, professor of dairy husbandry and animal nutrition at the U of M Saint Paul campus, was born today in 1846.

This Week's Events

Monday

Tuesday
Blue Man Group

Wednesday
Blue Man Group

Thursday
Saint Paul Almanac Soul Sounds
Open Mic
Blue Man Group

Friday
Blue Man Group
Cinco de Mayo Festival
Festival of Nations

Saturday
Downtown Saint Paul Farmers'
Market
Blue Man Group
Cinco de Mayo Festival
Festival of Nations
The Saint Paul Chamber Orchestra
Summer Flower Show
Summit Avenue Walking Tours

Sunday
Downtown Saint Paul
Farmers' Market
Blue Man Group
Cinco de Mayo Festival
Festival of Nations
Summer Flower Show
Summit Avenue Walking
Tours

> "For other people the work that has come to be called interracial has been a real insight into the most pressing of our present-day social problems, that one of race."
>
> MARION CUTHBERT, *African American educator, YWCA official*

Cinco de Mayo dancers

Frogtown, 1996 ● HOLLY DAY

We had only been living in Saint Paul for a couple of months when my husband told me he'd found somebody else. "Someone from work," he said. "Can I keep my stuff here until I find a new place?"

I put off telling my mom for a couple of weeks, not wanting her and my dad to worry about me and my one-year-old son. When I finally did tell her, I had to repeatedly assure her that my freelance work was actually bringing in enough money to live on, even though it was far from true. "He's still got his stuff here," I told her, thinking that that would put her somehow at ease, knowing he would have to come back and see me at some point. "His office is still set up in the other bedroom."

My mother laughed incredulously. "I can't believe you didn't just put all that crap out on the street," she said. "How about if I come over tonight, fix dinner for the two of you, see what we can do about that spare bedroom?"

She showed up a few hours later with a stack of cardboard boxes in tow. "I say we put his crap in here, and whatever doesn't fit, we put out by the trash," she said. I protested, saying that he would be back to pick his things up in just a couple of days, but she wouldn't have anything to do with it. "If you're paying the rent, you should get to use the whole apartment," she said firmly. "Just think of how much work you'll get done when your desk isn't in the middle of the living room, surrounded by baby toys and laundry?" She was right, of course, and by the end of the evening, all of my ex's things had been stuffed into a teetering pile of cardboard boxes by the front door. She helped me move my desk and computer into my brand-new office, an office with a window that looked out over downtown Saint Paul, the flickering lights of the tiny convenience store across the street blazing perpetually in the foreground. It was a beautiful room, with a beautiful view, and it was mine.

At the end of the week, the landlord showed up for the rent, and I only had half of it. I didn't even have to explain to the gruff old man who always reminded me of Popeye with his Greek fisherman's cap and knobby physique that I was alone now. He just asked me to give him whatever I had on hand and asked if I'd have the rest in a couple of weeks. "I'll have it by Friday," I promised, and I would have it; I had little trickles of money from small jobs coming in, and I had just signed on with a new agent who was directing a bunch of small jobs my way.

The landlord shrugged at my explanations. "Take your time," he said and winked at my infant son crawling around on the rug close behind me. "No rush."

That night, I put my son to bed and went to work until the wee hours of the morning, as I would continue to for years afterward. Every night I spent in that apartment on Thomas Avenue, my infant son snoring peacefully in the other bedroom, I would look out my window at the Saint Paul skyline and think how much I loved being there. Of all the places I'd ever lived, I felt that this place was truly mine. ●

MAY 2014						
S	M	T	W	T	F	S
				1	2	3
4	5	6	7	8	9	10
11	12	13	14	15	16	17
18	19	20	21	22	23	24
25	26	27	28	29	30	31

On May 8, 1914, Saint Paul received a total of $75,000 from Andrew Carnegie to build three public libraries: Saint Anthony Park, Arlington Hills, and Riverview.

MONDAY

5

Cinco de Mayo

TUESDAY

6

Mary MacGregor, singer best known for her 1976 recording "Torn Between Two Lovers," was born today in 1948.

WEDNESDAY

7

THURSDAY

8

FRIDAY

9

SATURDAY

10

SUNDAY

11

Mother's Day

Sister Carmella Hanggi, Cathedral School principal who founded the nation's first school safety patrol, was born today in 1875.

This Week's Events

Monday
Summer Flower Show

Tuesday
Summer Flower Show
The Saint Paul Chamber Orchestra

Wednesday
Summer Flower Show

Thursday
Saint Paul Almanac Soul Sounds Open Mic
Summer Flower Show
20th Annual Great River Gathering

Friday
Summer Flower Show
The Saint Paul Chamber Orchestra

Saturday
Downtown Saint Paul Farmers' Market
Summer Flower Show
Summit Avenue Walking Tours

The Saint Paul Chamber Orchestra
TU Dance
Mother's Day Bonsai Show

Sunday
Downtown Saint Paul Farmers' Market
Summer Flower Show
Summit Avenue Walking Tours
The Saint Paul Chamber Orchestra
Mother's Day Bonsai Show
Saint Paul Civic Symphony Mother's Day Concert

Elkanah Odembo, the ambassador of Kenya, visited Saint Paul on May 8, 2012, for two events sponsored by the local Books For Africa project.

© Jack Steinmann

Renovations in the Union Depot station in May 2012. The station opened to the public in December.

Midway Memories ● ELI FREBERG

My Hamline-Midway neighborhood is the kind of place where childhood memories are made. Sure, Wisconsin Dells, a Caribbean cruise to the Bahamas, and Disney World all have their fair share of excitement and joyous wonderment. But nothing can compare to the warm feeling you get as sticky chocolate ice cream drizzles down your fingers, while you watch your sister try to feed the dog some of hers. The simple rushes of adrenaline as you speed away on your tarnished red mountain bike, the fading orange sun glaring off the chrome handlebars. In the winter, glistening white snow forts protect from compacted snowballs that sting like bees. Baseball games under the bright floodlights of Midway ballparks, making you feel as if you are at Target Field, standing right next to Justin Morneau. Buying rich, creamy Milky Way candy bars at Lloyd's Pharmacy, then stopping at the library to pick up Tintin comics. Spending time with loved ones, be it shouting "Uno!" as the last card leaves your hand, getting a plastic birdie stuck in your inexpensive racket, or figuring out a puzzling crossword. These are all memories that might not seem big and amazing, but they are the most important. ●

© Jack Steinnman

A Mother's Hope ● NICHOLAS "NICK" METCALF—
CETANZI (YELLOW HAWK)

Proud back with a chest high in the air
Swaying with desire
Never knowing when to bend
Afraid to break
Walking into the wind
Bowing to the ravages of life
A life of hurling lessons
Mistakes that grow into other mistakes

Proud back with a chest high in the air
Swaying with desire
How do I stop this?
How do I bend?
What do I allow?
Questions tearing a grown person asunder
Begging God, doubting that there is one
Abandoned again for worthier causes
Pleading for respite but finding none

Proud back with a chest high in the air
Swaying with desire
Familiar with a man's desire
A lot of fives feed young, hungry bodies
Those dirty fives keep clothes on young backs
Stinky fives keep a roof over children's heads
Desperate that my children's dreams be realized
Dreams that look past this circumstance

Proud back with a chest high in the air
Swaying with desire
Stopping for the briefest of moments
Catching glimpses of a stranger passing dirty shop windows
Recognizing this is not the dream that I once dreamed

Proud back with a chest high in the air
Swaying with desire
Hanging on
Hope is all I have left

MAY 2014

S	M	T	W	T	F	S
				1	2	3
4	5	6	7	8	9	10
11	12	13	14	15	16	17
18	19	20	21	22	23	24
25	26	27	28	29	30	31

Sitting Bull, a Lakota leader from the Standing Rock Reservation, arrived in Saint Paul on May 14, 1884, to make a case for immediate government help for his people.

MONDAY
12

TUESDAY
13

WEDNESDAY
Buddha Day
14

THURSDAY
15

FRIDAY
16
Nathaniel McLean, pioneer newspaperman and real estate dealer, was born today in 1787.

SATURDAY
17

SUNDAY
18
Joel E. Whitney, pioneer daguerreotype and a wet plate photographer, was born today in 1822.

This Week's Events

Monday
  Summer Flower Show

Tuesday
  Summer Flower Show
  Bring It On: The Musical
  Seniors in Mind

Wednesday
  Summer Flower Show
  Bring It On: The Musical

Thursday
  Saint Paul Almanac Soul Sounds
    Open Mic
  Summer Flower Show
  Bring It On: The Musical

Friday
  Summer Flower Show
  Bring It On: The Musical
  RetroRama

Saturday
  Downtown Saint Paul Farmers'
    Market
  Summer Flower Show

  Summit Avenue Walking
    Tours
  Bring It On: The Musical
  The Saint Paul Chamber
    Orchestra

Sunday
  Downtown Saint Paul
    Farmers' Market
  Summer Flower Show
  Summit Avenue Walking
    Tours
  Bring It On: The Musical
  Urban Expedition: Brazil

> "I am easily bored, and, after I have written one kind of book, I like to try another kind. Each book is a new problem, and I come to it with the zest of a new adventure."
>
> CAROL BRINK, *Saint Paul writer*

© Ken Friberg/RatRaceStudios.com

A train runs along the Mississippi with the Robert Street Bridge in the background.

Roblyn Avenue, 1953 ● MARIANNE McNAMARA

The first thing I saw when Dad turned our car down Grandma's street in Merriam Park was the sky-high catalpa tree in her front yard. It was the only "cigar tree" on the block, and when I spied it, I knew we were almost there. It was a beautiful tree, with frilly white flowers in the spring that magically became long, brown seedpods in late summer.

A visit to Grandma's guaranteed delicious treats. Her cakes were confectionary works of art. She swirled frosting into high, fluffy peaks, then added fat walnuts and fresh flowers. When I was born, on my mother's twenty-fifth birthday, Grandma brought a beautiful cake to Miller Hospital, trimmed with pink flowers from her garden. Strawberry shortcake, mounded with vanilla whipped cream, was her specialty. I was sure she baked the best cookies in all of Saint Paul.

Small and thin, Grandma had short, silver-brown hair and coffee-brown eyes that crinkled at the corners when she smiled. She was proud to be a Democrat and a Catholic, in that order. Grandma lived through the Great Depression, and that experience taught her to be strong and independent.

When school was out for the summer, it was time for my week with Grandma. There was always an endless supply of Juicy Fruit gum in the top drawer of the sideboard in her dining room. I wasn't allowed to chew gum at home, but I inhaled the sugary sticks at Grandma's house. She treated me to bubble baths topped off with puffs of fragrant talcum powder. Best of all was sleeping in Grandma's wide, safe bed. I snuggled deep into the space next to her while she told me stories about her childhood until I drifted off to sleep.

Grandma had a green thumb and could make anything grow. My favorite flowers were the tall hollyhocks that bloomed beside her garage. Grandma taught me how to make hollyhock dolls, clever flower ladies in ball gowns and turbans. To make them, we gathered handfuls of blossoms and buds in different colors. When they were finished, I arranged make-believe dance parties in a shady corner of the back yard. Sometimes I floated the pink and purple ladies in a chipped enamel wash pan Grandma kept at the back door.

A door in the spare bedroom at Grandma's led up winding steps to the attic where she kept a baby doll with eyes that click-clacked open and shut. My dad gave Grandma the doll as a keepsake before he left for overseas during World War II. I'd beg to play with the doll, and Grandma always said yes. Later, we would carefully wrap her in tissue and pack her in the trunk for next time.

Grandma is gone now, and other people live in her house. But that towering catalpa tree is still there, watching over her tiny bungalow summer and winter. Life has come full circle, and I'm a grandmother myself. I use Grandma's recipes when I bake cakes and cookies, but they never taste as good as hers did. There's a blue-eyed granddaughter named Nora for me to spoil and love, and her brand-new baby sister, Annie, born last spring when the catalpa tree bloomed.

Grandma's Frosting

This old-fashioned cooked icing recipe makes a sweet, fluffy frosting.

Mix and cream thoroughly
½ cup shortening
¼ cup butter

Add
¾ cup sugar
Mix until it is no longer grainy. Set aside.

Combine
3½ tablespoons flour
¾ cup milk
Cook until thick, stirring constantly. When cool, add by tablespoon to first mixture. Beat after each addition.
Add 1 teaspoon vanilla. Beat well.

Photo courtesy Marianne McNamara

Marianne as a little girl, on the porch of her grandmother's Roblyn Avenue home.

MAY 2014

S	M	T	W	T	F	S
				1	2	3
4	5	6	7	8	9	10
11	12	13	14	15	16	17
18	19	20	21	22	23	24
25	26	27	28	29	30	31

The restored Joyce Kilmer Memorial Fireplace in Como Park was rededicated on May 19, 2011. It was built in 1936 as a memorial to poet Alfred Joyce Kilmer.

MONDAY

19

TUESDAY

20

WEDNESDAY

21

THURSDAY

22

FRIDAY

23

SATURDAY

24

James Oppenheim—American poet, novelist, and editor—was born today in 1882.

SUNDAY

25

This Week's Events

Monday
Summer Flower Show

Tuesday
Summer Flower Show

Wednesday
Summer Flower Show

Thursday
Saint Paul Almanac Soul Sounds
Open Mic
Summer Flower Show

Friday
Summer Flower Show
The Saint Paul Chamber Orchestra
Fourth Friday at the Movies

Saturday
Downtown Saint Paul Farmers'
Market
Summer Flower Show
Summit Avenue Walking Tours
The Saint Paul Chamber Orchestra

Sunday
Downtown Saint Paul Farmers'
Market
Summer Flower Show
Summit Avenue Walking Tours

Dusk

Her 80th birthday—"Surprise!"
She smiles from the party photo,
    her last.
As a kid, rushing home after
    basketball,
barely beating curfew,
I'd nuzzle her.
I smell her now,
rosebud salve and a perfume
    I can't recall,
but warm and home and Mom.

D. Stephen Elliott

The Ireland family, including
a young John—the future
archbishop—stepped off
a steamboat at Saint Paul's
Jackson Street levee on May
20, 1852. They first lived in a
hastily built shack at Fifth and
St. Peter.

(© Bob Muschewske/370SummitStPaul.com)

*Hmong spoken word artist Tou SaiKo Lee at an event in the Western
Sculpture Garden*

Whether you're new to Saint Paul,
a longtime resident, or simply a visitor, here's . . .

The Saint Paul Art Tour You
Weren't Expecting ● JODY HUBER

First, let's take the word "art" and think beyond the museum or gallery wall. (Minneapolis has plenty of both.)

How would you characterize Saint Paul? Do the words "venerable" and "dignified" usually come to mind? That's fine, but what about "playful" and "quirky"?

Okay, before you start thinking, *C'mon, where's this going, I've got things to do,* let me quickly add that my art tour is a mere sam-

© Kristi Abbott/KristiAbbott.com

Remix of a panel from her work, Jack and Jill, *made for a promotional Saint Paul Art Crawl postcard*

pling of what Saint Paul has to offer. Not to mention, it may surprise you. What's more, every stop on my little tour is *free*.

Ready?

First Stop: Art in Our Neighborhood Parks

PUBLIC ART

More and more public art is popping up all over Saint Paul, as artists collaborate with the city, businesses, even residents. So look up, around—and down. There's even poetry imprinted in sidewalks. Here are just two of my favorite places to enjoy art outdoors:

NORTH HIGH BRIDGE PARK *(on Smith Avenue at entry to High Bridge)*: Look for the oversized (and that's putting it mildly) Adirondack chair. "Green Chair" (*artist: Joel Sisson*) appears all the more giant-like sitting in such a tiny charming pocket of a park. And as domineering as this 2,500-pound chair is, you can't resist staring at "The Watcher" (*artist: Zoran Mojsilov*), a gravity-defying, curvy pile-of-stones sculpture that looks like the remains of some prehistoric animal's tail, frozen mid-lash. Nor would you want to leave this park without stepping through "Community Gates" (*artist: Craig David*), a contemplative, Stonehenge-like garden created in part (and I love this) from leftover pavers and curbstones. The bonus? This wee park sits right atop the bluffs, so you can look down on the activity on the Mississippi River.

WESTERN SCULPTURE PARK *(on Marion Street off of I-94)*: Hard to miss any park with a rabbit just sitting there, boldly staring at you. That is, if you, too, are 14 feet high. "Max Rabbitat" (*artist: Mary Johnson*) is not your usual 4,000-pound rabbit with hubcap eyes, so get up real close. It's embedded with delightful bits of yard-sale mundanity. Cookie cutters, puzzle pieces, clothespins—and I found at least one action figure and a spoon. Nearby, shooting up past the trees, is "Walking Warrior 1" (*artist: Melvin Smith*). This elegantly spare steel man looks like he stepped out of a cubist painting, then grew 33 feet high to loom over the park, as if guarding it.

So now imagine what else is in this concourse of a park that pulls you in with its whimsy, dotted with fantastical towering shapes. But there are delightful smaller-scale pieces, too. Ones you can sit

Max Rabbitat *by Mary Johnson*

atop, climb on, or crawl through. (Or if that embarrasses you, your kids can.)

Second Stop: Art in Downtown Saint Paul

ARCHITECTURE

"Ah, to build, to build! That's the noblest art of the arts . . ." said poet Henry Wadsworth Longfellow. "Architecture is inhabited sculpture," said sculptor Constantin Brancusi. And who's going to argue with these guys?

If you live here, you know Saint Paul has more than its share of magnificently preserved and restored structures. Whole districts are on the National Register of Historic Places. Architecturally, you have a host of styles, from Richardsonian Romanesque and Italianate to Beaux Arts and Art Deco. The Capitol and the Cathedral of Saint Paul are stunning examples indeed. But I insist you also visit the following, all within easy walking distance of one another:

First, there's Union Depot (on Fourth Street), followed by Merchants National Bank, now the Brooks building (on Jackson Street). Then scoot down Jackson to the Pioneer-Endicott building, the temporary home of the Minnesota Museum of Art, (featuring American artists, from 1860 to the present). Then, take in the most strikingly beautiful block in all of the Twin Cities (yes, not just Saint Paul): Rice Park, flanked by the Landmark Center, Saint Paul Hotel, Ordway Center for the Performing Arts, and the Saint Paul Public Library/James J. Hill Reference Library. And don't forget to go inside. I can't begin to describe the splendid detail of their interior spaces.

Third Stop: Art in Hidden Falls Park

(off Mississippi River Road)

NATURE

Nature has inspired artists forever, so you can't tell me that nature isn't art, purely by itself. Well you can, but I won't be listening.

At first glance, Hidden Falls on the Mississippi River looks like it could easily be the subject of a Hudson River School landscape painter from the mid-1800s. Or as if Huck Finn could wander through at any minute. It's a pleasant throwback to a quieter, slower-moving century. (The park still lists horseshoe pits as one of its amenities.)

Massive cottonwood trees hang right over the river— trees that look like a giant tried to pull them out by the roots, but got just so far and gave up. Big old rocks (stone's answer to beach chairs) are just a few flip-flop lengths from the Mississippi River, a surprisingly decent way to sit and watch barges, paddleboats, and ducks go by. I should know—I've been doing it for years. I never tire of it.

So where is art in Saint Paul? It's all around you. I like how writer Saul Bellow put it: "What is art, but a way of seeing?" Clearly there is so much more of it for you to see. And when you do and it delights you, tell others. ●

© Tom Dunn/Tom DunnPhoto.com

Saint Paul Building Executive Suites at Fifth and Wabasha

Cheery vintage PennSalt advertisement for Dichlorodiphenyl-trichloroethane (DDT), finally banned in the United States in 1972

JUNE

Danger Days ● JOYCE SUTPHEN

Back in the old danger days,
when we were kids, we stood
on the front seat of the Chevy Impala—
no seat belts to hold us back,
our mother's arm the only thing
between us and the dashboard,

though sometimes they strapped us
into contraptions hooked over
the back of the seat, our chubby legs
dangling down, our small hands
gripping the frame—all set to be
launched through the windshield!

And it is one of the wonders of
American life that most of us
survived to drive those cars to the
outdoor movies so we could watch
Easy Rider while the crop-dusting planes
passed low overhead and the mosquito

control-trucks sprayed DDT down
the streets of our town, a trail of kids
on bicycles following behind. And it
probably never occurred to us what
a Lawn Jart could do—we were too busy
worrying about the end of the world.

(From After Words, *Red Dragonfly Press, copyright © 2013 by Joyce Sutphen)*

JUNE 2014

S	M	T	W	T	F	S
1	2	3	4	5	6	7
8	9	10	11	12	13	14
15	16	17	18	19	20	21
22	23	24	25	26	27	28
29	30					

On May 27, 1919, Walter Deubener of Saint Paul received a patent for a grocery bag with handles that he invented for his store.

MONDAY

MAY

26

Memorial Day

Kermitt Ervin Wheeler, African American attorney for the U.S. government and minister, was born today in 1930.

TUESDAY

MAY

27

Jerry Kindall, major league baseball player, was born today in 1935.

WEDNESDAY

MAY

28

THURSDAY

MAY

29

FRIDAY

MAY

30

SATURDAY

MAY

31

SUNDAY

1

Tony Sanneh, professional soccer player, was born today in 1971.

This Week's Events

Monday
Summer Flower Show

Tuesday
Summer Flower Show

Wednesday
Summer Flower Show
Saint Paul Almanac Lowertown
Reading Jam

Thursday
Saint Paul Almanac Soul Sounds
Open Mic
Summer Flower Show

Friday
Summer Flower Show

Saturday
Downtown Saint Paul Farmers'
Market
Summer Flower Show
Summit Avenue Walking Tours

Sunday
Downtown Saint Paul
Farmers' Market
Summer Flower Show
Summit Avenue Walking
Tours
Grand Old Day

Untitled

It's warmer now than it was.
This simple comparison does
More for one's mood
And whole attitude
Than a glass of wine. Why? Just
because.

Garrison Keillor

Women's bike race at the Nature Valley Bicycle Festival in Downtown Saint Paul

Tornado ● GREG WATSON

Just beyond the hem of the lake's blue skirt
the sky turned suddenly jaundiced,

a weighted stillness, not quite your own,
descended, and even the black pine

and birch hovered motionless
in a calm that bore no calm at all.

And for what must have been the briefest
of moments you gazed, a child of seven,

transfixed on the sinewy black thread
of the storm, its form swaying,

tearing the fabric of the horizon,
throwing bits of cloud and gravel dust

as dogs and kids scurried into small, white cabins
which suddenly looked as though they were

made to be thrown all along, something
stolen from the set of someone else's epic.

And years later you would not remember
how it was you were pulled indoors,

or whose arm it was that lifted you
with the force of a blow, bringing you to safety,

nor how the storm at once lifted, lifted,
like a needle from a phonograph

above the roofs of trees still trembling;
and when you looked out again

it was through brown sheets of mud
slapped across the windows,

the dark fragrance of earthworms
seeping through the slats,

beyond which the world shone as green
and peaceful as it ever would again.

Summer storm above Saint Paul, as seen from the High Bridge

JUNE 2014

S	M	T	W	T	F	S
1	2	3	4	5	6	7
8	9	10	11	12	13	14
15	16	17	18	19	20	21
22	23	24	25	26	27	28
29	30					

A century ago, architect Clarence Johnston designed an adapted Tudor Revival style for the Summit School, 1150 Goodrich Avenue.

MONDAY

2

TUESDAY

3

WEDNESDAY

4

Shavuot

Susie Scanlan, Saint Paul epee fencer and member of the 2012 U.S. bronze-medal team, was born today in 1990.

THURSDAY

5

FRIDAY

6

SATURDAY

7

SUNDAY

8

Jane Frazee, actress who appeared in many musicals, was born today in 1918.

This Week's Events

Monday
Summer Flower Show

Tuesday
Summer Flower Show
Saint Paul (Seventh Place) Farmers' Market
Nooks and Crannies Tours

Wednesday
Summer Flower Show
History Pub Crawl

Thursday
Summer Flower Show
Saint Paul Almanac Soul Sounds Open Mic
Saint Paul (Seventh Place) Farmers' Market
Music in Mears

Friday
Summer Flower Show
Last Day of School K–12
The Saint Paul Chamber Orchestra

Saturday
Downtown Saint Paul Farmers' Market
Summer Flower Show

Summit Avenue Walking Tours
The Saint Paul Chamber Orchestra
Hamline-Midway Heartland Festival
Saint Anthony Park Arts Festival

Sunday
Downtown Saint Paul Farmers' Market
Summer Flower Show
Summit Avenue Walking Tours
The Saint Paul Chamber Orchestra

On June 1, 2000, meatpackers at the Dakota Premium Foods plant in Saint Paul carried out a successful seven-hour sit-down strike to protest a dangerous speedup on the production line.

© Tom Reynen/tom-reynen.artistwebsites.com

The new light rail in Lowertown, Saint Paul

Slow Boats and Fast Water ● CAPTAIN BOB DECK

Early in the morning on June 21, 2007, my son Cullen encountered a rowing scull, crewed by five young women in the Saint Paul Harbor and pinned by a heavy current of the Mississippi River. This crew team had misjudged the current and was trapped against the Padelford wharf barge.

Cullen was a crew chief on the *Betsey Northrup* at Harriet Island that morning and getting ready for a charter. Caterers were preparing food in the galley and setting tables on the lower deck. Bartenders were stocking the bar and cleaning the boat. Cullen was moving between the engine room of *Ugh the Tug* and the *Betsey*, keeping the *Northrup* crew on task. Outside the river was rising with a strong, swift current.

At one point in his work, Cullen glanced upstream through the main deck windows. There he saw a rowing scull hugging the bank above the Padelford wharf barge. The crew seemed to be struggling to maneuver the craft away from the bank. Nearby, a small outboard-powered chaperone boat was following the scull, and it too appeared to be confused. While Cullen watched, the scull continued to flounder.

Ahead of the scull, a broken tree branch banged into the wharf and rolled beneath it. The swirling current created a strong eddy, which sucked large objects under the wharf. Cullen had a feeling the rowers weren't going to make it back into the channel. He ran back through the *Betsey*'s main cabin and headed for the end of the wharf barge. By the time he got there, the current had turned the rowers sideways and slammed them into the barge: all he could see of the rowers were their fingers clinging to the edge. A couple of the oars had already been torn loose and disappeared.

Later, Cullen told me what happened when he discovered the pinned rowers: "The *Betsey Northrup* passenger barge was docked facing upstream. The crew boat found itself flat across the gap between the rake end of the wharf barge and the *Betsey*. I put a couple of caterers in charge while I ran to get more people to help."

As he turned to summon help, the coxswain and the escort boat driver were yelling at Cullen that they did not need help and would get themselves free. "As I hustled back to the office door, I could hear the chase boat driver telling the crew to pull themselves hand over hand out toward the channel. When I heard that, I ran as fast as I could.

"By the time Steve Bowell and I got back, the situation was chaotic. The scull had rolled under the water and the rowers were dangling from the edge of the barge. One of the caterers started throwing ring buoys into the river where the women could reach them. I told everyone to grab someone, then dropped to my knees and grabbed the nearest victim. She was the woman who was in the stern, the coxswain, who had been telling me that they would get themselves free.

"The crew boat was sucked under the bow of the *Betsey*; we could hear it slowly rolling back under the *Betsey*'s hull. After we rescued the rowers, we were standing with them in front of the office and watched it snap in half on the bow of our other boat, the *Anson Northrup*, then float downstream. The five women we rescued were very shook-up. We gave them water and coffee before they walked down Harriet Island to their boat club on Raspberry Island."

In recognition of the rescue, Saint Paul mayor Chris Coleman honored Cullen and Steve Bowell when he officially proclaimed January 16, 2010, as Padelford Riverboats Day. Now Cullen is a Padelford captain learning the same lessons about small boat behavior that I learned as a young riverboat pilot. ●

Photo courtesy Bob Deck

Captain Bob Deck (R) with his son Cullen, on the bridge of the Betsey Northrup *paddleboat*

JUNE 2014

S	M	T	W	T	F	S
1	2	3	4	5	6	7
8	9	10	11	12	13	14
15	16	17	18	19	20	21
22	23	24	25	26	27	28
29	30					

Lyman Dayton, an East Side pioneer, drove a Territorial Road surveyor off his land on June 12, 1855, saying the man had no right to be there.

MONDAY

9

TUESDAY

10

Jim Beattie, 6'9" heavyweight boxer, was born today in 1942.

WEDNESDAY

11

THURSDAY

12

FRIDAY

13

SATURDAY

14

SUNDAY

Father's Day

15

This Week's Events

Monday
Summer Flower Show

Tuesday
Summer Flower Show

Saint Paul (Seventh Place) Farmers' Market

Nooks and Crannies Tours

Wednesday
Summer Flower Show

History Pub Crawl

Thursday
Summer Flower Show

Saint Paul Almanac Soul Sounds Open Mic

Saint Paul (Seventh Place) Farmers' Market

Music in Mears

Friday
Summer Flower Show

Broadway Songbook: Comden and Green

Saturday
Downtown Saint Paul Farmers' Market

Summer Flower Show

Summit Avenue Walking Tours

Broadway Songbook: Comden and Green

Sunday
Downtown Saint Paul Farmers' Market

Summer Flower Show

Summit Avenue Walking Tours

Broadway Songbook: Comden and Green

> "The principle that ownership is stewardship, that the man who possesses superfluous goods must regard himself as a trustee for the needy, is fundamental and all-pervasive in the teaching of Christianity."
>
> FATHER JOHN A. RYAN,
> *teacher and writer*

© Tom McGregor/mcgregorart.com

Spires at Dusk, *detail*

The Cathedral—June Thirteenth

● MARGOT FORTUNATO GALT

Because the vistas end in arches
    that do not change
And the grillwork of sails
    forecasts a season of palms
The dove holds a steady hover
    over the crossroads of death
My heart beats erratically
I have been afraid
    of harsh words
    of hounds quarrying
    the cat of my aging.

Because the stone shines golden
    through erratic chords
And the mundane world
    falls away like shorn hair
The lilies in stained glass
    stride forth like embattled veterans
I lower myself into the flood
My heart holds steady
A strong hand carries me,
    leaf riding the crest.

The interior of the Cathedral of Saint Paul

Grandma's Arms

● COLLEEN CASEY

Grandma's brown arms
wrapped around the world
and held it tight,
close to her bosom,
close to her heartbeat.

Grandma's brown arms
always listened,
paid attention,
knew just how tight
to squeeze,
and when to let go.

Grandma loved fierce,
fiercer than anyone.
In her brown arms
I know
I was pressed to a force
that felt with me,
fought *with* me,
floundered, never.

Wise with life,
wise with love,
wise with hurt,
Grandma's brown arms
wrapped around the world.

JUNE 2014

S	M	T	W	T	F	S
1	2	3	4	5	6	7
8	9	10	11	12	13	14
15	16	17	18	19	20	21
22	23	24	25	26	27	28
29	30					

On June 21, 1990, a small cross was burned in an African American family's yard at 290 Earl Street. The eventual arrest led to a famous U.S. Supreme Court ruling.

MONDAY

16

TUESDAY

17

Shirley J. Larkin, founder of the Larkin Dance studio, was born today in 1934.

WEDNESDAY

18

THURSDAY

19

Juneteenth

Mary Hartung, who became first woman editor of the U of M's *Minnesota Daily* in 1917, was born today in 1899.

FRIDAY

20

SATURDAY

21

Summer Solstice

SUNDAY

22

This Week's Events

Monday
Summer Flower Show

Tuesday
Summer Flower Show
Saint Paul (Seventh Place) Farmers' Market
Nooks and Crannies Tours
Summer History HiJinx Craft Activity

Wednesday
Summer Flower Show
History Pub Crawl
Summer History HiJinx Craft Activity

Thursday
Summer Flower Show
Saint Paul Almanac Soul Sounds Open Mic
Saint Paul (Seventh Place) Farmers' Market
Summer History HiJinx Craft Activity
Music in Mears

Friday
Summer Flower Show
Summer History HiJinx Craft Activity

Saturday
Downtown Saint Paul Farmers' Market
Summer Flower Show
Summit Avenue Walking Tours

Sunday
Downtown Saint Paul Farmers' Market
Summer Flower Show
Summit Avenue Walking Tours

Untitled

The echo was in the stone
long before any voice
emerged, the instinct of departure
born long before
the body.

Greg Watson

The American Queen, *the largest passenger steamboat in the world, passes by the former Saint Paul central post office building.*

Thank You for Calling the Radisson
Saint Paul ● KATHRYN KYSAR

During the summer of 1980 between my sophomore and junior years at Hamline University, I worked as a telephone operator on the 3 to 11 p.m. shift on the last existing cord board in Saint Paul, at the downtown Radisson Hotel. The toggles and cords were mounted in a long, narrow black desk with metal-rimmed holes in a vertical wall panel. Two operators sat side by side, clicking the cloth-wrapped cords into room-numbered holes to connect the calls. To listen in, we flicked a small toggle at the bottom of the cord, but we did not do this—at least, not very often.

We were expected to greet every caller with a cheery "Thank you for calling the Radisson Saint Paul!" As we became tired each evening, our voices became more nasal, like Lily Tomlin's character Ernestine, the cord-board operator who always said, "Is this the party to whom I am speaking?" It took less energy and air to talk through our noses.

Like Ernestine, the phone department supervisor must have been complimented on her legs back in the 1940s, as she still wore short black skirts, heels, and rolled-under hair. Every evening she'd call us several times from home between the TV shows she was watching, unable to imagine that we could do our work without her assistance.

The kindly older woman I worked with was round from sitting and fond of the puppy pictures in the *National Enquirer*. As a newly minted feminist, I read Anaïs Nin, Violette Leduc, Monique Wittig, and other obscure French authors. We spent our entire shift in the small, stuffy room, getting up only to use the restroom. A television was mounted in one ceiling corner, so we could monitor the pay-for-TV movies. Again and again, the alien burst forth out from a crewman's chest, then later, full grown, unhinged its saliva-dripping jaws to fight with the sweating and undershirt-clad Sigourney Weaver.

I was by far the youngest phone operator. The other women chatted about soap operas and read *Good Housekeeping*, *Better Homes and Gardens*, and gossip magazines they'd flip through between calls in the hot basement room. Halfway through our shifts, we ordered grilled sandwiches from the room service menu to break the boredom, the movie droning in the background, the gruesome alien being reborn again and again. I usually kept my mouth shut, having little to discuss with the other operators, but I relished the click of the plugs as they slid into place, the interweaving black snakelike cords, the snap of the released plug, the physical rhythm of the work.

I quit at the end of the summer to return to my classes at Hamline and take a job across the street at the Midway Motel, but to this day I cannot pass the Crowne Plaza without saying in a nasal voice, "Thank you for calling the Radisson Saint Paul!" ●

JUNE 2014

S	M	T	W	T	F	S
1	2	3	4	5	6	7
8	9	10	11	12	13	14
15	16	17	18	19	20	21
22	23	24	25	26	27	28
29	30					

Henry Van Liew opened the People's Theater, the first building dedicated to entertainment in frontier Saint Paul, on June 27, 1857.

MONDAY

23

TUESDAY

24

Tom Reid, bar owner and radio voice of The Wild hockey team, was born today in 1946.

WEDNESDAY

25

THURSDAY

26

Robert Kelly, painter and visual artist, was born today in 1958.

FRIDAY

27

SATURDAY

28

SUNDAY

Ramadan Begins

29

This Week's Events

Monday
Summer Flower Show

Tuesday
Summer Flower Show
Saint Paul (Seventh Place) Farmers' Market
Nooks and Crannies Tours
Summer History HiJinx Craft Activity

Wednesday
Summer Flower Show
History Pub Crawl
Summer History HiJinx Craft Activity
Saint Paul Almanac Lowertown Reading Jam

Thursday
Summer Flower Show
Saint Paul Almanac Soul Sounds Open Mic
Saint Paul (Seventh Place) Farmers' Market
Music in Mears
Summer History HiJinx Craft Activity

Friday
Summer Flower Show
Summer History HiJinx Craft Activity
Fourth Friday at the Movies

Saturday
Downtown Saint Paul Farmers' Market
Summer Flower Show
Summit Avenue Walking Tours

Sunday
Downtown Saint Paul Farmers' Market
Summer Flower Show
Summit Avenue Walking Tours

"There is a certain type of writer that likes to take everything out from under the table—stuff that no one wants to look at—and say, 'Let's look at this.' For better or worse, that happens to be what fascinates me."

DAVID MURA,
Japanese American writer

© Bob Muschewske/370SummitStPaul.com

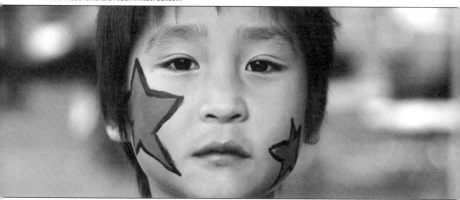

The True Box of Life ● STUDENTS OF GORDON PARKS HIGH SCHOOL: RHODA BALFOUR, DWIGHT DAVIS, LUIS GUADAR-RAMA, ANTHONY HARE, ZING LO, JASMINE TOLIVER, TAYLOR VANG, CINDY XIONG, KENDRICK JOHNSON, AND NA YANG

Kofi Bobby Hickman was an artist in residence in Jennifer Bangoura's writing class at Gordon Parks High School. The following piece was compiled from the writing of students in that class and is formatted to use as a group performance or dramatic reading. Kofi was instrumental in the feeding of these hungry young minds.

KENDRICK:

> Have you ever had a
> Snake in your life?
> Have you ever had a
> Snake in your grass?

CINDY: Kofi Bobby Hickman taught us about the three snakes of life: the cobra snake—it lures you in; the rattlesnake—it warns you; and the garter snake—it bites you without warning.

DWIGHT: We can relate snakes to our situations in life. . . . In life we take interest in beautiful things like a cobra. The cobra's scales reflect and shimmer in the light that might draw us closer to admire. We are blinded by the cobra's beauty so much so that we don't notice the fangs that have sunk into our lives.

Open your eyes to true beauty, but be aware of the traps of life. Like the cobra, the python can catch you by surprise. It might seem harmless at first, but when you unknowingly let the python get a start, wrapping you up as its prey, just like in life, it's hard to untangle the mess we make.

LUIS: The cobra is two faced. It's a snake that gets your attention, puts on a show. When it has a chance, however, it will bite and spit venom—meaning stab you in the back. In my perspective, the cobra seems to be friendly, but his goal is to bite. It lures you in until it has a chance to attack. I'm comparing the cobra to real life and people.

TAYLOR: We have all had situations where we find out that people who say they are our friends are not. The rattlesnake warns you about this. I used to have a friend; we were great friends, but she

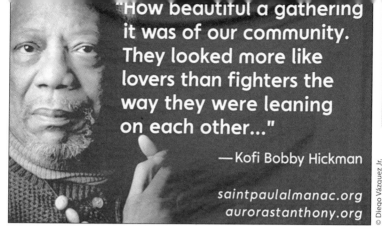

The Kofi Bobby Hickman banner at University and Western Avenues. Banner photo by Tobechi Tobechukwu. Banner designed by Shaquan Foster and Michael Waite.

started a rumor about me. I was in middle school, and because of that I was dumb and fought her. Well, actually, we didn't really fight because our teachers came and talked to us about the situation. When I think of it now, it was really immature. I should not have trusted her so easily. The warning signs were right there and I was blind to them.

RHODA: Have you ever been trapped inside of a box? This box I speak of happens to be no ordinary box. The box I refer to is a true box of life. What snakes are in your life? But not physical snakes, all right?

CINDY: Sometimes I feel as if I'm always stuck in a box, but that's only because I think of my situation in a negative way, and the invisible box is me. Kofi made me think critically about the situation I was in, my relationships with certain people, school, and how I feel fatherless.

ANTHONY: An everyday situation that Kofi helped me with is watching out for the snakes in my life. Letting me know there is always a way out of a bad situation—if you think outside the box—has also been helpful. It's interesting how mean and evil people take on certain characteristics such as that of a reptile. The snakes in life are the cobras and the rattlesnakes. They'll either let you know they will mess you up or they will lure you into their world unexpectedly.

ZING:

> Let me out of here.
> Someone help me.
> Get me out of here.
> Someone once said to me
> How'd you get in there?

KENDRICK:

> Mom told me to make
> Good choices in life.
> But I slithered myself so far from
> Her words and saved her option for last.

NA LEE: I am still stuck in the box. I'm really pushing myself to graduate. Because of my work schedule, however, I get really tired so I tend to slack off and don't come to school.

ZING:

> I'll help you if you help me.
> I'll get you out if you help me.
> Help me help you and you will be free.

JASMINE: A snake I've had in my life was someone full of drama. She pretended to be my friend but didn't like me and found stupid reasons to fight me. That's a box I was in, and I got out of it staying away from her and not talking to her. I started ignoring her. She would go left and I would go right.

TAYLOR: What I've learned is not to trust people so easily and tell them secrets easily. I've learned that there are true friends and fake friends—you just have to be aware of which you have.

NA LEE: Kofi Bobby Hickman taught me about the box, characters, and snakes.

RHODA: Snakes play a role and are identities in your life.

CINDY: Hearing Kofi talk made me motivated in a way to succeed at the things in life that I've always dreamed of. . . . It's very hard for people like me to open up because sometimes you will fear rejection and it feels like when you open up, nobody listens. That's when Kofi Bobby Hickman taught me it can all be written down on paper. ●

Teaching from the Heart ● KAYE THOMPSON PETERS

As with most love affairs, it happened by chance and caught me by surprise. After our first few dates, I realized that my life had led me to this moment, that I was right where I belonged: in front of 150 students every day at Central High School.

Unlike many of my colleagues, who had begun their professional lives as teachers, my love affair with teaching is an autumn romance. I had spent twenty years doing other things. First, I was an aide to a senator and then a newspaper reporter. When I looked at the next chapter of my life, still on a mission to make the world a better place, I thought of teaching as an opportunity to cultivate thinkers.

Little did I know then how little I knew. I was an adept learner in the master's program at the University of St. Thomas and quickly found my own philosophy of education (constructivist, which means I believe in setting up situations where students construct their own meaning). I got straight As and a student teaching placement at Central, where my eldest daughter was a junior and where I wanted to be. I rocked at student teaching (so said my supervising professor) and was immediately hired in January 1998 by Mary Mackbee to teach two sections of regular senior English and one section of ninth grade honors. Then my real education began.

My students were my teachers—every day. The gangly, towheaded boy whose family kicked him out on the day he turned eighteen, the kid to whom everyone looked for direction as to whether we were going to study *Macbeth* or pretend to be on *The Jerry Springer Show*, the two boys who fought each other in the middle of class over a grudge from the streets, the waif-like girl who preferred sitting under the table rather than at it and refused to do homework. I learned quickly to never get into a power struggle, to speak with respect outside the door to any student who needed calming or correcting.

"I really respect you," a math teacher told me midway through my second year. "You never send anyone to the office."

"You can do that?" I responded.

My third year, I began teaching the junior International Baccalaureate class and faced another whole set of challenges. These kids were far smarter and better educated than I had been in high school, but there were a fair number of math and science types who were uncomfortable with the ambiguity of literature. They wanted me to give them an answer—*the* answer—to what a metaphor meant, or the significance of the goldfish in Gabriel Garcia Marquez's *One Hundred Years of Solitude*. When I turned the question back to them, asking them what they thought, I got excruciating evaluations that said I didn't know my content. I learned to stand firm, be confident in what I believed was good teaching, and refused to cave in with an "answer." I still have the little note one of them brought me the next year, thanking me for "being the kind of teacher I needed."

I also learned how to let go and have fun with students who were willing to risk looking foolish on the chance that they might learn something. I learned that in surrendering power, I gained authority. I learned to trust my students, just as they needed to trust me. Sometimes it looked like chaos, with plastic swords and arms waving, but those were the moments when I could see their faces come alive and I knew they were learning. I learned to let them be themselves.

Somewhere along the way, I fell in love. Whether talking with a student after class about *Agamemnon* or coaxing a sweet but reluctant ninth grader to make his paragraph longer than one sentence, I felt more myself than in any of my previous careers. On a good day, it was like weaving a tapestry with the students, full of rich threads of thought. On a bad day . . . I had my colleagues and "book clubs," where we would worry about the kids who were struggling and laugh at ourselves.

When people ask what makes Central so special to me and my colleagues, I tell them that our principal, Ms. Mackbee, treats us like professionals. My response never fails to draw a blank stare. You see, most people don't realize how belittled and disrespected we teachers feel in a district, state, and country that act like we need fixing. In this "education reform" age, it is unusual to have a principal who treats us with respect and like we know what we are doing. Just like our students, we rise to her expectations. Central is a mosaic of color and culture that reflects a cross section of my adopted city. Graduates who return to it tell of a world far less rich than the one inside our cinderblock walls. It is a school where there is a place for everyone—and all are welcomed. Ms. Mackbee, refusing to "place children," says every child has a right to fail or to succeed, to follow his or her own dreams.

In recent years, as the reform movement has increasingly tried to reduce teaching to statistics, I have become heavily involved with my union, the Saint Paul Federation of Teachers, because when you love something, you fight for it. Through my union and the leadership of our president, Mary Cathryn Ricker, I have a voice and a seat at the table to discuss education policy. I have been part of creating a strong support program for new teachers and tenured teachers, and feel I have the right to speak up on behalf of my students. Their learning conditions are my working conditions. We have a common interest in this age of testing and data. I owe them my humanity and my voice.

The clean, white lines of Central turn rosy in the early morning light, my favorite time of the school day. All things are possible. In the fall of 2013, a new ninth grade class climbed the steps to become learners in that morning light. For the first time in fifteen years, I was not there to greet them. I am starting fresh with a new group of students in New Delhi, half a world away, where my classes will average eighteen students and I will have a smart board and a computer for every child. But Central will be in my thoughts and my heart. This is my love letter to the school that embraced my children and me—and to the students and educators who taught me how to open my heart. ●

Courtesy Central High School

Students stream into Central High School during "Opening Week," 2012.

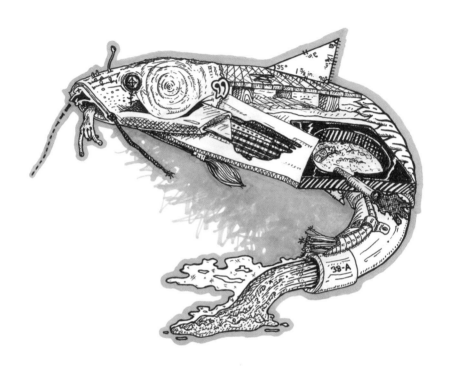

JULY

Good River Feeling Bad ● J. OTIS POWELL?

Her voice is deep water
Though she's too shallow this year for ships
Her body more round than angular
When I ask her questions I get more
Answers than I know what to do with
She says her name in whispers
I know her by many names
And by the ranges she explores
When she sings
I know her by how she changes tunes
And carries her heart to the sea
Bare feet
Wide bottom
She stands like Betsy and Billie and Ma Rainey
Belting blues in wordless conundrums
When she returns to actual lyrics
She sings:
The blues is a good river feeling bad
Her song carries ever-changing sameness
While everything about her transforms
Banks
Depths
Ecology
Water
Running River
Reclaiming place

JULY 2014						
S	M	T	W	T	F	S
		1	2	3	4	5
6	7	8	9	10	11	12
13	14	15	16	17	18	19
20	21	22	23	24	25	26
27	28	29	30	31		

On July 2, 1904, several local youngsters were taken to the Saint Paul police station for shooting off large fireworks and discharging pistols.

MONDAY JUNE 30

TUESDAY 1

Mother Seraphine Ireland, educator and school founder, was born today in 1842.

WEDNESDAY 2

THURSDAY 3

Thomas Boyd, writer and bookstore owner, was born today in 1898.

FRIDAY 4

Independence Day

SATURDAY 5

SUNDAY 6

This Week's Events

Monday
Summer Flower Show

Tuesday
Summer Flower Show

Saint Paul (Seventh Place) Farmers' Market

Nooks and Crannies Tours

Summer History HiJinx Craft Activity

Nine Nights of Music Outdoor Concert

Wednesday
Summer Flower Show

Summer History HiJinx Craft Activity

Thursday
Summer Flower Show

Saint Paul (Seventh Place) Farmers' Market

Music in Mears

Summer History HiJinx Craft Activity

Saint Paul Almanac Soul Sounds Open Mic

Friday
Summer Flower Show

Summer History HiJinx Craft Activity

Saint Anthony Park Parade

Saturday
Downtown Saint Paul Farmers' Market

Summer Flower Show

Summit Avenue Walking Tours

Sunday
Downtown Saint Paul Farmers' Market

Summer Flower Show

Summit Avenue Walking Tours

Hmong international Sports Tournament and Freedom Festival

> "My freedom of conscience is the bottom line. I think that the larger issue of freedom of conscience is more important than an individual state statute of trespass."
>
> ELIZABETH MCKENZIE, *member of Sisters of St. Joseph of Corondelet*

© Barbara Dodge/CameraMaven.net

Wall Street in Lowertown, Saint Paul. Not too many bankers in sight.

Eating Philosophy ● SANDRA ERSKINE

Waitresswalking
across the bridge
still smell like kitchen.
Want to serve you
my seven spice butter sauce
blueberry eyes
freshly baked buns
grated parmesan hair.
I float not boat over the
syrup sweet river,
once again resisting the jump.
Anxious for your
carrot fingers
banana split dessert,
I cross Plato Boulevard.
A sign reads
"love is a serious mental disease."
Straight up mashed potato hill,
the reflection of your binoculars
in the window
is bright as hollandaise.
Garnished with cherries,
vanilla flavored anticipation
leads me to your front door.

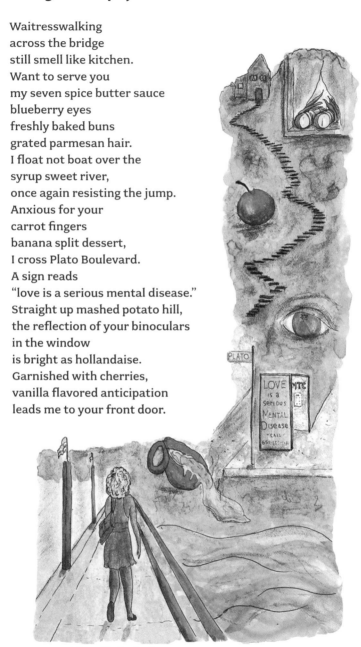

© Serena Mira Asta/AstaArt.com

© LMNOP/www.goo.gl/E7b17

LMNOP 6·16·13

My Como Zoo Funeral ● JAMIE HAGG

I want mini donuts at my funeral
nothing fancy, just a van
owned by a retired couple
who won't skimp on the sugar
and for the kids, all-you-can-ride wristbands.
A merry-go-round with traditional calliope,
no additional cost for adult riders.
Courtesy of my estate—
funky little motorcycles that go up and down
pop-a-wheelie style,
and a Scrambler for the older ones.
Then while the priest
is busy with "ashes to ashes
through the valley . . ."
the kids can scream with glee
to be done with me.
And when the carnies are tired
and the little ones too,
give them each an Icee
so their lips can be
as blue as mine.

JULY 2014

S	M	T	W	T	F	S
		1	2	3	4	5
6	7	8	9	10	11	12
13	14	15	16	17	18	19
20	21	22	23	24	25	26
27	28	29	30	31		

On July 7, 1902, the Afro-American Press Association opened its national meeting at Saint Paul's Pilgrim Baptist Church, then located at Cedar and Summit Avenues.

MONDAY

7

TUESDAY

8

Cleora Clark Wheeler—a "designer-illuminator" specializing in bookplates, greeting cards, and wedding invitations—was born today in 1882.

WEDNESDAY

9

THURSDAY

10

FRIDAY

11

SATURDAY

12

Susan Maria Blu, voice actress in animated movies and voice and casting director, was born today in 1948.

SUNDAY

13

This Week's Events

Monday
Summer Flower Show

Tuesday
Summer Flower Show
Saint Paul (Seventh Place) Farmers' Market
Nooks and Crannies Tours
Summer History HiJinx Craft Activity
Hmong international Sports Tournament and Freedom Festival
Seniors in Mind
Nine Nights of Music Outdoor Concert

Wednesday
Summer Flower Show
Summer History HiJinx Craft Activity
History Pub Crawl

Thursday
Summer Flower Show
Saint Paul (Seventh Place) Farmers' Market
Music in Mears
Summer History HiJinx Craft Activity
Saint Paul Almanac Soul Sounds Open Mic

Friday
Summer Flower Show
Summer History HiJinx Craft Activity
Summer Movies

Saturday
Downtown Saint Paul Farmers' Market
Summer Flower Show
Summit Avenue Walking Tours
Dragon Festival and Boat Races

Sunday
Downtown Saint Paul Farmers' Market
Summer Flower Show
Summit Avenue Walking Tours
Dragon Festival and Boat Races

> "I have rarely seen a happy person walking a dog, but rather a burdened sort, a put-upon soul who is merely accomplishing a rote, sometimes humiliating, chore."
>
> JOE SOUCHERAY, *Saint Paul radio show host and columnist*

© Tom Dunn/TomDunnPhoto.com

Going to the Library ● GLORIA BURGESS LEVIN

Early on, my library card was one of my most precious possessions. This small piece of heavy card stock, about three by four inches, was my passport to the adventure of other worlds, and also to my own adventures. My first card was issued at the bookmobile that came on Fridays to my elementary school, Chelsea Heights, near Como Park. I still remember my first trip to the bookmobile. Not knowing what I was doing, and with few adults to help, I looked at book-jacket pictures in the adult fiction section. The one I liked best was of a man dressed in black on a funny-looking mountain. When I brought it to the librarian, she told me the book was too hard for me, and gently led me to the picture book section where she helped me make other choices.

But that book-jacket picture was engraved into my mind, and I never forgot it. Years later, when I was reading at a much more advanced level, I went back to the Cs, always remembering where I had found it. Searching through the book jackets, suddenly there it was: A. J. Cronin's *Keys to the Kingdom*, a novel about a missionary priest in China. This book has had a continuous influence throughout my life. Even as a child, I became a kind of missionary for libraries and books. After gaining parental permission, I took every child on our block to get his or her first library card. It was exciting to start these kids on their reading journeys!

My favorite library was Hamline Branch Library, located on Minnehaha Avenue a half block east of Snelling. A small, unassuming brick building, it housed treasures. In the summertime, the book-reading program was always a big draw. I was good at reading books. In fifth and sixth grades, I read six books a week, and the summer was no different. I could easily have read more, but six was the limit to check out. I would plow through two the first day, and then ration out the other four over the next six days. People called me a bookworm, and I was proud of that epithet, even as I cringed at some of the other nicknames kids gave me. Hamline Library had so many more books than the bookmobile: shelf after shelf, a whole building's worth of books to revel in.

Hamline Library had other gifts too. In the summer the building was cool and hushed. On many afternoons it was a quiet oasis of tranquility. Sometimes I would go to the encyclopedia shelves. Getting them off the shelves was a challenge for a little girl like me. The *World Book* was the best. What wondrous knowledge was inside those book covers! I would pick one at random, settle myself at one of the huge heavy library tables, and lose myself in reading whatever caught my eye. I drank in the serenity and quiet that accompanied these hours, forever melding together learning and peacefulness. My love of learning was nurtured by that fortunate juxtaposition.

I became very efficient at checking out books. First I opened the books to their back covers with the book card in its envelope, and then I stacked the books one on top of the other. That way, the librarian could quickly pull out each card and stamp the due date in purple ink. It was fun to see which books were the most popular, as shown by how many due dates were stamped and how close the dates were in time to one another.

Going home with a stack of heavy books was another matter. I walked the half block to the bus stop on Snelling and waited for the 4A or 4B bus. Sometimes the wait was as long as twenty minutes, and there was no bench to help ease the weight in my arms. If it was blistering hot, I would slip into the blessedly cool drugstore on the corner, Lloyd's Pharmacy. But I was always anxious about missing the bus. So I would peek out the door every few minutes to see if it was coming—the air conditioning bill must have been a little bit higher on my library days! Safely on the bus, I would peruse my treasures, planning the order in which to read them. Once decided, I'd begin right then and there, delicious summer days and nights of reading ahead of me. ●

© Ferdinand Uebel, 1950.
Courtesy Minnesota Historical Society

Ferd. Uebel, July 19/50.

JULY 2014

S	M	T	W	T	F	S
		1	2	3	4	5
6	7	8	9	10	11	12
13	14	15	16	17	18	19
20	21	22	23	24	25	26
27	28	29	30	31		

On July 14, 1992, William "Corky" Finney was appointed as Saint Paul's first African American police chief.

MONDAY

14

TUESDAY

15

Charles E. Flandrau, pioneer judge, was born today in 1828.

WEDNESDAY

16

THURSDAY

17

Charles James, African American activist and three-time president of the Saint Paul Trades and Labor Assembly, was born today in 1866.

FRIDAY

18

SATURDAY

19

SUNDAY

20

This Week's Events

Monday
Summer Flower Show

Tuesday
Summer Flower Show
Saint Paul (Seventh Place) Farmers' Market
Nooks and Crannies Tours
Summer History HiJinx Craft Activity
Nine Nights of Music Outdoor Concert

Wednesday
Summer Flower Show
Summer History HiJinx Craft Activity
History Pub Crawl

Thursday
Summer Flower Show
Saint Paul (Seventh Place) Farmers' Market
Music in Mears
Summer History HiJinx Craft Activity
Saint Paul Almanac Soul Sounds Open Mic
Sunset Affair Gala

Friday
Summer Flower Show
Summer History HiJinx Craft Activity
Summer Movies
Highland Fest
Home Expo and Art Fair

Saturday
Downtown Saint Paul Farmers' Market
Summer Flower Show
Summit Avenue Walking Tours
Highland Fest
Home Expo and Art Fair
Rondo Days

Sunday
Downtown Saint Paul Farmers' Market
Summer Flower Show
Summit Avenue Walking Tours
Highland Fest
Home Expo and Art Fair

> "This is a time when workers are being exploited and are fighting back, trying to make their lives more stable and secure in this difficult period in the global economy where inequality is growing so sharply."
>
> **PETER RACHLEFF,**
> *activist and labor historian*

© Tony Ernst/gamelaner on Flickr

Artist Ta-coumba Aiken and a team of hundreds broke the official Guinness Record for Largest Picture Made of Lite-Brite with a 596,897-peg sculpture.

Selby Avenue, 1970 ● MARCIE RENDON

As a teenager I drove grain trucks, pickup trucks, and Massey Ferguson tractors for farmers in the Red River Valley. I hauled oats, corn, and soybeans and drove alongside combines as wheat poured into truck beds. I plowed fields and threw straw bales. While not an idyllic life by any means, it was a life of sunshine and even golder harvest moons.

In 1970, on a whim, I set off for Saint Paul with ninety dollars in my pocket, two pairs of jeans, and a couple tee shirts. A relative helped me find an attic room on Laurel Avenue. I got my first "every-two-weeks-paycheck" job working for American Family Insurance on University Avenue by the building that reads "Minneapolis-Saint Paul." I don't think I lasted the summer.

The 21 bus took me down Selby every evening on my way home from work. I was a country girl used to walking, so sometimes I walked. No one warned me otherwise. Selby-Dale was a hotbed of illicit activity in 1970. It was also an era of sex, drugs, and rock and roll. Selby Avenue is where it all happened.

Girls hung out on the corners. I would greet them, have a chat. I didn't know they were "working" until one night an undercover cop pulled up and my new friend went running. Her wig flew off and tens and twenties fluttered to the ground in the twilight glow. While the cop stooped to pick up the bills, I too took off running. I wasn't sure why I was running, but it seemed like the smart thing to do.

Hippies hung around Selby and Western. With long hair and embroidered bell bottoms, they sold pot, smoked pot, or had pot parties in the cheap apartments of that area. There were young runaway girls from the girl's reform school in Sauk Center. Some were running from harsher lives than mine in suburbs like Edina and White Bear Lake. I once walked into a party on Western Avenue where a kids' swimming pool was filled with naked hippies body-painting each other in the glow of black lights. I didn't join in.

Like I said, I don't think I lasted the summer with the insurance company. There was a pimp I met when eating my daily tuna sandwich, the one meal I could afford by that time. I was sitting in a back booth at the deli on Selby listening to the jukebox while Otis Redding sang about sitting on the dock of the bay. Charlie Pride was trying to get to San Antone, and I was reading the help wanteds. This pimp had my best interests at heart. He told me about the Saint Paul American Indian Center, and that maybe I should go there and see if they could help me find another job.

At the Indian Center, I met advocate Paul Shultz. He found me a job at Burlington Northern Railroad in downtown Saint Paul. He also got me rent money so I could move into a real one-bedroom apartment on Western Avenue, right behind the Angus Hotel, which is now Blair Flats. The hotel at that time was rent by the hour, or week, or moment—all depending on what you wanted. I discovered a tunnel in my building basement that went into the beer cooler of the hotel's bar. Paul Shultz also arranged for Mrs. White Rabbit to teach me how to make frybread tuna sandwiches so I could stop hanging out at the deli after work. A noble plan. ●

© Clifford M. Renshaw/Minnesota Historical Society

The Angus Hotel at 165 North Western Avenue, 1971. See a photo of the building today on page 340.

JULY 2014

S	M	T	W	T	F	S
		1	2	3	4	5
6	7	8	9	10	11	12
13	14	15	16	17	18	19
20	21	22	23	24	25	26
27	28	29	30	31		

Bootleggers Abe Wagner and Al Gordon were gunned down in broad daylight by two hit men at the Green Dragon Café, 469 North Snelling Avenue, on July 25, 1932.

MONDAY

21

TUESDAY

22

Dr. Eva-Jane Ostergren, 42-year practitioner on Saint Paul's East Side and first woman Chief of Staff at Mounds Park Hospital, was born today in 1914.

WEDNESDAY

23

THURSDAY

24

FRIDAY

25

Midge Decter—neoconservative journalist, editor, and author from Saint Paul—was born today in 1927.

SATURDAY

26

SUNDAY

27

This Week's Events

Monday
Summer Flower Show

Tuesday
Summer Flower Show
Saint Paul (Seventh Place) Farmers' Market
Nooks and Crannies Tours
Summer History HiJinx Craft Activity
Nine Nights of Music Outdoor Concert

Wednesday
Summer Flower Show
Summer History HiJinx Craft Activity
Saint Paul Almanac Lowertown Reading Jam
History Pub Crawl

Thursday
Summer Flower Show
Saint Paul (Seventh Place) Farmers' Market
Music in Mears
Summer History HiJinx Craft Activity
Saint Paul Almanac Soul Sounds Open Mic

Friday
Summer Flower Show
Summer History HiJinx Craft Activity
Summer Movies
Fourth Friday at the Movies

Saturday
Downtown Saint Paul Farmers' Market
Summer Flower Show
Summit Avenue Walking Tours

Sunday
Downtown Saint Paul Farmers' Market
Summer Flower Show
Summit Avenue Walking Tours

> The Saint Paul Community Design Center's East Side Conservation Corps received a Junior Ranger Award from First Lady Laura Bush on July 27, 2005.

© Tony Ernst/gamelaner on Flickr

Nirmala Rajasekar, vocalist and veena player in the group "Butterfly," who plays with bandmates Gao Hong on pipa and Michelle Kinney on cello

Old Rondo • DONTE COLLINS

we were Ferris
wheel watchers
firefly fighters
dollar store cap gun
robbers
cops and
Sunday creased collars
private school scholars
giving the church basket
the dollars our mothers
slipped into our pockets
seconds before.
we held doors for our elders
and snuck to receive communion
even though our tongues
hadn't reached their stage of holy
water guns weren't allowed
in our homes
but balloons were
so we soaked our summers
in Battleship,
bottled water
sipped through
naive nine-year-old lips
at horizon sunset sitting on
J.J. Hill
waiting for those street lamps
to call us home before our mothers did
and when she slept
we ditched our
screen doors
danced in the rain
rinsed out our grass stains
and became the night's
nickname they called us kids
we called ourselves bigger
than most things our size
sneaking girls beneath the

playground slide
first kisses were a lot
like gut laughter everything
was funnier when you weren't
supposed to smile
they told us to mind our
manners
fold our fingers
crisscross applesauce
for dinner
did you wash your hands
before dishing them greens
did you help your mother
pick them greens
we were scabbed knees
and bubble gum fiends
all cocked up on
Mike and Ikes
and Now and Laters
sounded a lot like
a metaphor for
childhood
for the way we grew up
through adversity

Illustrations © Leann E. Johnson/lea-way.com

and anniversaries
of jazz parades
and street signs
I guess before they built
that freeway,
there was a
colony of houses
lined up like
heritage on
an auction block
about to meet their
God the largest black
community in Saint Paul
was cut down
like it hadn't deserved
the land it slept on for so long
like it hadn't raised its children
under corner store stories
front porches
and grandma's front lawn
I bet if they knew we
hid beneath the bridges
they built
they would tear
those down too
they would tell us kids
to grow up
like high rises
through minority roofs
we were minorities' proof
that if you raise
your fireflies in the
heart of the dark
they will earn their
light in the form of a spark
in the form of a million matches
attempting to set flame the desert
until every grain is a
diamond worth giving a name
so they called us kids

we called ourselves
the reason this neighborhood lives
the reason you can clear your conscience
and throat and enjoy the right to breathe
our pigment permanent in cement silhouettes
so our street lamps never have to leave
our tattered shoes and
collard greens
our mothers
awoke us at dawn
told to walk
down the block
to Golden Thyme
given enough money for
a coffee and a Krispy Kreme
and if I remember to bring
four creams and four sugars
she would always
blow me a wink
that meant
the top of the world
or at least the
Ferris wheel peak

ev 1/2　　　　　Co-op

The Welcoming Energy of
Lowertown ● DEBORAH MCLAREN

The final stop on the new Green Line light rail in Saint Paul is historic Lowertown: easy to get to, very walkable, and connected by the Morgan, Bruce Vento, and Gateway bike trails. Originally called "Lowertown Landing," the port was the first point of access to the Twin Cities from the Mississippi River, a bustling hub of factories, warehouses, railroads, and banking and distribution buildings that served the entire Upper Midwest from 1860 to 1920. Lowertown's boundaries are Seventh Street to Kellogg Boulevard from north to south, and from Robert Street to the Kellogg Bridge from east to west.

Lowertown's old brick buildings, many of them Revivals and Victorians from the late nineteenth and early twentieth centuries, are now home to a vibrant community of artists and many small independent businesses. People in Lowertown exude a welcoming energy, and their laid-back, offbeat vibe propels the ongoing neighborhood renaissance. The Saint Paul Saints baseball team chose Lowertown as the site for its new stadium, designed to be one of the greenest stadiums in the country when it opens in 2015.

Lowertown is the place to visit on weekend mornings between late April and November, when a bustling farmers' market offers a dazzling array of local food and crafts that originate from within one hundred miles of Saint Paul. Farmers offer fresh vegetables and cut flowers; other local merchants sell artisan chocolates, salsas, cheeses, and meats from nearby farms. A pop-up bagel shop serves coffee and lemonade, and there's often entertainment—music, storytelling, and magicians. In the winter, a scaled-down outdoor market continues, with an indoor wing across the street in Golden's Deli, where delicious offerings of honey, maple syrup, and bakery items are sold.

Across the street from the market, the Northern Warehouse building is home to the main community hub of Lowertown, the Black Dog Coffee and Wine Bar, offering locally sourced and often organic soups, sandwiches, beer, and unusual wines, with monthly exhibits by local artists on its walls and an impressive roster of people performing blues, folk, and many genres of jazz. Here, neighbor-

Illustration © Amy Joy Hosterman

hood residents gather for games and friendly socializing, or to work on sketch books and canvases. The *Saint Paul Almanac* hosts poetry readings and spoken word performances at the Black Dog throughout the year, rebroadcast on local cable channel SPNN.

The Northern Warehouse is also home to the Japanese Tanpopo Noodle Shop and, also at street level, the AZ Gallery, which offers a diverse spectrum of exhibits, including Saint Paul Public School children's art shows. Opened in 2013, and within a block of the farmers' market, the Three Sisters Gallery offers a quality range of local crafts, art, jewelry, and furniture. Turn up in Lowertown for First Friday evenings, the spring or fall art crawls, and the annual Northern Spark festival to meet the artists themselves.

Music festivals throughout the summer and fall take place at Mears Park, the location for the Jazz Festival, Concrete & Grass Festival, American Guitar Festival, Roots Festival, and free concerts every Thursday of the summer, as well as movie nights. Golden's Deli and the nearby lounge bar/restaurant Senor Wongs—with a delightful Mexican-Asian fusion menu—host Lowertown's open mic nights, with Golden's also offering a comedy open mic.

Visitors and locals alike find plenty of places to eat around Mears Park at restaurants such as the Barrio Tequila Bar, Bin Wine Bar, the Bulldog pub, Faces-Mears Park, and Trattoria da Vinci. Serious diners revere the nearby Heartland Restaurant for cutting-edge cocktails and cuisine made from indigenous and cultivated ingredients from the American and Canadian Midwest. Owned by award-winning chef Lenny Russo, the Heartland—and its adjoining Farm Direct Market deli—offer menus that change daily, depending on what farmers bring to the back door. Three neighborhood bars—Kelly's Depot Bar, the Gopher Bar, and the Hat Trick Lounge—offer visitors a uniquely local pulse.

Several unusual theaters, small venues, and performing arts festivals also call Lowertown home. Bedlam Theater—a longtime leader in Minneapolis's independent arts scene—is opening a new space as a "theater nightclub," although you might catch one of their acts outside, on the street or in the park. The Northern Warehouse houses the Nautilus Theater, dedicated to the development of new operas and other forms of music theater. Flamenco and belly dancing happen at Studio Sendero in the Jax building. Winner of

City Pages's Best Pub Crawl, the seventh annual Lowertown Santa-Con will again flood the streets with Santas and elves in December in 2014

Trains, light rail, and city buses stop at Lowertown's newly restored Union Depot, a destination in itself. One of the great architectural achievements of the city, the Depot's grand concourse and waiting room last saw passenger trains arriving and departing in the early twentieth century. On Wednesday nights at the Depot, you can play oversized versions of Jenga, dominos, chess, and checkers on the polished floors, with "regular size" games happening on tabletops along the walls. Christos Greek Restaurant inside the Depot offers excellent food as well as drink specials at happy hour. And when it's time to head home—or back to your hotel—the light rail just outside is ready to take you there! ●

© Tom Dunn/TomDunnPhoto.com

Artists' drawing circle in the Black Dog Coffee and Wine Bar. Almost all of the artists pictured contributed artwork to this Almanac.

Pulling Weeds ● GEORGIA A. GREELEY

I finally got that one patch of garden done,
walked past it the next day and found green growing things,
not beautiful, dark, crumbly soil warming in the sun—
it was full of weeds twice the height of those I'd pulled the day
  before.
I got angry. Did it again. Yanked those plants up by the roots
and delighted in stuffing them, handful by handful,
down into that black claustrophobic garbage bag.
Next day they were back, knee high,
crowding my roses, coralbells, and bleeding hearts.
I went berserk, stamping and pulling and swearing—
neighbors looked the other way as they passed.
Shoulder height! Next day they were shoulder height,
with no garden to be seen, just a patch of golden,
gone-to-seed weeds waving in the sun.
I cried. Took out the tiller, uprooted and buried everything,
tossed grass seed in the dirt, watered, and stood guard all night.
I sensed the creeping Charlie hiding in the grass, cringing.

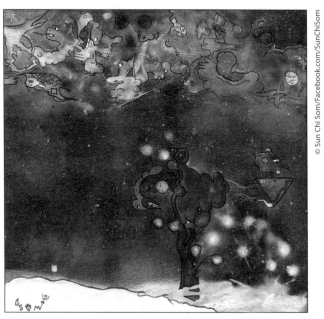

Planet Next

© Laura Erickson/LauraErickson.com

AUGUST

Mother ● LINDA BACK MCKAY

She is waiting by the front door.
Her wings whir, invisible as the August breeze.
She hovers, almost motionless there,
held in place by air. The oaks are singing
tangled songs through serrated leaves,
asphalt appears liquid under the harsh
beat of the sun. The air is metallic.
I am just behind the screen,
standing as still as I can. I want
to take her in my cupped hands
and keep her with me. I want to feed her
tidbits of sugar and wafer, the holy
communion of our lives, our bodies
inside and outside of our souls,
hopelessly connected, two full moons,
circling each other in endless flight.

AUGUST 2014

S	M	T	W	T	F	S
					1	2
3	4	5	6	7	8	9
10	11	12	13	14	15	16
17	18	19	20	21	22	23
24	25	26	27	28	29	30
31						

The Junior Pioneer Association was formed at a meeting in Saint Paul on August 1, 1889.

MONDAY

JULY

28

Jim Smith, an East Side community builder and advocate for a just and caring society, was born today in 1944.

TUESDAY

JULY

29

Eid Al-Fitr

WEDNESDAY

JULY

30

THURSDAY

JULY

31

FRIDAY

1

T. H. Lyles, prominent Saint Paul African American businessman and community activist, was born today in 1853.

SATURDAY

2

SUNDAY

3

This Week's Events

Monday
Summer Flower Show

Tuesday
Summer Flower Show
Saint Paul (Seventh Place) Farmers' Market
Nooks and Crannies Tours
Summer History HiJinx Craft Activity
Nine Nights of Music Outdoor Concert

Wednesday
Summer Flower Show
Summer History HiJinx Craft Activity
Seniors in Mind
Circus Juventas Summer Show
History Pub Crawl

Thursday
Summer Flower Show
Saint Paul (Seventh Place) Farmers' Market
Music in Mears
Summer History HiJinx Craft Activity
Saint Paul Almanac Soul Sounds Open Mic
Circus Juventas Summer Show

Friday
Summer Flower Show
Summer History HiJinx Craft Activity
Summer Movies
Circus Juventas Summer Show

Saturday
Downtown Saint Paul Farmers' Market
Summer Flower Show
Summit Avenue Walking Tours
Circus Juventas Summer Show

Sunday
Downtown Saint Paul Farmers' Market
Summer Flower Show
Summit Avenue Walking Tours
Paws on Grand
Circus Juventas Summer Show

© Bob Muschewske/370SummitStPaul.com

Melvin Carter III with his daughters. Melvin is the state's director of the Office of Early Learning.

Getting Paid to Play Basketball ● LAWRENCE DANIELS

Dedicated to Mel Riley

I have played sports all of my life, but the one sport I have always wanted to play at a high level is basketball—and be paid for it. In my quest to go pro, I have played all over the state of Minnesota, including the University of Minnesota field house, where I was able to sharpen my skills and learn the game with some of the best Division I players in the state.

It was 1986 when my dream came true: I was getting paid to play basketball! My own gym! Well, not really—the City of Saint Paul owned the building. But I was the caretaker.

Frogtown was the neighborhood where I was perfecting my skills playing round ball at Scheffer Recreation Center. (It wasn't the NBA, but maybe next year!) I was the Recreation Leader; the job was not only dribbling a basketball, but much more. There were great little minds to inspire, give guidance to, and keep safe. It was all in a day's work. On Monday, it was time to open those doors and let their minds run free. Who knows, with the wings they carried on their backs, the sky was the limit! I pictured a doctor, a judge, and a CEO of a Fortune 500 company. Why stop there? The President of the United States of America!

Monday night was open gym, from 3 to 10 p.m. The cut-off time for young kids was 5:30 p.m.—anyone under eighteen years old had to leave the gym. From time to time, I would tell the "Kats" from the neighborhood that even though the sign said "Scheffer Recreation Center," it was, for that time between 5:30 and 10 p.m., my gym! Oh boy, was it my gym. Sweet spots! One through seven I had mastered! Full court or half, it didn't make a difference. All you heard all night was swish and "Who got him?"

The year 1987 was a great time to be a Recreation Leader; there were opportunities to have different events at the center. We had volunteers helping from the neighborhood. Their help made it easier for me to work on new ideas for Scheffer playground.

One of the duties of a Recreation Leader was to create opportunities for all who came through the doors, keeping young minds thinking about their hidden skills and participating in activities they may not experience anywhere else.

Arts and crafts, especially papier-mâché, were a big deal for ages three through thirteen, and sometimes we would even get some of the older kids involved.

On one of my shopping days for arts and crafts material for the center, I stopped in a Fashion Bug store and talked with the manager to see if she would be interested in sponsoring a show I was thinking about organizing. She said sure, just let her know when.

The first annual fashion show at Scheffer Recreation Center was aired on public access that year with the help of a Kat named Copeland who was producing the show and was a member of the St. Paul Neighborhood Network station (SPNN). We had always talked about collaborating on a project of this magnitude, and we succeeded. The fashion show was a real hit!

After that, I organized a spelling bee contest. I would like to think it inspired young minds to go on to do bigger and better things.

Today I am riding the 67A bus route, and every time I ride it, down Thomas Avenue on my way to my mom's house, I see the Scheffer Recreation Center where I worked. I think about how life would have turned out if I were still getting paid to play my favorite sport. It wasn't the NBA—but I still got paid to play basketball! ●

© James Nutt, AIA/NuttDraws.blogspot.com

AUGUST 2014

S	M	T	W	T	F	S
					1	2
3	4	5	6	7	8	9
10	11	12	13	14	15	16
17	18	19	20	21	22	23
24	25	26	27	28	29	30
31						

The new Robert Street Bridge in downtown Saint Paul was opened with a gala celebration on August 6, 1926.

MONDAY

4

TUESDAY

5

Lizz Winstead, comedian, was born today in 1961.

Hiroshima/Nagasaki Remembrance Day

WEDNESDAY

6

THURSDAY

7

FRIDAY

8

SATURDAY

9

See Vang Thao, early woman Hmong attorney, was born today in 1965.

SUNDAY

10

Hascal Brill, longtime Saint Paul judge, was born today in 1846.

This Week's Events

Monday
Summer Flower Show
Circus Juventas Summer Show

Tuesday
Summer Flower Show
Saint Paul (Seventh Place) Farmers' Market
Nooks and Crannies Tours
Summer History HiJinx Craft Activity
Nine Nights of Music
Circus Juventas Summer Show

Wednesday
Summer Flower Show
Summer History HiJinx Craft Activity
History Pub Crawl
Circus Juventas Summer Show

Thursday
Summer Flower Show
Saint Paul (Seventh Place) Farmers' Market
Music in Mears
Summer History HiJinx Craft Activity
Circus Juventas Summer Show
Saint Paul Almanac Soul Sounds Open Mic

Friday
Summer Flower Show
Summer History HiJinx Craft Activity
Irish Fair
Circus Juventas Summer Show

Saturday
Downtown Saint Paul Farmers' Market
Summer Flower Show
Summit Avenue Walking Tours
Irish Fair
Circus Juventas Summer Show

Sunday
Downtown Saint Paul Farmers' Market
Summer Flower Show
Summit Avenue Walking Tours
Irish Fair
Circus Juventas Summer Show

© Patrick McCutchan/PatrickMcCutchan.com

Actors dressed in period costumes at the opening of the Union Depot station, December 8, 2012

Spider in the Car ● DAVID BORNUS

Driving up Snelling
After the reading at Ginkgo,
Relaxing toward home.
What is that, in the headlights? A leaf? A piece of fuzz?
Another headlight—no, a spider! Long brown legs on the
    windshield.
Hit the wipers, get rid of it. It doesn't move—inside with me!
Nowhere to pull over in traffic. My hands chained to the wheel.
    Eyes on the road.
Yet I cannot look away. If I lose him, he'll drop down onto my lap.
Look at traffic.
Look at spider.
Where is a red light when you need one?
Groping below the seat for napkin, carefully multitasking.
    Watching spider, watching traffic.
Found napkin. Now, I am ready.
Napkin on steering wheel. Nonchalant. I slowly raise napkin.
    The spider tenses. Closer . . .
Now! Got him! Or did I? Watch the road!
Squeeze the napkin into a hard ball. Don't think about him
    escaping in my hand.
In the dark, can I be sure? Squeeze the napkin ball again, toss it
    onto the floor, away from my legs.
I got him, didn't I? But there are no spider guts on the windshield.
I feel crawling on my leg. I hope I'm imagining it.

© Samantha Esguerra

Artifacts from Rondo ● NORITA DITTBERNER-JAX

Pete gave us the bricks for the patio
from the pile in his back yard,
bricks he inherited from Margaret Wilson
when she moved to Florida at 97.

Margaret Wilson—Aunt Margaret to me
and a thousand others, black and white,
not five feet tall, cream-colored suit,
matching hat and heels.

She built the rambler in 1958
in the heart of the Black neighborhood.
Rondo Avenue—saxophones, player pianos,
leafy streets and spindled porches,
torn down for the freeway.

Aunt Margaret couldn't save the house
but took the bricks from the street;
neighborhood boys piled them
in the back of the station wagon
and she drove them to the back yard
of the new house where they stayed put.

So the bricks in our front yard were the bricks
in her back yard, were the cobbles
of Rondo, cut one by one, hewn
by hand into anchors strong enough
to withstand hooves of horses,
the wheels of carriages, model Ts
and Aunt Margaret's station wagon.

A few have come to rest on Goodrich.
Late afternoons we take our places
on the patio and look out over the open
field of the school yard. A footnote
in the life of the city, two lawn chairs
and a small table.

AUGUST 2014

S	M	T	W	T	F	S
					1	2
3	4	5	6	7	8	9
10	11	12	13	14	15	16
17	18	19	20	21	22	23
24	25	26	27	28	29	30
31						

▌ "Love life as if it was the end, because you never know what comes knocking at your door."

MARY LY, *Hmong actress*

MONDAY

11

Rick Aguilar, Latino businessman and multicultural marketing consultant, was born today in 1963.

TUESDAY

12

WEDNESDAY

13

THURSDAY

14

FRIDAY

15

SATURDAY

16

SUNDAY

17

This Week's Events

Monday
Summer Flower Show
Circus Juventas Summer Show

Tuesday
Summer Flower Show
Saint Paul (Seventh Place) Farmers' Market
Nooks and Crannies Tours
Summer History HiJinx Craft Activity
Nine Nights of Music
Circus Juventas Summer Show

Wednesday
Summer Flower Show
Summer History HiJinx Craft Activity
History Pub Crawl
Circus Juventas Summer Show

Thursday
Summer Flower Show
Saint Paul (Seventh Place) Farmers' Market
Music in Mears
Summer History HiJinx Craft Activity
Circus Juventas Summer Show
Saint Paul Almanac Soul Sounds Open Mic

Friday
Summer Flower Show
Summer History HiJinx Craft Activity
Circus Juventas Summer Show

Saturday
Downtown Saint Paul Farmers' Market
Summer Flower Show
Summit Avenue Walking Tours
Circus Juventas Summer Show

Sunday
Downtown Saint Paul Farmers' Market
Summer Flower Show
Summit Avenue Walking Tours
Japanese Lantern Lighting Festival
Circus Juventas Summer Show

© Patrick McCutchan/PatrickMcCutchan.com

Actors dressed in period costumes at the opening of the Union Depot station, December 8, 2012

The Fantastic Four ● DAVID R. WEISS

Okay, I am *not* a superhero, but I *will* lay claim to something more than mere delusions of grandeur. Like the superheroes of our imagination, I am an otherwise ordinary-looking individual. And, like them, on occasion I manifest extraordinary powers to preserve our freedom and democracy . . .

So it was that four of us circled ourselves in the early dawn, at the edge of an empty Saint Paul parking lot, on a Tuesday morning in August. The gentle breeze and clear skies seemed innocuous. But the *stillness*, the stillness might've signaled to an attentive onlooker that something unusual, something *extraordinary* was about to happen.

And then it did.

Our leader, her red hair beckoning flames in the morning sun, spoke first. And her words called the rest of our voices forth into an incantation fit for flying capes and masked crusaders:

"I . . . solemnly swear that I will perform the duties of election judge according to the law and the best of my ability and will diligently endeavor to prevent fraud, deceit, and abuse in conducting this election. I will perform my duties in a fair and impartial manner and not attempt to create an advantage for my party or for any candidate."

"Oh," you say.

No. Not "Oh." In the vivid vocabulary of Vice President Joe Biden, this is a "*big f***ing deal.*" I mean, four of us, *complete strangers*, meet in an empty school parking lot at 6 a.m.—and thirty minutes later engage ourselves in a ritual recitation that transforms us from mere neighbors into *stewards of democracy*. With these words we become keepers of an electoral process for which many around the globe still yearn.

True, mostly we just push papers. Register new voters. Collect signatures in the registration roster. Hand out receipts at one table and then collect them at the very next table in exchange for a ballot. And see to it that the ballots, duly marked, make their way into the big black box that today becomes the voice of our combined citizenship.

So capes, tights, and masks would probably be overkill. But on this day, in the humble (and sporadic—it was a primary election, after all) procession of citizens who cast their votes, the highest ideals of our democracy are being practiced. Setting campaign rhetoric aside but with competing visions of the common good still claiming our silent allegiances, on *this* day we do something all too *un*common on our planet: *We settle our differences peacefully.*

And on this day, as the sun rises, a whole assortment of us step out of our otherwise ordinary lives to become election judges for a day. If "superhero" is an overstatement, it is only just barely so. After all, in a democracy the real superpower is helping to ensure that every vote, every voice, is heard. ●

© William Birawer/WilliamBirawer.com

AUGUST 2014

S	M	T	W	T	F	S
					1	2
3	4	5	6	7	8	9
10	11	12	13	14	15	16
17	18	19	20	21	22	23
24	25	26	27	28	29	30
31						

"Having moved from Pittsburgh to St. Paul, I felt I could hear voices for the first time accurately."

AUGUST WILSON,
African American playwright

MONDAY

18

Adam Granger—guitarist, teacher, author, and Prairie Home Companion musician—was born today in 1949.

TUESDAY

19

WEDNESDAY

20

THURSDAY

21

FRIDAY

22

Henry Castle, author of *History of St. Paul and Vicinity*, was born today in 1841.

SATURDAY

23

SUNDAY

24

This Week's Events

Monday
  Summer Flower Show

Tuesday
  Summer Flower Show
  Saint Paul (Seventh Place) Farmers'
    Market
  Nooks and Crannies Tours
  Nine Nights of Music

Wednesday
  Summer Flower Show
  History Pub Crawl

Thursday
  Summer Flower Show
  Saint Paul (Seventh Place) Farmers'
    Market
  Music in Mears
  Minnesota State Fair
  Saint Paul Almanac Soul Sounds
    Open Mic

Friday
  Summer Flower Show
  Minnesota State Fair
  Fourth Friday at the Movies

Saturday
  Downtown Saint Paul Farmers'
    Market

  Summer Flower Show
  Summit Avenue Walking
    Tours
  Minnesota State Fair

Sunday
  Downtown Saint Paul
    Farmers' Market
  Summer Flower Show
  Summit Avenue Walking
    Tours
  Minnesota State Fair

Dragonfly

You are soul-weigher, tiny
devil's horse, doctor
of snakes. You are strength
of late summer, double-barred
cross of courage and speed,
rendered flightless
with two pebbles
and a string
of child's hair.

Paige Riehl

© Faye Sparks

Black Hawk helicopters over the Saint Paul skyline

How Sweet It Was! ● RONALD CRAIG SPONG

"Ronny, time to get up!" It was 4 a.m., and my sixth birthday surprise was about to be revealed on this summer day in 1949. After a bowl of my grandmother's hot oatmeal, I accompanied my grandpa, Albert Vikla, in his old Ford coupe to the family's business, Mays, Inc., at 1481 Marshall Avenue in Saint Paul. As we turned into the alley, the sun's first rays warmed the building's brick façade in soft hues.

We entered through the rear loading dock, and immediately I smelled the pungent odor of ammonia. Walking across the creaky warehouse floor, we paused by a stairwell leading to the basement. Grandpa descended to check the ammonia refrigeration plant and make sure it was not leaking. Then he led me through large rubber-fringed, swinging doors into a cavernous room. Bright overhead lights revealed rows of stainless steel mixing machines and vats lining one side; on the other side, heavily latched doors led to freezers.

My uncle, Edmund Vikla, was working in his office at a rolltop desk. In the late 1920s, he had been certified by the University of Minnesota's dairy sanitation program in ice cream manufacturing. Working first as the Mays' bookkeeper, he later bought out the company's owners as the economy slipped deeper into the Great Depression. The 1930s were a financial rollercoaster ride for the business, and the close-knit Vikla family pitched in to help. Years later my mother, Edna, recalled those difficult years when she and my aunts Vicky, Ann, and Austine took turns selling Mays ice cream at a little shop on West Seventh Street not far from their home in Saint Paul's Little Bohemia neighborhood.

By 8 a.m. that birthday morning, the busy compressors, conveyors, and mixers hummed as the production of ice cream and other frozen treats began. I watched, fascinated by the workers' choreographed movements filling endless containers of the frozen confections. Each mixer on the assembly line poured concoctions of fragrant flavors, including vanilla, strawberry, chocolate, and Uncle Ed's unique version of "Rocky Road."

Up and down the line, wheeled carts packed with containers of ice cream squeaked as they were rolled into the huge freezers. Further chilling was necessary before the ice cream could be loaded onto refrigerated trucks bound for local markets, hotels, concessionaires, and catered events all over the Twin Cities. Mays was especially well known for its high-quality ice creams molded into specialty forms, such as edible animals, for children's birthday parties and Christmas decorations.

I idled away some time in Uncle Ed's office, doodling and spinning around on his massive oak swivel chair, until Grandpa called me to help. My chore was to open small boxes of wooden sticks for Grandpa to set in Popsicle molds. Chilled water and flavored syrups would be mixed in the vats, followed by the dipping of the metal molds holding the wooden sticks. Emerging at the other end of the refrigerated line, the molds would release their now frozen Popsicles to be packaged. On other days, different molds and ice milk recipes were used to create Fudgesicles and Dreamsicles.

Those sights, sounds, smells, and sweet tastes became very familiar as I returned to the family business again and again. In the 1960s, Mays, Inc., was sold to a major competitor, Vander Bies, Inc. Until then, my grandparents' basement freezer continued to be the source of delicious reminders of those childhood summers spent with Grandpa and Uncle Ed at Mays. ●

Photo courtesy Spong family

Mays, Inc., at 1481 Marshall Avenue

AUGUST 2014

S	M	T	W	T	F	S
					1	2
3	4	5	6	7	8	9
10	11	12	13	14	15	16
17	18	19	20	21	22	23
24	25	26	27	28	29	30
31						

▶ "Writing is innate. You can be trained but you have to have inner desire and an ability with words."

ELEANOR OSTMAN, *newspaper columnist, cookbook author*

MONDAY

25

Steve Dress, teacher and union activist, was born today in 1932.

TUESDAY

26

WEDNESDAY

27

THURSDAY

28

FRIDAY

29

Charles Elfelt, early Jewish settler and clothing-store owner, was born today in 1828.

SATURDAY

30

SUNDAY

31

This Week's Events

Monday
Summer Flower Show
Minnesota State Fair

Tuesday
Summer Flower Show
Saint Paul (Seventh Place) Farmers' Market
Nooks and Crannies Tours
Nine Nights of Music
Minnesota State Fair

Wednesday
Summer Flower Show
History Pub Crawl
Minnesota State Fair

Thursday
Summer Flower Show
Saint Paul (Seventh Place) Farmers' Market
Music in Mears
Minnesota State Fair
Saint Paul Almanac Soul Sounds Open Mic

Friday
Summer Flower Show
Minnesota State Fair

Saturday
Downtown Saint Paul Farmers' Market
Summer Flower Show
Summit Avenue Walking Tours
Minnesota State Fair

Sunday
Downtown Saint Paul Farmers' Market
Summer Flower Show
Summit Avenue Walking Tours
Minnesota State Fair

The "Afro-American Arch" at Sixth Street and Summit Avenue was dedicated on August 28, 1896. It honored the African American Civil War casualties and was on the parade route of the national GAR encampment.

© Julia Singer/WriteWorks.net

Why did the chicken cross the road? To get to the State Fair of course!

MINNESOTA STATE FAIR A TO Z! ● DEBRA FRASIER

Count twelve days back from Labor Day and you can always figure out the starting date of the Minnesota State Fair, the largest fair in the United States. Texans argue about that, of course, but I've seen both, and Minnesota's is not only the biggest but also *the best*. Actually it wasn't until I brought my child to the fair that I learned to see the fair properly. That was twenty-four years ago, and I now have two firm rules. First: travel the fair slowly and don't try to see everything. Second: sitting on benches, eating, and watching people is acceptable fair-going! If you can accept these two guidelines, we can go together, at least in spirit!

First, let's drive to the parking lot and take a bus shuttle. For me, that is where the fair stories start. Listen to everyone around you. We'll be at the gate by 8 a.m.

First stop: coffee and hot chocolate! I head for the Farm Union Building, straight up from the Snelling entrance, stopping at the information booth to pick up a "Find Your Fabulous Fair Alphabet" game card. (If we collect two fair words for each letter of the alphabet, we can trade in the card for a blue ribbon!) Note: **F**arm **U**nion! Enter the word "**F**arm" on the game card by "F" and "**U**nion" on the line for "U." (Be grateful. Words for the letter "U" are hard to come by.)

Now let's head to the animal barns: **C**ows first, where we can sip coffee and watch **H**olsteins munch slowly, then on to the Poultry Building to hear the last morning cock-a-doodle-doos. Next is the Agriculture Building, where a glass of fresh-pressed **A**pple **C**ider is a must. Duck into the small vegetable showcase room to see "The Longest **B**ean," "The Largest **P**umpkin," and "The Very Best **Z**ucchini." Check on the day's flower competition, which I hope is one of my favorites: **G**ladiola Day, or the Miniature Bouquet arrangements, or **P**eony Day. This building also showcases Minnesota's seed art exhibition, a serious business in Minnesota. From Senator Al Franken to **E**lvis Presley, the portraits are meticulously spelled out in corn, millet, and a zillion other seeds you've never seen before. Don't miss the array of vintage seed and corn cloth sacks on display on the wall, as well as the **S**carecrows that dot this area.

Exit north. Look up! Want a **S**pace **N**eedle ride? Is the heat getting to you? Then make a detour to the oldest ride at the fair: Ye Old Mill. Expect nothing fancy, but, as a boat carries you through a tunnel of cool water, relax enough to laugh at the absurd tiny troll dioramas that have not been altered in decades.

Emerge refreshed, and then head to the Creative Arts Building to see the hand-Knitted sweaters, stitched Quilts, and slices of cakes and cookies missing tiny bites where the judges took their tastes. Pick up a free Pencil at the Education Building, then head north to the home of Minnesota's 4-H club members. (There are swarms of 4-H participants living upstairs for their overnights at the fair.) Find out how many tablespoons of sugar are in a can of soda amid the dozens of project displays. Don't miss one of the showtimes for the original musical created by 4-H high school students each year. This is my favorite live act at the fair, and times are listed at the information desk.

Right across the street from the Education Building, step under the tall trees decorated with letters. This is the Alphabet Forest, my home at the fair! Need any more words on that game card? Spin the wheel and win a word, toss bags for a word, or ask a famous Minnesota children's author to loan you a word. All authors are ready to make a project with you and give autographs. You might find a host of Minnesota Book Award winners such as David LaRochelle, Lauren Stringer, Laura Purdie Salas, or Nancy Carlson, winner of

© Debra Frasier

the University of Minnesota's Kerlan Award. Chris Monroe and her mischievous star, *Monkey with a Tool Belt*, has been seen swinging through the trees at the Alphabet Forest! Young adult readers might meet some of our state's Newbery Honor Medal winners including Joyce Sidman or Margy Prieus.

Wait, there's more! Stir up a word in the **W**ord **K**itchen, make an alphabet necklace, or color a Ferris wheel of letters—everything is free! When you are ready, present your A-to-Z-filled game card to the red-aproned volunteer on the log cabin's porch and receive your own 2014 blue ribbon to take home from the Minnesota State Fair!! Now step around to the photo booth at the back of the cabin and spell out your name with the giant Fair Letters. Snap a photo to send to your friends and family.

Pick up another game card if you want, as we've barely begun. Go slowly, sit often, eat a lot, and watch the people. When you are ready, there is the Art Building to see, the Pet Show, the Eco Building—and don't miss visiting the campers and tractors on display. Be sure to check out the Midway rides, both Kid Way and the wild Big Midway, where there are also games. Pick up a home-improvement gadget, see the hawks swoop at the DNR building, and try food on a stick. An entire alphabet of unbelievable foods and sights on sticks awaits: **A**lligator, **O**strich, **W**alleye, **K**ey Lime Pie, **F**alafel. Tired of sticks? Go straight for the roasted corn on the cob, across from the grandstand. If you don't want butter, you have to shout, *"No butter!"* and a steaming ear of corn will be peeled and handed to you.

During the State Fair, I can usually be found checking game cards at the Alphabet Forest. In 2014, we will be celebrating our fifth year of serving up words to fairgoers. Come find me before 8 p.m., because after that I head off to the Minnesota State Fair Campground, where I actually live in a borrowed trailer for twelve days. At the campground, we shower in the restrooms built into the base of the giant water tower. At 10 p.m., when you might be watching the fireworks from the grandstand, a crowd of us stands in our pajamas, holding our toothbrushes and watching the sky sparkle with proof that another day at the fair has ended.

I hope to meet you at the Minnesota State Fair this year. Look for me somewhere between A and Z, and remember what we say at the Alphabet Forest: "Leave the fair with more words than you brought!" ●

Mama Bear ● BARBARA LANGER THUKRAL

Unlike Julius, I am not having surgery to correct my clubfeet in a few hours, and so I run. Each pounding step on the treadmill brings me closer to the hospital. Left foot. Right foot. Harder. Faster. I run to try to calm myself. I run because I have two feet and I can.

The morning passes, and my husband and I arrive with Julius at Children's Hospital. In the pre-op room, the anesthesiologist meets with us and offers Julius a sedative. I take this opportunity to swallow the sedative my doctor prescribed for me, and both of us breathe a bit more easily. There are a few smiles, laughs, a couple of photos, and then it is time. I put on my gown, hairnet, booties, gloves, and mask, and become a walking vision of blue cotton candy.

When I turn around, there is Julius on a stretcher and we begin the long walk to surgery. Earlier I had vowed to my husband that I would not cry in front of Julius. In this hospital, many families are caught in similar circumstances, walking down hallways with children, praying, hoping, wondering if they will be okay. This should be a comforting thought, but I may as well be alone on the moon. I feel like the only parent who has ever sent their child to surgery, and I remind myself to walk, smile, and trust.

I turn to the Mama Bear within me, willing her to hold me upright. Left foot, don't fail me now. Right foot, keep pressing on. Down a brightly lit, sterile hallway; through a set of locked doors; turn, down another hallway; thoroughly disoriented, we arrive. There I see bright lights, machines, another bed, more people than I had anticipated. Quickly, two attendants slide Julius off the stretcher onto the tall bed.

"We are going to put this mask on your face, Julius. It will make you look like an airplane pilot. I need you to breathe very deeply when the mask is on your face, and this will help you go to sleep. Can you do that?" says the anesthesiologist.

Julius nods. They put the mask on his face. I look into

© Serena Mira Asta/AstaArt.com

those beautiful chocolate-brown eyes and smile. The brave look of my nervous little boy makes my heart throb with pain. He smiles, though the tears in his eyes betray him.

"I love you with all my heart, Julius. I am so proud of you. Daddy and I will be waiting just next door when you are all done. We will see you so soon."

He gives me a goofy peaceful smile; the drugs are kicking in. Dazed eyes begin to weigh down, dreamily, coaxed into a deep sleep, the way they did when as a nursing baby he used to fall asleep in my arms eight years earlier.

"I love you too, Mama."

For a moment he seems to settle in, but then begins thrashing. He fights the sleep. Turning his head from side to side, he pushes the nurses away, pulling the mask off his face, so agitated, they aren't able to control him. Fear is flashing from his eyes. I hold his hands tightly and get down close to his ear. What do I say to my baby who is about to head into the unknown? How do I help settle him, when I need to be settled myself?

My chest begins the vibrations of a hum. I start softly but my lips and voice take over, the music comes naturally off my tongue, and there in an operating room full of people, I sing,

Too-ra-loo-ra-loo-ral, Too-ra-loo-ra-li,
Too-ra-loo-ra-loo-ral, hush now, don't you cry!
Too-ra-loo-ra-loo-ral, Too-ra-loo-ra-li,
Too-ra-loo-ra-loo-ral, that's an Irish lullaby.

Silence. Sleep has won the battle.

The nurses and doctors look at me and nod. Time to go. Time to leave my child in the hands of strangers, trusting that they will do their job well; that not even for a moment will they take their eyes off his monitors.

For good measure, Mama Bear speaks.

"This little boy is my whole world. He has to be okay," I say. If there is a hint of threat in my voice, it is intentional, a voice the doctors and nurses likely hear several times each day. Something guttural, instinctive. Something a mother would say.

I turn around, walk out of the surgical suite in perfect stride, and burst into tears. ●

Twenty-one Pounds ● IBé KABA

Twenty-one years.
It took twenty-one years to call myself an American.
Twenty-one years not to feel like a hypocrite
When I sing the national anthem.
Twenty-one years to share the same nationality as my children.

Long before they apple my eye,
I came on a B2 visa, allowed only six months to stay.
Went to high school, went to college, got a job.
Paid federal, state and local taxes.
To be more than a spectator
Come first Tuesday in November,
Volunteered in a presidential election.

When the towers fell I too trembled with fear,
But America became hostile to anyone with a name like Ibrahim.
Fifty states or a five-by-five cell—
What's the difference between jail and immigration limbo?
One doesn't guarantee three free meals a day.
Not allowed to work, to eat,
I sold my blood by the pint,

A man and his words: IBé Kaba

The only legal way
To earn my means while I waited.

Tell me, what would you do to reach America?
I know men who gave all four of their limbs,
Mothers who gave up their first born . . .
You'll need a lawyer, plenty of patience,
Two senators and a pocketful of money.

Apparently fingerprints expire.
A valid driver's license is not a valid form of identification.
It was an alternate universe that sounded like Babel:
In the land of Egyptians you better know history.
Criminal history, driving history, credit history—
What is the measure of "good moral character"?

Boehner, Roberts, Obama—
What are the three branches of the US government?
Thirteen colonies, ten amendments, countless wars;
The name of the governor,
Who wrote the Declaration of Independence,
The "Star Spangled Banner."

I passed the test!
On the telephone, blared the news across the Atlantic!
August 22, 2012, forever etched in the tapestry of my being,
I stood at the Landmark Center in Saint Paul:
Necktie, black shoes, black suit.
Next to white people, black people, brown people.
Right hand on my chest,
Left hand in the air,
Repeat after me, she instructed,
"I hereby declare, on oath, that I absolutely . . .
Will support and defend . . ."
No longer an alien, I claimed my rights as a human being!
Once and for all no longer subject
To checking in with the INS whenever I changed my address.

How did it feel to finally become a US citizen?
Like twenty-one pounds off my shoulders.

SEPTEMBER

Six-Foot-Tall Sugarcane ● NIMO H. FARAH

She covers her expressions with a shawl,
modest, but heaven is at her feet
and I fear God through her.
So I sit on the floor massaging her swollen ankles.
The combination of third and first world
burdens continue to weigh her down.
She was once a six-foot-tall sugarcane, but now
she and I are the same height
and my heaven is seven inches shorter.

Photo © Bob Muschewske/370SummitStPaul.com

SEPTEMBER 2014

S	M	T	W	T	F	S
	1	2	3	4	5	6
7	8	9	10	11	12	13
14	15	16	17	18	19	20
21	22	23	24	25	26	27
28	29	30				

"I love the rainy day, the quiet room, the books, the pictures and the glowing fire."

ARTHUR UPSON,
19th century Saint Paul poet

MONDAY

1

Labor Day

Richard Arlen, movie actor from Saint Paul, was born today in 1898.

TUESDAY

2

WEDNESDAY

3

THURSDAY

4

FRIDAY

5

SATURDAY

6

Daniele Gaither, comedian from Saint Paul, was born today in 1970.

SUNDAY

7

This Week's Events

Monday
Summer Flower Show
Minnesota State Fair ends

Tuesday
Summer Flower Show
Saint Paul (Seventh Place) Farmers' Market

Wednesday
Summer Flower Show

Thursday
Summer Flower Show
Saint Paul (Seventh Place) Farmers' Market
Saint Paul Almanac Soul Sounds Open Mic

Friday
Summer Flower Show

Saturday
Downtown Saint Paul Farmers' Market
Summer Flower Show
Summit Avenue Walking Tours

Sunday
Downtown Saint Paul Farmers' Market
Summer Flower Show
Summit Avenue Walking Tours

Downtown Saint Paul's "Family Night" on September 4, 1952, featured sales and free street-car rides.

© Jim Teske

Downtown Saint Paul reflecting on itself

The Alleyway to Kent Street ● PATSY KAHMANN

When I moved to Kent Street in Saint Paul, my mother was excited to visit. The house had been designed by the same architect who built the Glensheen Mansion in Duluth. My mom was from Duluth.

She loved chance connections like that, and she particularly loved the history around Kent Street. Old alleyways had been restored to their former, though weathered, glory. City crews and volunteers had chipped away the concrete and exposed one-hundred-year-old bricks, some in better shape than others.

I didn't get the same rush from the broken bricks, stubbing my toe on one. "Pick up your feet, honey." Such a mom thing to say. I avoided the alleys when I could, though friends insisted on walking the shortcut to Sweeney's Saloon, while I counted broken bricks along the way.

But that was August and now it was Halloween, Mom's favorite holiday. There, in a crowded room at a huge hospital after her frantic helicopter ride from the rooftop of a small-town hospital, we sang to her, as she had done for us. My eight brothers, three sisters, and I hummed a simple mantra learned from her so long ago. "Bye, bye. Off to dreamland, little one," she would croon. "Bye, bye, bye . . ." Her steady voice over and over chanted the mournful tune, soothing out the rough edges of restless babies.

Now it was our turn. "Bye, bye. Off to dreamland."

"Della," the nurse said gently. "Your daughter is going to take your rings off and keep them for you. The medicine is making your hands swell. You can have them back tomorrow," she lied.

I shoved the rings in my pocket, a shallow, unsafe place, but I could not deal with the rings right then.

Three rings. A white gold wedding band with the missing diamond that had fallen out of the setting the year Dad died. A Black Hills gold souvenir. And her treasured Mother's Ring, a Christmas present from all twelve of us kids. The jewels were tiny with two rows of birthstones, January's garnet for Dad and Mom's opal bookending the others.

I stroked her hands—her lovely, hardy hands, looking fragile without the rings. I wanted to burn this picture into my brain, how beautiful her hands were.

Bye, bye. Bye, bye, bye. This was not a day for miracles.

That night I navigated the cobblestone alley to Sweeney's. It was closed. I turned around and wandered home, reaching into my pocket for the comfort of Mom's rings, to touch something that still held her energy. My pocket was empty.

I searched everywhere for the rings, retracing my steps, calling the hospital, ripping up the car mats. I couldn't bring myself to tell my siblings at the funeral.

Afterward I drove home to empty Kent Street. Sweeney's beckoned, and even though falling snow had turned to freezing rain, I stepped into the alley. The stones were slippery and I could imagine hearing Mom's voice: "Pick up your feet, honey." I actually looked down. At my feet.

There in the crevice between two broken bricks something shimmered.

I stood there unable to move, afraid the vision would disappear. Icy rain burned my face and still the rings stayed there, glistening from the cleansing. A garbage truck approached. I quickly knelt down and plucked the trio from their baby cave. No dents, no scratches, nothing marred the rings; they were perfectly preserved. How many vehicles had driven down this alley in the days since Halloween? Still, the rings lay, untouched, a quiet miracle waiting in plain sight. ●

© Carla Kennedy

SEPTEMBER 2014

S	M	T	W	T	F	S
	1	2	3	4	5	6
7	8	9	10	11	12	13
14	15	16	17	18	19	20
21	22	23	24	25	26	27
28	29	30				

The West Side Theater Project—an artist-driven, community-inspired organization—opened its third production, *Once Upon a River*, on September 14, 2012.

MONDAY

8

TUESDAY

9

Robert J. Pruden, staff sergeant who won a Medal of Honor for valor in Vietnam, was born today in 1949.

WEDNESDAY

10

THURSDAY

11

Charles A. Stickney, early Saint Paul manufacturer, was born today in 1876.

FRIDAY

12

SATURDAY

13

SUNDAY

14

Kathryn Murray—writer, artist, and political activist—was born today in 1934.

This Week's Events

Monday
Summer Flower Show

Tuesday
Summer Flower Show
Saint Paul (Seventh Place) Farmers'
Market
Seniors in Mind

Wednesday
Summer Flower Show

Thursday
Summer Flower Show
Saint Paul (Seventh Place)
Farmers' Market
Saint Paul Almanac
Book Release Party

Friday
Summer Flower Show

Saturday
Downtown Saint Paul Farmers'
Market
Summer Flower Show
Summit Avenue Walking Tours

Sunday
Downtown Saint Paul
Farmers' Market
Summer Flower Show
Summit Avenue Walking
Tours
Golden Thyme Jazz Festival

Today

Today
someone sat
on the
   sidewalk breathing
   in
   car exhaust
thinking
about
cigarettes

Gozong Lor

Borderland at the Raymond Avenue Bridge ● LISA STEINMANN

Train tracks, a complicated braid of lines
between twin cities on opposite horizons,
separate south and north sides of the neighborhood.
This borderland,
this old corridor of industry, steel polished
by hundred-ton traffic, graveled and aching with heavy noise
can only be crossed on foot.
It's a good place to stop and watch train cars
painted over in a neon language,
uncoupled, back and forth, words
from some traveling sentence.

It's a good place to see sky where birds punctuate
the power lines until the trumpet sounds.
Most people obey the warning signals
and stick to the tripp-trapp bridge. They avoid
the tracks and stop-for-no-one progress of trains.
They don't notice scraps of spring-fed ponds,
red-gold prairie grass and tree-tangled grapevine.
This borderland is left for neon-vested workers,
wanderers, runaways and the coyotes,
always just the two of them, heading east at dusk.

© Jack Steinmann

Raymond Avenue train yards in the St. Anthony Park neighborhood of Saint Paul

#84 Westbound ● ELIZABETH DINGMANN

Four high school girls
wearing shorts in March
to prove they can.

Two young men
in tight jeans
and T-shirts,
flirting, knees angled
side by side.

One family the bus passes
is dancing,
mother, father, two small children,
living room lights on, curtains wide
open against the night, their lives
warm orange square by square.

SEPTEMBER 2014

S	M	T	W	T	F	S
	1	2	3	4	5	6
7	8	9	10	11	12	13
14	15	16	17	18	19	20
21	22	23	24	25	26	27
28	29	30				

▶ "One time a guy handed me a picture. He said 'Here's a picture of me when I was younger.' Every picture is of you when you were younger."

MITCH HEDBERG,
Saint Paul comedian

MONDAY

15

TUESDAY

16

WEDNESDAY

17

THURSDAY

18

FRIDAY

19

SATURDAY

20

William Henry Illingworth, Saint Paul photographer specializing in stereographs and portraits, was born today in 1842.

SUNDAY

21

International Day of Peace

This Week's Events

Monday
Summer Flower Show

Tuesday
Summer Flower Show
Saint Paul (Seventh Place) Farmers' Market

Wednesday
Summer Flower Show

Thursday
Summer Flower Show
Saint Paul (Seventh Place) Farmers' Market
Saint Paul Almanac Soul Sounds Open Mic

Friday
Summer Flower Show

Saturday
Downtown Saint Paul Farmers' Market
Summer Flower Show
Summit Avenue Walking Tours
F. Scott Fitzgerald Walking Tour

Sunday
Downtown Saint Paul Farmers' Market
Summer Flower Show
Summit Avenue Walking Tours
F. Scott Fitzgerald Walking Tour

On September 21, 1805, explorer Zebulon Pike and his expedition passed by the future site of Saint Paul and noted that he saw three bears swimming across the Mississippi.

© Bob Muschewske/370SummitStPaul.com

The Sweet Potato Lady (Deborah Torraine)

● SHERONDA ORRIDGE

When I see sweet potatoes, I often think of Deborah Torraine. Deb was a community organizer in the Twin Cities. She always referred to herself as a cultural worker; she was a mentor to new and emerging artists, and the Director of Community Engagement for the *Saint Paul Almanac*.

Deb liked to garden, and one year she decided to plant sweet potatoes, despite everyone's warning. People told her she would never be able to grow them in Minnesota because of the climate. It doesn't stay hot for long in the Twin Cities.

Regardless of people's advice, she decided to plant them anyway. The first year she planted the sweet potatoes, they turned out really small, but she was very proud of her accomplishment. As each year passed, the sweet potato plants flourished, producing bigger spuds.

Each year, Deb paid attention and reflected on what went right and what went wrong, and then she made the necessary adjustments. One year, she grew sweet potatoes around fourteen inches long, the biggest sweet potatoes she had ever grown. Deb didn't need instant gratification. She knew in her heart that if she put love and attention into everything she set out to do, eventually she would reap a great harvest. Pretty soon other gardeners, inspired by her success, attempted to grow sweet potatoes as well.

Deb took the same approach in organizing communities as she did in planting her sweet potatoes, which was to plant seeds, nurture, and reflect. Deb passed away unexpectedly in June of 2011, and the community is still suffering the great loss. Even though she has transitioned, her work lives on in everyone she knew, because she left a legacy and a blueprint of how to continue her work.

The Spicy Sweet Potato Fries recipe is dedicated to Ms. Deborah Torraine because, just like these fries, she was spicy and sweet. ●

Spicy Sweet Potato Fries

Ingredients
4 large sweet potatoes
Cinnamon
Nutmeg
Cayenne pepper
1½ to 2 cups of canola or olive oil
Sweet Baby Ray's Hot and Spicy Barbecue Sauce

Directions
Peel and wash the potatoes, and then slice them into french fries. Sprinkle cinnamon, nutmeg, and cayenne pepper (to taste) on the potatoes. Heat the oil in a 12-inch skillet until the oil is hot. Place the potatoes into the hot oil, cooking them until they turn soft and golden brown. Remove them from the oil and drain them on a plate covered with paper towels. Serve them with the barbecue sauce, and enjoy.

© Diane Dodge

Deborah Torraine

SEPTEMBER 2014

S	M	T	W	T	F	S
	1	2	3	4	5	6
7	8	9	10	11	12	13
14	15	16	17	18	19	20
21	22	23	24	25	26	27
28	29	30				

On September 22, 1861, some boys stole a horse and carriage during a Saint Paul church service. They were arrested after police found the contraband at Lake Como.

MONDAY

22

Fall Equinox

TUESDAY

23

WEDNESDAY

24

Chester Oden, African American WWII veteran and owner of Road Buddy's Café at 799 University Avenue, was born today in 1911.

THURSDAY

25

Rosh Hashanah

FRIDAY

26

William Hamm, second-generation family executive of Hamm's Brewery, was born today in 1858.

SATURDAY

27

SUNDAY

28

This Week's Events

Monday
Summer Flower Show

Tuesday
Summer Flower Show

Saint Paul (Seventh Place) Farmers' Market

Wednesday
Summer Flower Show

Thursday
Summer Flower Show

Saint Paul (Seventh Place) Farmers' Market

Saint Paul Almanac Soul Sounds Open Mic

Friday
Summer Flower Show

Fourth Friday at the Movies

Saturday
Downtown Saint Paul Farmers' Market

Summer Flower Show

Summit Avenue Walking Tours

Sunday
Downtown Saint Paul Farmers' Market

Summer Flower Show

Summit Avenue Walking Tours

The library of the Ramsey County Medical Society was established on September 23, 1897, after Dr. Eduard Boeckmann donated the profits from his patent for a method of preparing surgical sutures.

© Tom McGregor/mcgregorart.com

The Backwater

Choose Your Adventure: A Saint Paul Guide for College Students and Twenty-Somethings ● ABE LEVINE

Yes, Saint Paul is the mellow sister city to Minneapolis, prime family-raising territory and, from the mansions on Summit to the bluffs gazing over the river, a place to walk and contemplate. But whether you've got a week or four years here to explore, Saint Paul is also a place where you can be adventurous, curious, and free.

Whether moving through the urban or open landscape, you're gonna need a metal horse to cut it up. Zip over to Capital Deals on the West Side for colored rims and banana seats; this all-kinds-of-reused-stuff and tune-up shop will have what you need to pave new lines across the city. Cycles for Change on University Avenue offers tools if you want to do the work yourself. From fixing a flat to doing a complete overhaul, Cycles has courses and staff to support you in greasing your gears. It also hosts a Women and Transgender Night every Tuesday from 5 to 8 p.m.

In the territory of the University of St. Thomas and many a student residence there, careen down Marshall Avenue, past Izzy's Ice Cream and Rising Sun Martial Arts Supply, then hang a left onto East Mississippi River Boulevard via Otis Avenue. Along the boulevard, note a series of parks and unmarked spots to traverse with a best friend, lover, or pet, all reliable companions for working out those existential crises that tend to accompany deep discussions. Stop at Hidden Falls for a close look at the Mississippi River or continue for a couple miles along the boulevard's massive oak trees to Crosby Regional Park. There, shaded pathways wrap around lakes and wetlands and ultimately lead to Fort Snelling State Park.

Returning from the wilderness—or avoiding it altogether—you can find plenty more places to get away from the classroom. Paul Ndayizeye, a 2012 University of Minnesota graduate who grew up in Saint Paul, says, "If I were to pick one strip of Saint Paul to visit, it definitely would be Grand Avenue." Ndayizeye suggests Billy's, Bonfire Wood Fire Cooking, and Tavern on Grand if you're over twenty-one. The best date spot has got to be the Barbary Fig near Dale. Head chef and owner Boss Hadj, in addition to offering meticulously prepared Moroccan cuisine, will indulge you in saucy conversation better than fine wine. You can chill on the patio or take the meal upstairs, and afterward enjoy waffle cones at the Grand Ole Creamery. Further north, on Selby Avenue, you'll find the

Muddy Pig and the Happy Gnome, which serve a large selection of local brews, craft beers, and good eats. If you want a martini or a fancy place to let your parents take you for dinner, there's Moscow on the Hill or W.A. Frost. With senses mildly impaired, be sure to explore Subtext Bookstore downstairs in the Blair Arcade building for that treehouse-feel reading space of your childhood. Boys, girls, and gender non-conforming folks are all allowed!

Shaquan Foster, a student at Saint Paul College, recommends Saint Paul coffee shops and cafés as "great for thinking and finding yourself, reading, or writing." Many cafés offer music, poetry readings, and meeting spaces as well as good coffee. Selby Avenue traditionally has been home to Black-owned businesses. At Golden Thyme Coffee on Selby and Milton, you can sit down with Billie Holiday—that is, an espresso with dark chocolate, caramel, milk, and whipped cream. Golden Thyme reflects the intergenerational clientele of many Saint Paul places: here you can overhear community elders and even legislators discussing politics and sit beside teachers from the local high school grading papers. On Thursday nights, performance poet Tish Jones hosts Soul Sounds performances, an open mic, and music. Be prepared: the atmosphere, including discus-

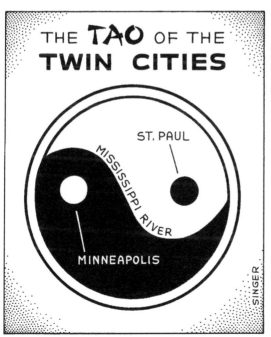

© Andy Singer/AndySinger.com

sions, can be electric. Nearby is the Hallie Q. Brown/Martin Luther King Community Center, home of the Penumbra Theater Company. Founded in 1976, the theater is dedicated to stories told by, for, and about African Americans. It has helped to launch the careers of various playwrights, including Pulitzer Prize winner August Wilson, and its performances reach over 40,000 people each year.

Other cafés to try: Kopplin's on Marshall near St. Thomas; the original Dunn Brothers on Grand near Macalester; Expresso Royale on Fairview near St. Catherine's; and Groundswell on Thomas near Hamline University.

If you want to cross the river—and I don't mean to Minneapolis—head downtown and take the Wabasha Bridge to the West Side community of Mexican and Hispanic businesses and organizations. Cruising down Cesar Chavez Street you'll find El Burrito Mercado, a large family-owned market selling tamales, hot dishes, and Mexican groceries, with an area to sit and chow, and smaller *tiendas* featuring pottery and various handicrafts. The Paul and Sheila Wellstone Center hosts dances, rallies, and gardening fairs, and also offers volunteer opportunities. Other well-known spots to eat are Boca Chica and Jerabek's New Bohemian Coffee House and Bakery. If you're staying late into the night, bring your headlamp and swing on over to the Wabasha Street caves. Thursday is swing dance night!

Certain places like Mickey's Diner downtown are living Saint Paul history, as old as Sven and Ole jokes, and Mama's Pizza, Carbone's, and Red's Savoy make up the Minnesota triangle of pizza. The Town House on University is a well-known LGBTQ-friendly bar; evening events range from drag shows to dollar drink nights. For all kinds of live rock and jazz music, hit the Turf Club, an old 1940s dance bar still located on University just west of Snelling. Looking for something completely different? Recent Macalester grad Morgan Sleeper recommends going downtown with a group, then splitting into teams to try and find "the quickest route from the St. Paul Hotel to Mears Park staying in the skyways the whole time." Don't know what a skyway is? Time to find out! For reference, see www.stpaul.gov/DocumentCenter/Home/View/18775.

If you haven't had a chance to get out beyond your campus and into the communities, take a risk and check out one of these places or another of your own wanderings. You might be surprised at what's waiting for you. ●

Books of St. Anthony Park ● LISA NILLES

St. Anthony Park Public Library surely ranks as one of the state's most picturesque buildings. It sits atop a hillside at an intersection, positioned to see and be seen. A meticulously landscaped lawn sweeps up to the red brick exterior. Seven huge, nearly floor-to-ceiling Palladian windows define the building's face. Eager to see the inside, I climbed the steps and opened the door, hoping to find a single room as large as the footprint of the building, filled with large tables. Instead, I found the spacious interior chopped into several small spaces by low bookshelves. Even worse, all sound in the library was amplified by the high ceiling. I could hear the librarian cough, the computers whir and click, and the patrons whisper. The "s" sound of every whispered word was particularly magnified. This library, beautiful on the outside and ugly on the inside, reminded me to not judge a book by its cover.

Fortunately, I knew where to find an antidote to the disappointing interior of the St. Anthony Park Public Library. I headed to Micawber's bookstore. It was just as I remembered from a visit years ago, and I sighed with relief when I saw the rustic wood floors,

© Debra Forbes/HOARYHEAD on Flickr

Saint Anthony Park Library

dark shelves, and comfortable leather chairs. Books were handsomely displayed on the shelves in small collections, often with the cover facing out, like works of art. I pulled an especially attractive book down from the shelf, appreciating its heft in my hands. The cover felt like dolphin skin: strong, velvety, and soft.

I spent the rest of the afternoon browsing in Micawber's. Dimly lit, with two window air conditioners laboring to keep it cool, the bookstore was a comfortable respite from the bright heat outdoors. ●

The library in the 1920s

Solipsist
© Mike McColl

One No Matter What ● LOUIS ALEMAYEHU

Granpa: Daniel Jones, 1889—1975

If you looked into my grandfather's face,
Where all the times and trials had come to rest,
Into his *eyes*.
You would see that all the world merges into
One Dream,
One Linking Unity,
Like the Earth, the Sun,
the Righteous Rain,
One Sacred fluidity,
One perfect, complex simplicity
One exquisite, eternal moment, unbelievably
One gorgeous movement
Of coming and going, coming and going,
Moving slowly, slowly on this wheel of time,
Caked with a muddy Love,
Carrying our One Soul
To a New Birth.

Autumn winds drag leaves from the trees,
clog the streets in a dreary finale.
Bare branches crisscross the heavy sky.
Icy rain spatters, ink-blots the pavement.
I settle at the window, stare into thick black
search the woolly lining of the night for win

The city of Saint Paul seen from Dayton's Bluff, east of downtown
© Ryan Chernik/RyanChernik.com
Opposite: © Katie Howie

Postcard to Saint Paul
from a Bus ● ELENA CISNEROS

I go by your tall boxes of light
And captured lakes
Buses, taxicabs and cars
From the window I see
The streamline of new machinery down the heart
Of a stolen city
Carrying bodies of old machinery
And despite the concrete and hidden grass
I love you and always will

	OCTOBER 2014					
S	M	T	W	T	F	S
			1	2	3	4
5	6	7	8	9	10	11
12	13	14	15	16	17	18
19	20	21	22	23	24	25
26	27	28	29	30	31	

The Fire Fighters Memorial was formally dedicated on the State Capitol grounds in Saint Paul on September 30, 2012.

MONDAY

SEPTEMBER

29

TUESDAY

SEPTEMBER

30

Christian Lund, Norwegian-born founder of Northland Ski Manufacturing Company, was born today in 1880.

WEDNESDAY

1

William Dawson, banker and first Irish American Saint Paul mayor, was born today in 1825.

THURSDAY

2

FRIDAY

3

SATURDAY

Yom Kippur

4

SUNDAY

World Teacher's Day ● Eid Al-Adha

5

Larry J. Kitto of Saint Paul, a Santee Dakota lobbyist for Native American issues, was born today in 1946.

This Week's Events

Monday
Summer Flower Show

Tuesday
Summer Flower Show
Saint Paul (Seventh Place) Farmers' Market

Wednesday
Summer Flower Show

Thursday
Summer Flower Show
Saint Paul Almanac Soul Sounds Open Mic

Friday
Summer Flower Show
Medtronic Twin Cities Marathon Health and Fitness Expo

Saturday
Downtown Saint Paul Farmers' Market
Summer Flower Show
Medtronic Twin Cities Marathon Health and Fitness Expo

Sunday
Downtown Saint Paul Farmers' Market
Summer Flower Show

Garaad Sahal became the Saint Paul Police Department's first Somali American officer on October 4, 2012.

© Justin Strom/PaintAddict.com

Fall

The Fall After ● JULIA KLATT SINGER

The fall after my father died
his buddy Gene came for the dog.
It was way before dawn, too dark to see
the hands on my alarm clock.
I heard his truck though, in the gravel
heard the sound of the back door, opening.
Heard him whisper, *come here girl*, and she
did. She ran to him, her tags all a-jangling—
even though my mother and I had forgotten
it was the opener, she hadn't.

The house was quiet that weekend.
It always was, when Dad had taken her hunting.
But this, living without the sounds of him,
living without the sounds of her, and
living too with the memory of his voice,
Gene's voice, a man's voice,
saying, *come here girl.*
I didn't know what to do with all those
sounds, now that they were gone.

It was late Sunday night when Gene returned.
He shyly let the dog back in, stood
on the back stoop, under the porch light,
a dead pheasant in his hand, which my mother took.
She tried to talk him in
for a cup of coffee, which he refused.
He said he was sorry, sorry about this—

This being everything.
The bird he was giving my mother, that
she would have to pluck and clean and dress,
that his oldest friend was dead, that
he was still hunting, still breathing, still standing
here, on their back porch, talking to her.
He said he was sorry, he should have called,
but he didn't realize he was coming for the dog
until it was too late or too early
for that.

You'll Never Know ● MARGARET HASSE

Alex dresses up in a sweet black suit
for his Central High senior picture
holding his trumpet as if
he will raise it
like a silver night-blooming moonflower
to play "Sweet Georgia Brown" or "Almost Blue."

Alex has sat in on jazz gigs in New Orleans, San Francisco, D.C.,
and Saint Paul.

He attends summer jazz camps, jazz competitions, jazz schools,
listens to Smithsonian Jazz Orchestra records.
He once ate ice cream
named Jazz,
ate an apple
named Jazz,
hopes there'll be a car
branded Jazz,
wears a cologne with notes of jazzy fragrance from a blue bottle.
When he shakes his silver ID bracelet
his own name flashes on one side,
Louis Armstrong on the other.

Alex, I ask, what is it with you and jazz?
If you have to ask, Mom, he says, quoting his hero,
you'll never know.

© Mike Hazard/thecie.org

Margaret's son,
Alex Grothe,
onstage with
Douglas Ewart

OCTOBER 2014

S	M	T	W	T	F	S
			1	2	3	4
5	6	7	8	9	10	11
12	13	14	15	16	17	18
19	20	21	22	23	24	25
26	27	28	29	30	31	

▸ "Place matters. Stories matter. Stories may be as important as food for survival."

KIMBERLY NIGHTINGALE,
Saint Paul Almanac founder

MONDAY

6

TUESDAY

7

WEDNESDAY

8

THURSDAY

9

FRIDAY

10

SATURDAY

11

James Knox Taylor, supervising architect of the U.S. Department of the Treasury, was born today in 1857.

SUNDAY

12

This Week's Events

Thursday
Saint Paul Almanac Soul Sounds
Open Mic

Friday
Saint Paul Art Crawl

Saturday
Downtown Saint Paul Farmers'
Market
Saint Paul Art Crawl
Fall Flower Show

Sunday
Downtown Saint Paul Farmers'
Market
Saint Paul Art Crawl
Fall Flower Show

Alone

Standing.
Waiting.

So much depends upon
being
asked
to dance.

Caroline Bassett

**The Everywoman Suffrage
Association, an African
American group, held its first
meeting on October 12, 1914,
and elected Saint Paul's Nellie
Griswold as its first president.**

© Michael Klement/KlementGallery.com

Growing Up on Beaver Lake ● CYNTHIA SCHREINER SMITH

In 1962, when I was seven, my father announced, "We're moving." He did not consult my mother nor had he asked any of us kids for our opinion. Our family *had* grown too large for our small home in Dayton's Bluff, however.

The house Dad bought was on Case Avenue just inside the eastern border of Saint Paul. When folks heard where we were moving, they'd ask him, "Why do you want to live way the heck out there in the middle of nowhere?" They questioned my father's sanity. "For heaven's sake," they'd say. "It'll take you over fifteen minutes to get downtown to work!" I was sad to be leaving my friends, and indeed, compared to Dayton's Bluff, Case Avenue was almost like living out in the country.

But the new house was awesome! We had a white picket fence around a *big* yard. It had three whole bedrooms. It was stucco. It was—pink! A pink stucco house just like the movie star Jane Mansfield had! I found out years later that my brother was not as thrilled with that color as his younger sisters. In high school, he'd have his buddies drop him off blocks away so none of them would discover his humiliation of residing in a pink stucco house.

Just outside our front door was Beaver Lake, a small body of water with a wild, untamed shoreline. The eastern border of Saint Paul runs right through it. Across the lake you could see the exotic, new suburb of Maplewood—a place populated mostly by farmers and a few industrious intellectuals from 3M.

Living on Beaver Lake was the best part of our new home. The gnarled old trees around the shore made for great climbing. A gully leading to the lake brought out our inner Evel Knievels as we flew across the chasm on our bikes. In winter we'd ice-skate and sled down the big hill, sailing out onto the ice. In summer we fished for bullheads, carp, and sunnies.

The dense, lakeside foliage provided a sumptuous buffet of cherry and plum trees, along with wild boysenberry, strawberry, and raspberry bushes. There were even hazelnuts. We ate and ate until we were as green as the raw nuts. But while we were snacking outside all day, Mom was inside slaving away on a nice roast beef and mashed potato dinner. She never could figure out why we didn't each much supper. Sometimes, to make up to Mom, we'd walk to the swamp on the northern shore to pick cattails and milkweed pods.

We'd glue them onto long-playing records along with some maca-roni, spray-paint them silver, and give Mom the coolest gift ever.

The wildlife we saw there were creatures we never saw in Day-ton's Bluff: skunks, muskrats, salamanders! And true to its name, Beaver Lake was home to several beavers. We loved watching them build their dams. One day my older sister decided to wade into the lake to get a better look. She found out the hard way the lake was also home to some very hungry leeches.

As the city grew, the increased housing around the lake called for improvements in the lakeshore. The swamp of cattails and milk-weed was dredged and replaced with a little beach. The gully was filled, the trees were cleared, and the bushes of tasty fruits and nuts were replaced with sod. The wildlife fled as its habitat disap-peared. There were no more beavers in Beaver Lake.

Today, beautiful Beaver Lake is a safe, family-friendly area. But the kid in me, to paraphrase singer John Prine, will always be glad that I got to grow up in the untamed jungles of east Saint Paul. ●

© Brett Fechheimer

Downtown Saint Paul from the air, with Beaver Lake in the foreground

OCTOBER 2014

S	M	T	W	T	F	S
			1	2	3	4
5	6	7	8	9	10	11
12	13	14	15	16	17	18
19	20	21	22	23	24	25
26	27	28	29	30	31	

There was a "free fight" on the levee between deckhands from steamboats and the Saint Paul police on October 18, 1861.

MONDAY

13

Indigenous People's Day

Dr. Justus Ohage, Saint Paul public health leader who performed the first surgical gallbladder removal in history, was born today in 1849.

TUESDAY

14

WEDNESDAY

15

Esther Jerabek, teacher and Minnesota Historical Society librarian, was born today in 1897.

THURSDAY

16

FRIDAY

17

SATURDAY

18

SUNDAY

19

Aurilla Furber, writer and poet, was born today in 1847.

This Week's Events

Monday
Fall Flower Show

Tuesday
Fall Flower Show

Wednesday
Fall Flower Show

Thursday
Fall Flower Show
Saint Paul Almanac Soul Sounds
Open Mic

Friday
Fall Flower Show

Saturday
Downtown Saint Paul Farmers'
Market
Fall Flower Show
ZooBoo

Sunday
Downtown Saint Paul Farmers'
Market
Fall Flower Show
ZooBoo
Victorian Ghost Stories

Umbilical Cord

I stand here passively
listening to the thoughts
that swirl in my mind
gathering a thought of strength
    and continuity
working for life balance feeling
    no shame
I walk tall
I stand soft
I listen with my heart
I'm the poet Dreamer on verge
    of reality
Red is my path for I dream of a
    true coming
of the understanding and
    acknowledgment
of a true existence of my people

Richard Merlin Johnson Jr.

Northern Cardinal (Cardinalis cardinalis)

When You Have Double the Words in Your Head ● POLYXENI ANGELIS

For Aglaia, who understood the journey

My parents, young and poor and beautiful, unearthed in each other, amid the ruins in Athens and the ghosts of her philosophers, a fierce and inflamed courage I will never know, when a postcard came from Saint Paul on which a relative had scrawled, *There's a better life here.*

My mother walked a tightrope between hysteria and fear as a young clerk in a fabric store on University Avenue pointed to the Woolworths one store down and said, "They sell cigars there." Our brows furrowed in confusion until I finally understood. "No, she wants a *Singer sewing needle*," I said, forcing a smile as the constant, young, composed interpreter. Later that evening, as my mother hemmed some rich lady's dress, she finally laughed, and to this day she shrugs and asks how anyone could confuse a sewing needle with a cigar. I learned not to defend that young clerk, because once, I said, "They do kind of sound alike if you say them a certain way," and got her famous *don't you dare be a traitor* look.

My father was a house painter, but he took me to old Como Zoo every week and often entertained the carnies there with his jokes, though he didn't speak a word of English. I felt their thick fingers on my waist as they lifted me onto some old, paint-chipped car or boat or horse, and watched as he amused them with his worry beads. They laughed and nodded, their big bellies jiggling under their discolored tee shirts, bummed cigarettes from him, winked and whistled at his foreign gestures in some machismo language I didn't understand. We roamed the animal building where the smell was so overpowering we breathed through our mouths, watched the caged monkeys throw their feces at each other for fun (PETA didn't exist yet), our fingers and lips stained red from the dyed pistachios we broke open with our teeth. I whispered my secrets to Toby the giant tortoise as I rode on his back. My father is now buried close to that zoo, and the wind carries the roar of the lions in his direction.

Me, I navigated through a world of small-boned blond girls with names like Heidi and Patty and Kimberly, names that tasted sweet in my mouth, as I spent years mumbling under my breath, "My name is not Polly." I watched the pale-skinned boys with the Norwegian and German names and imagined marrying them, the strong and silent type I still gravitate toward, so unlike the temperamental and loud Greek boys I still run from. When the girls with the sugary names picked on me, I swore at them in Greek, and they laughed harder, even as I yelled "I have double more words in my head than you do." Sometimes my native language embarrassed me; I remember how my cheeks burned. I took my comfort in McDonald's french fries, and my mother, shaking her head and asking how I got so chubby as I crammed a dozen in my mouth at once, touted the benefits of the Mediterranean diet to anyone who would listen, forty years before it became trendy.

I still navigate through the blond girls, now leggy and thin, with perfect white teeth, sporting yoga pants and perky ponytails, and when I feel petty and jealous I tell myself that I still have double the words in my head. ●

© Than Tibbetts/thanland.com

Monkey high-five at Como Zoo

OCTOBER 2014

S	M	T	W	T	F	S
			1	2	3	4
5	6	7	8	9	10	11
12	13	14	15	16	17	18
19	20	21	22	23	24	25
26	27	28	29	30	31	

The grand opening of Josie and William Lehmann's Castle Royal nightclub, 215 South Wabasha, which was carved out of the West Side limestone river bluffs, was held on October 26, 1933.

MONDAY

20

TUESDAY

21

WEDNESDAY

22

Jimmy Damiani, longtime owner of Damiani and Sons grocery at Seventh and Payne on Saint Paul's East side, was born today in 1915.

THURSDAY

Diwali

23

FRIDAY

United Nations Day

24

SATURDAY

Muharram Begins

25

SUNDAY

26

This Week's Events

Monday
Fall Flower Show

Tuesday
Fall Flower Show

Wednesday
Fall Flower Show
Saint Paul Almanac Lowertown
Reading Jam

Thursday
Fall Flower Show

Friday
Fall Flower Show
ZooBoo
Fourth Friday at the Movies

Saturday
Downtown Saint Paul Farmers' Market
Fall Flower Show
ZooBoo
Dia de los Muertos Family Day

Sunday
Downtown Saint Paul Farmers' Market
Fall Flower Show
ZooBoo
Victorian Ghost Stories

Untitled

If your dog married my dog
we would be related
and I would bring you meals
when you were ailing
and insist that you come out with
me
to simply sniff the air.

Susan Olsson

© Amber Michel/AAphotographyinMN.com

Windglow! *by Shelley Rohlf and Ella Thomson includes a skyline of Saint Paul and a flaming heart focal point—Lowertown as "The Heart of Saint Paul."*

Ora Lee O'Neal Patterson ● KATE CAVETT

The following oral history is excerpted from *Voices of Rondo: Oral Histories of Saint Paul's Historic Black Community* and is used by permission. *Voices of Rondo* won the 2006 Minnesota Book Award.

My father,[1] John O'Neal, was a Pullman Porter. That meant he was gone from home a lot. He had a short run to Brainerd from Saint Paul and back. The railroad was the reason why many Black men came here to Minnesota. They were good paying jobs up north, where they make a living for their family. The porters made good money back then, 1947, 1948. When I say good money I remember looking at one of my Dad's checks, way back when I was a little girl. And it was fifty-eight dollars. Can you imagine that?

It was rough, being a Pullman Porter, especially during the time that I was in high school, because the Pullman Porter's Association/ [Brotherhood of Sleeping Car Porters][2] was really under fire with A. Philip Randolph[3] heading it. And Frank Boyd[4], who was like the general chairperson of the Pullman Porter's Union, he worked out of his house, in the 400 block on Mackubin.

The union did not have any money. I remember one Christmas I had the nicest Christmas present. It was an Olympia typewriter, kind of gold and yellow with gold on it. I thought, *Oh this is so nice. Now I can practice my typing at home.* So my dad let me know that he had bought that typewriter for me so I could do work for the

---

1. Father John O'Neal was born November 3, 1896, and passed September 6, 1967.

2. The Brotherhood of Sleeping Car Porters was the union of Pullman Porters located in Frank Boyd's home at 443 Mackubin.

3. A. Philip Randolph (April 15, 1889–May 16, 1979) was a labor and civil rights leader. In 1925, he organized the Brotherhood of Sleeping Car Porters, the first union of predominately Black workers to be granted a charter by the American Federation of Labor. In 1957, he was elected vice president of the AFL/CIO.

4. Frank Boyd (1881–1962) moved from Kansas to Minnesota in 1904 and began as a Pullman Porter in 1907. After WWI, Boyd was instrumental in the organization of a Saint Paul branch of the Brotherhood of Sleeping Car Porters Union. In 1987, a park on Selby Avenue and Virginia Street was dedicated to him—the only public monument to a labor leader in the city of Saint Paul.

Pullman Porter's Union! [Laughs] I thought it was a gift! [Laughs] So I did a lot of the work, addressing envelopes.

That's where I think I picked up my spirit of volunteerism. Just doing that volunteer work with the Pullman Porters and Frank Boyd, and doing their papers. Daddy would bring them home for me and I would type them and he would take them back to Frank Boyd. By using me to do the typing, that helped them to get by because they couldn't pay anyone to do it.

And then what was so hard was watching my dad—because the Brotherhood of Sleeping Car Porters under A. Philip Randolph were taking a lot of heat. I don't really understand to this day the whole story about it, but all I know was what took place in the churches, and the Brotherhood of Sleeping Car Porters was accused of being Communist, because of A. Philip Randolph and some of the tactics that he used.

I'll never forget when I got highly involved in politics during the McCarthy campaign. I ended up moving over then to support Hubert Humphrey and my dad was so happy. He said to me, with tears in his

© Patrick McCutchan/PatrickMcCutchan.com

Actor dressed in a Pullman porter period costume at the opening of the Union Depot station, December 8, 2012

Ora Lee O'Neal Patterson

eyes, he said, "You know, in 1948, I was selected to be a delegate to the convention." And he said, "They did not want us to be delegates to the convention, especially the Brotherhood of Sleeping Car Porters. So what they did with me . . ." He said, "Now I want you to always remember this." He said, "I was on the run going up to Brainerd and they planted watches on me and said that I was taking watches and selling them and bringing them back from Canada." And he said, "Nothing was further from the truth. So I got my delegate seat taken away from me because of that; because I was a member of the Brotherhood of Sleeping Car Porters. That's the reason."

I said, "Well, why didn't you fight it, Daddy?" He said, "You couldn't fight the system at the time. And the union wasn't strong enough even under A. Philip Randolph. It just wasn't." And he said, "What happened to me," he said, "A lot of things happened to other men, too, that were Pullman Porters." And he said, "I am so happy that you are involved with politics. I am so happy." And every poster I would bring home of Hubert Humphrey, he had it in his room. When he died in 1967, he had a big picture of Hubert Humphrey on his wall. All the pictures I brought home from the convention, he had hanging in his room and he was so proud. Just proud of the fact that I had gotten involved, to make a change. And you know, "One person can't make changes, but just think, my daughter is involved in politics, something that was taken from me. And she's involved to the extent that she's doing all of these things. And he would say "I'm so proud of you. I'm just so proud of you." So that was good.

I figure that I'm this extension of what my father was. All he was, was just an activist. And not a popular activist and he was not one that was well known. Those people who were well known people were of course the doctors, the lawyers. People like that, who got recognition. If you were a police chief, deputy police chief, or if you were one of the Black firefighters, you were in that camp. But Pullman Porter and the unions were the unrecognized leaders. I am so proud of my father, John O'Neal. ●

City Critters in Saint Paul ● Z LU ALEXANDER

Wildlife thrives in Saint Paul.

This morning, I roused two Red Tail Hawks feeding on Mouse in my back yard. They flew off over our neighborhood community garden and disappeared beyond the rooftops. Hawks are frequently seen perched atop light posts along the I-94 corridor.

While I was out driving, Deer leapt across Shepard Road, then vanished into the woods. Golden Eagle burst out from the ditch, swooped across my windshield, and flew away. Then traffic stopped completely as a rafter of Wild Turkeys meandered across the thoroughfare.

At night, Red Fox trotted along Ayd Mill Road, where heart-faced Opossum smiled from the curb. A lingering aroma evidenced I had just missed an encounter with Skunk. And Saw-whet Owl stared down from his stoplight roost on Maryland Avenue.

As I walked the river at Crosby Farm, Bald Eagle devoured a fish on the beach only a hundred feet ahead, while Barred Owl slept in a giant Cottonwood high above.

I rescued Painted Turtle off Robert Street and went looking for his perfect new home. As we approached Como Lake, Turtle clawed the air and stretched far out of his shell, urging me to hurry. Released, he moved as fast as he could to get away into the water. Then something beautiful happened: Turtle turned around, floated, and looked at me for several moments. It felt like a "Thank You" before he slowly turned and disappeared into the deep. Great Blue Heron glided overhead to land on a boulder at the edge of the bay. Woodchuck munched grass along Lexington Parkway.

In Como Zoo, Peacock and Lunar Moth maneuvered together. Moth fluttered down close to Peacock, then up out of range. Peacock reached for Moth, and withdrew. Rhythmically, they danced and danced. Then, lightning fast, Peacock snapped its neck and swallowed Moth whole.

The garden is a wonderful place to interact with wildlife. Goldfinches eat Swiss chard, and drink from puddles captured in the bumpy leaves after a rain. Rabbit sleeps in the hedge all day before emerging at dusk to nibble leafy greens. Garter Snake awaits prey in the Strawberry patch. Hummingbird arrives at the same time each day to extract fresh nectar from blossoms. And, Bald Faced Hornet responds to Love: even though more aggressive than Afri-

can Bees, he did not hurt me as I admired him up close and personal on a Sunflower.

As I rode the Metro 21A along Selby Avenue, Dragonfly hitched a ride on my hand. I enjoyed his iridescent companionship all the way to my bus stop.

In June, Warbler filled my yard with honey-sweet song while attracting a mate. By July, I'd renamed him "Rattlesnake Bird," as song turned to scold when anyone came within ten feet of their nest.

Passing through my back yard, Pileated Woodpecker stopped to drum for lunch in the dead tree stripped bare by Squirrel; moving mostly upside down, tagalong Nuthatch followed close behind.

Last winter, Crows squawked relentlessly until I brushed fresh snow off the body of their dead relative, then perched around me in silence for a long while. They took more than two weeks to grieve.

One of my favorite wildlife encounters in Saint Paul happens only during warm months. As I brush my teeth before bed each summer evening, peering out the open upstairs window overlooking the garden, I see a pair of Bats buzz the screen, as if to say, "Hello!" •

A deer in Fort Snelling State Park © Philip Kaiyalethe
Opposite: Great Horned Owl © Jon Holtz/JonHoltzPhotography.com
Next page: Great Blue Heron © Jon Holtz/JonHoltzPhotography.com

NOVEMBER

Ice on Como Lake in the winter
© Jack Steinmann

Como Lake Haiku ● LISA STEINMANN

Blue morning circuit,
the lake ice forming. Two swans
with cygnet stop by.

NOVEMBER 2014

S	M	T	W	T	F	S
						1
2	3	4	5	6	7	8
9	10	11	12	13	14	15
16	17	18	19	20	21	22
23	24	25	26	27	28	29
30						

Eisenberg Fruit, a discounted food business located at 170 East Tenth Street since 1937, closed its doors on October 27, 2012.

MONDAY
OCTOBER
27

Christopher Columbus Andrews, author of Saint Paul history, was born today in 1829.

TUESDAY
OCTOBER
28

Homer Dodge Martin, impressionist artist, was born today in 1836.

WEDNESDAY
OCTOBER
29

THURSDAY
OCTOBER
30

FRIDAY
OCTOBER
31

Halloween

SATURDAY
1

All Saints' Day/Day of the Dead

SUNDAY
2

Daylight Saving Time Ends

This Week's Events

Monday
Fall Flower Show

Tuesday
Fall Flower Show

Wednesday
Fall Flower Show

Thursday
Fall Flower Show
Saint Paul Almanac Soul Sounds
Open Mic

Friday
Fall Flower Show

Saturday
Downtown Saint Paul Farmers'
Market
Fall Flower Show

Sunday
Downtown Saint Paul Farmers'
Market
Fall Flower Show

Untitled

I am so confused
that last night I slept
on the other side of the bed
because I thought someone
had taken my place.

Jennifer Pennington

▌"The guy who takes a
chance, who walks the fine
line between the known and
unknown, who is unafraid
of failure will succeed."

GORDON PARKS, *African American
photographer and writer*

© Mike Hazard/thecie.org

*"I think he's the happiest human being I have ever seen," says writer and
doctor Tim Rumsey. "We celebrated Carl Bentson's fiftieth birthday on
October 27, 2012, with an exhibit of his drawings at the Saint Paul Gallery on
West Seventh Street. It was one happy party."*

The Preeve ● DEL MEATH

I had been working as a residential counselor at a Ramsey County facility for the developmentally disabled for about five years when I ran into an old friend. He asked where I was working. I told him the Lake Owasso Residence, and his face brightened. He had lived there as a child.

I was convinced that he was confusing Lake Owasso with some other piece of property, but his story caused me to spend the next year and a half researching its history. In the end I managed to uncover a part of local history that should never be forgotten . . . and it all happened right here in Saint Paul.

The year was 1914, and the "White Death," tuberculosis, was ravaging the city of Saint Paul. In a massive effort to save the children from this dread disease, the Anti-Tuberculosis Committee, under the direction of Dr. H. Longstreet Taylor, organized a fundraiser called "Tag Day" to acquire money to purchase a piece of property outside the city where endangered children could be treated.

Tuberculosis was epidemic. It was a killer disease. It was incurable, and it could be caught from a single cough. People were terrified. Hospitals refused admission. Many nurses refused to work with the victims, and people around the world were dying by the thousands. In 1910 the death rate from tuberculosis in the United States was 147,627. Two thousand, two hundred and seventy of those people lived in Minnesota.

In Saint Paul, Dr. Taylor convinced the city and county leaders of the need for a special facility close to the city where patients could be isolated while they were being treated. The death rate continued to rise. In 1916, in Saint Paul alone, 307 people would lose their lives to the disease. In 1917, 340 more people in Saint Paul would die from the White Death.

When Tag Day arrived, 100 prominent Saint Paul women, directing the efforts of more than 1,000 other women, took to the streets of the city and surrounding areas soliciting donations. Those willing to contribute had a small red and white tag pinned to their lapel. The citizens of the county responded by giving what they could afford to give. Some gave pennies, some gave dimes, and some gave dollars.

Some gave even more. When the day was over, nearly everyone in Saint Paul wore a tag, and the women had gathered $8,000 for their work. An additional donation of $7,000 from the "Empire Builder," James J. Hill, brought the total to $15,000. This enabled the newly founded corporation known as the Children's Preventorium of Ramsey County to purchase twelve wooded acres on the shore of Lake Owasso.

That piece of property became recognized worldwide for its fight against tuberculosis, and it is generally accepted that the lives of the 1,033 children who passed through its doors would have been lost had it not been for the care they received in that little institution. The "Preeve" closed its doors in 1953. The battle had been won. Modern drugs would replace fresh air and sunshine. The story was not over, however.

Those doors swung open again two years later. In 1955, the Preeve became the Lake Owasso Children's Home, a facility for the developmentally disabled. As the children aged, it became Lake Owasso Residence, serving the same purpose. In 2014 this Ramsey County Facility will mark 100 years of being devoted exclusively to the care, comfort, and safety of children.

© Flashlighters/courtesy Minnesota Historical Society

Dr. H. Longstreet Taylor in his office, Saint Paul, 1896

NOVEMBER 2014

S	M	T	W	T	F	S
						1
2	3	4	5	6	7	8
9	10	11	12	13	14	15
16	17	18	19	20	21	22
23	24	25	26	27	28	29
30						

Cafesjian's Carousel, as it is now called, was built by Philadelphia Toboggan Company a century ago. The Como Park ride has sixty-eight horses and two chariots, all hand-carved.

MONDAY

3

TUESDAY

4

Election Day

Frank Van Sloun, an American realist artist from Saint Paul, was born today in 1938.

WEDNESDAY

5

John Finnegan, open meeting advocate and longtime *Saint Paul Pioneer Press* editor, was born today in 1924.

THURSDAY

6

FRIDAY

7

SATURDAY

8

SUNDAY

9

This Week's Events

Monday
  Fall Flower Show

Tuesday
  Fall Flower Show

Wednesday
  Fall Flower Show

Thursday
  Fall Flower Show
  MSHSL Volleyball Tournament

Friday
  Fall Flower Show
  MSHSL Volleyball Tournament
  Saint Paul Almanac Soul Sounds
    Open Mic

Saturday
  Downtown Saint Paul
    Farmers' Market
  Fall Flower Show
  MSHSL Volleyball
    Tournament

Sunday
  Downtown Saint Paul
    Farmers' Market
  Fall Flower Show

> "The general public would read and support any amount of scholarly historical writing, if it were written in an interesting manner."
>
> HELEN WHITE, *writer and archivist*

© Tom McGregor/mcgregorart.com

River of Commerce

Reflections of the Riverfront ● TIM SPITZACK

November 4, 2011
12:30 p.m.
53 degrees; sunny; cool breeze

As I sit in the warm confines of my truck in the parking lot at Harriet Island Regional Park, the day outside my windshield looks glorious. The sun is shining brightly in a cloudless sky, the wind is fluttering a nearby American flag perched high on a pole, and the river is a sparkling blue. The baring trees and the swirling leaves are the only things that visibly differentiate this day from the more temperate days of weeks past, when summer ruled the land.

Once out of my truck, the cool breeze reminds me that it is indeed autumn. I pull the zipper of my jacket to my chin and walk briskly to a bench near the riverfront. There are more than a dozen similar benches scattered throughout the park, all empty, so I have my pick. I choose one that is near the middle of the park, one that affords me a good view of the river and the surrounding area.

It's not long before people begin to pass by. Some are young, some are old, and all are dressed for their activity. The runners and bikers wear light, breathable attire, while the walkers are covered in sweatshirts and polar fleece; some even don heavy winter jackets and puffy earmuffs. They all pass by without looking directly at me. They are engaged in conversation or the exertion of their sport, or they are deep in thought, as it should be along the river. An elderly couple walks by hand in hand, silent. A group of women follows them and I hear a fragmented three-second conversation about a difficult workplace situation. Nearby, a couple stands on opposite sides of a massive cottonwood tree. They hug its girth and try to clasp each other's hands, unsuccessfully. They step back, eye-up the tree, smile broadly, and continue on their way.

Upriver are the boats of the Padelford Riverboat Company, which this spring mourned the passing of its founder, Captain Bill Bowell. Downstream the boys at Upper River Services are busy moving barges around the harbor so a towboat can take them downriver. Around Thanksgiving each year, the last of the barges is gone, and about nine million tons of commodities will have been shipped to distant ports. Some of the crew on the last trip south will ride the season all the way to New Orleans and experience the height of autumn in nine states. In New Orleans today it is not much warmer than here—64 degrees—but the forecast calls for upper 70s in the coming days. Ours calls for lower 40s.

This past weekend, my brother-in-law posed the question: "Why do we live in Minnesota?" It's a fair question, especially from someone who grew up on the Iron Range and endured his share of brutal winter weather. It's a question that occupies our conversations these days as we brace ourselves for the approaching season. Many are hustling to get outdoor chores done before the snow arrives, and I'm no different from the rest. This week I purchased firewood, cleaned our windows and garage, and am planning to spend the upcoming weekend mulching the many leaves that are blanketing my yard.

Winter is coming, and with it the festive holiday season. Across the river I can see the Saint Paul Library on the skyline. On the other side of the library is Rice Park, which becomes a winter wonderland in December. It is home to Saint Paul's Christmas tree, thousands of holiday lights, and other seasonal decorations. This year's tree—a 65-foot-tall, 25-foot-wide, 50-year-old spruce—was donated by David and Therese Rice of Saint Paul.

I glance at my watch and see that my time has expired. A brittle, heart-shaped cottonwood leaf is shaken from the tree overhead and gently spins its way into the cold river. It floats with others in the quiet water near the river's edge. Waiting.

© Tom Dunn/TomDunnPhoto.com

NOVEMBER 2014

S	M	T	W	T	F	S
						1
2	3	4	5	6	7	8
9	10	11	12	13	14	15
16	17	18	19	20	21	22
23	24	25	26	27	28	29
30						

West Saint Paul, formerly in Dakota County, was annexed into the city and became the West Side neighborhood on November 16, 1874.

MONDAY

10

David French, teacher and researcher of plant and forest pathology, was born today in 1921.

TUESDAY

Veterans' Day

11

WEDNESDAY

12

Harry Blackmun, U.S. Supreme Court Justice from Saint Paul, was born today in 1908.

THURSDAY

13

FRIDAY

14

SATURDAY

15

SUNDAY

16

This Week's Events

Monday
  Fall Flower Show

Tuesday
  Fall Flower Show
  Seniors in Mind

Wednesday
  Fall Flower Show

Thursday
  Fall Flower Show
  Saint Paul Almanac Soul Sounds
    Open Mic

Friday
  Fall Flower Show

Saturday
  Downtown Saint Paul
    Farmers' Market
  Fall Flower Show

Sunday
  Downtown Saint Paul
    Farmers' Market
  Fall Flower Show

The Swedish Old Settlers Association organized on November 16, 1903, at 407 Jackson Street in Saint Paul with an initial membership of seventy-five.

© Saibal Ghosh/saibalghosh.com

Pigeons taking off over the Landmark Center in Downtown Saint Paul

The Birth of My American Babies ● ELDER RIVERA
HERRADORA, TRANSLATED BY KEVIN HERSHEY

One week before the babies were born, I took photos of Karen to see the size of her stomach. I took them from the front, and from her profile. One week passed, and the day of the birth came. That day I took pictures of Karen so that I would remember what she looked like. They explained to us the risks of a C-section and I still was not nervous or excited at all. I was only worried about my wife. Karen went to the operation room, and I was waiting for about twenty minutes. I was very curious, and I wanted to be in the room with her. When I entered, Karen was on top of the table and the doctors were working on her stomach. I was nervous for her because I saw her hand shaking. I was nervous, not excited, when I grabbed her hand. The doctor told me I could stand up when the first baby came out. The first one who came out was Krystal Alissa, my daughter. We named her that because her grandparents in Nicaragua had chosen this name. Later, they put her in her crib and a moment later the doctor told me that the boy had been taken out. This was Helder Warren. There was my second child!

How can I say how I felt? When I saw them, I was so excited. I said, "Look, Karen, there are our children!" I felt the need to have them both in my arms. I wanted to cry and my eyes turned very

red. It was so beautiful for me. We cleaned them and I put them next to my wife so she could see them because she was still lying in bed. There they were, fully formed. I still could not believe that these beautiful formed beings came out of Karen. I was still worried about her, however. The doctors did not tell me anything. The doctor said many things in English, but I felt calmer when she brought me to my wife. I felt that now we are a family. We are no longer two, but four. We had doubled in one day. ●

Detail © Sarah Wash/ErdeEcoArt.com

Photo courtesy Farah family

Nimo kissing Hooyo

Hooyo ● NIMO H. FARAH

she worries about time
I worry about distance
her tongue is tired
keep talking
my ears are lazy
keep listening
she guides me
to be
an emissary
I sacrifice
the afternoon
to drive her in this city
after a journey
she names things
we can't see
she named me
after a heaven
my home
since my beginning
mostly
we're each other's happiness
which is the meaning of
my name
happiness
her daughter

NOVEMBER 2014

S	M	T	W	T	F	S
						1
2	3	4	5	6	7	8
9	10	11	12	13	14	15
16	17	18	19	20	21	22
23	24	25	26	27	28	29
30						

▶ "Minnesotans really think they run the whole world. I love that."

LOUIE ANDERSON,
comedian and author

MONDAY

17

TUESDAY

18

WEDNESDAY

19

Roy Garza—Hispanic American active in United Way, CLUES, and Saint Paul politics—was born today in 1951.

THURSDAY

20

FRIDAY

21

SATURDAY

22

Nora Murphy, author, was born today in 1961.

SUNDAY

23

This Week's Events

Monday
  Fall Flower Show

Tuesday
  Fall Flower Show

Wednesday
  Fall Flower Show

Thursday
  Fall Flower Show
  Saint Paul Almanac Soul Sounds
    Open Mic

Friday
  Fall Flower Show

Saturday
  Downtown Saint Paul Farmers'
    Market
  Fall Flower Show

Sunday
  Downtown Saint Paul Farmers'
    Market
  Fall Flower Show

More than a thousand people gathered at Saint Paul's Summit Park on November 20, 1903, to dedicate a statue of Josias King, considered to be the first Civil War volunteer.

© Tom Dunn/TomDunnPhoto.com

Snowy day to get married in the Landmark Center in Downtown Saint Paul

Why I Write ● MARY KAY RUMMEL

Because my mother's mother carried her Irish language
across a stormy Atlantic to St. Paul

Because my great grandfather who lived to be 100
sang in Irish as he bounced us on his bony leg

Because on the front porch of my grandmother's house
the cousins, all named Mary, learned 100 names for green
from rebel songs

Because I lived sixty years before I learned my mother's father
died drunk under the hooves of a horse he was driving

Because my cousin, Sheriff O'Connell, who took bribes
from Chicago gangsters, gave money to my widowed grandmother

Because when I read about him in St. Paul histories
I thought saint not sinner

Because my father's tiny mother came from Galway
with a family too full of priests and nuns

Because she loved to talk in the way of Irish women
over tea and toast at small tables

Because I grew up in the quotidian music of women's murmuring

Because men were either silent or overbearing
I learned my life with Anne of Green Gables
and Little Women

the bus plying the Old Fort Road to school
became my Bridge at San Luis Rey

Because art and music were in the church
I thought beauty belonged to God

Because in the convent we were told to be silent
I picked up a pen

Because my granddaughters listen to my tales
their eyes pools where words sink and grow
the way I once listened to the old ones

Because words unwrite as they are written
unspeak as they are spoken

I do not want to die without writing
my unwritten watery universe.

Violinist Mattie Ernst, an instructor at the Center for Irish Music, plays in the Black Dog Coffee and Wine Bar on St. Patrick's Day.

		NOVEMBER 2014				
S	M	T	W	T	F	S
						1
2	3	4	5	6	7	8
9	10	11	12	13	14	15
16	17	18	19	20	21	22
23	24	25	26	27	28	29
30						

The Ford Building, an early motor vehicle manufacturing facility and showroom, was built at 117 University Ave. W. a century ago.

MONDAY

24

Cass Gilbert, architect who designed the Minnesota State Capitol, was born today in 1859.

TUESDAY

25

WEDNESDAY

26

THURSDAY

27

Thanksgiving

Dr. James W. Crump, longtime African American family practitioner and social activist, was born today in 1888.

FRIDAY

28

SATURDAY

29

SUNDAY

30

This Week's Events

Monday
Fall Flower Show

Tuesday
Fall Flower Show

Wednesday
Fall Flower Show
Hmong New Year

Thursday
Fall Flower Show
Hmong New Year

Friday
Fall Flower Show
Hmong New Year
Fourth Friday at the Movies

Saturday
Fall Flower Show
Hmong New Year

Sunday
Fall Flower Show
Hmong New Year

Around 2,500 workers marched to Saint Paul's City/County Courthouse on November 28, 1917, to support the union members striking against the owners of the streetcar system.

Saint Paul residents came out to see the newly rennovated and functioning Union Depot station, December 8, 2012.

The Bustle: An Episode of the Eighties

● CHARLES MACOMB FLANDRAU

Charles Macomb Flandrau was born in 1871 into a wealthy first family of Saint Paul (his father was Judge Charles E. Flandrau). Considered at the time to be as talented as F. Scott Fitzgerald and Sinclair Lewis, he lacked the drive needed to achieve the literary success of his more famous contemporaries. Flandrau authored six books, wrote articles for the *Saturday Evening Post*, and from 1915 on, served as theater critic for the *Saint Paul Pioneer Press*. Though he socialized with Scott and Zelda in Paris, Flandrau himself was more comfortable in the pre—Jazz Age world.[1] In this excerpt from *Loquacities* (D. Appleton and Company, 1931), he describes the upheaval in his late-nineteenth-century Saint Paul family caused when his father's *Pioneer Press* mysteriously disappears.

* * *

I hadn't forgotten these far-off things, but for years I hadn't thought of them, and as I sat there, I went on to remember the hectic, the historical and hysterical autumn evening when, while my father was reading the *Dispatch* in the library after dinner, he suddenly looked up and demanded that morning's *Pioneer Press*. . . .

"The *Pioneer Press*?" echoed my mother. "I'll get it for you. It's probably in the kitchen." But, most tediously, the *Pioneer Press* wasn't in the kitchen, and it wasn't in any of the three kitchen pantries. Furthermore, it couldn't be found in the dining-room or the parlour or any of the family's five bedrooms. . . .

"But I want it," my father insisted. "I want to read something in it—something of importance. If it hasn't been destroyed, it must be in the house. I don't suppose it just jumped off the dining-room table where I left it and strolled out of the front door."

"I can't imagine," began my mother. "I can't imagine," she repeated in a moment, but in a tone of noticeably less conviction. And then she suddenly sat down in the rocking-chair and by turning her back and frantically poking the fire, which didn't need poking, tried to conceal the fact that she had become feeble with laughter. But

---

1. Olivia Cole, "A Locked-up Life," review of *In Gatsby's Shadow: The Story of Charles Macomb Flandrau*, by Lawrence Peter Haeg, *The Times Literary Supplement*, March 6, 2005, http://www.powells.com/review /2005_03_06.html.

naturally my father caught her at it and, with the elaborate and glacial politeness that is ever the signal of suppressed rage, he said: "Really, my dear, I can't quite see what is so excruciating in the fact that I am being extremely annoyed."

"It's because—it's because it has all at once come over me that I know where it is," mother finally managed to gasp. She had given up and broken down completely.

"You know where it is?" father thundered. "Then why don't you get it for me—or at least tell me where it is and let me get it."

"Oh no—no," mother protested with something that was a cross between a sob and a moan. "You couldn't possible get it. You couldn't."

Charles Macomb Flandrau with his dogs, 1912

"If it wouldn't be too much trouble, will you kindly explain why not?" father then acidly inquired.

"You couldn't get it—you couldn't get it because—mother—is wearing—it," she then heroically brought out.

"Your mother, Mrs. McClure, is wearing a newspaper? How on earth can a woman wear a newspaper? Where is she wearing it?" father, in angry amazement, demanded.

"Oh, don't—don't," mother pleaded. "I can't in so many words tell you where she wears them, but with your legal brain," she wildly added, "I think you ought to be able to make a more or less accurate deduction. She wears them for bustles."

"Mrs. McClure uses the *Pioneer Press* for a bustle?" father hissed. "Oh, my God," he muttered as he clutched the arms of his chair and rolled his eyes. "Why, why, with the whole world filled to overflowing—teeming—positively bursting with potential bustle material, does she deliberately, wilfully, perversely choose the *Pioneer Press*—my *Pioneer Press*?"

"It's more economical," mother, having partly got control of herself, tried to explain. "And then, too, she's afraid of the wire ones—she doesn't trust them. After they've been worn a long time, they have been known to collapse and run into people's—and run into people. A *Pioneer Press* folded over a piece of tape and tied around the waist is perfectly safe. Sometimes, of course, it does get loose and fall off in the street, but she just kicks it aside and walks on, pretending it wasn't hers."

"But I want it—I want it right away," father wailed. "I realize, naturally, that I can't get it myself," he admitted with an attempt at sweet reasonableness, "but you can."

"But I won't," replied mother with spirit and decision. "I absolutely refuse to ask her to undress at eight o'clock in the evening merely because you have an uncontrollable desire—an uncontrollable desire to read her bustle. I think it's indecent." . . .

"Well, anyhow, she does go to bed at ten o'clock," he at last hopefully reflected.

"Yes—usually," mother agreed, but with considerably less optimism.

"You can get it then, can't you?" he asked.

"Oh, yes, I can get it then. I'll slip into her room, but after she's asleep, of course. It would upset her dreadfully if she knew."

That evening, however, "then," for some unaccountable reason, appeared to have determined never to arrive. It tarried, lingered, hesitated, changed its mind, got its second wind, and took a fresh hold. Nine o'clock struck, half past nine, and finally ten, at which father, bounding from his chair as if propelled by some hidden mechanism, began both ostentatiously and deafeningly to lock up. . . . He then blew out the lamps in the parlour and the hall and, standing in the dining-room doorway, exclaimed to grandmother, with a kind of hollow heartiness (she was now alone there): "Well— I don't know what you're going to do, but I'm going to bed."

"Are you?" murmured grandmother with no interest whatever—not even glancing up from her purple scallops. "I should if I were you. You can put out these lights—I can't reach them—and I'll go into the library. Finishing a piece of work like this always seems to excite me a little."

The hours from eight to ten had been merely so much time—a long time to be sure, but, after all, just time. From ten to one a.m., however, was pure, abstract, metaphysical, Einsteinian eternity, with a kind of beginning, perhaps, but with no predictable end. Father, after prolonged, undertoned, sepulchral urging, consented to undress, but refused to lie down or, for more than a minute or two, to sit down. In that most humorous of all human coverings, a nightshirt, he drifted interminably back and forth in the upper hall, scared me almost into screams by now and then suddenly sitting on the edge of my bed just as I was falling asleep, and creaked up and down the front stairs and past the library door four different times. The first three of these expeditions were productive of a single, reiterated, cryptic, intensely bitter phrase. Thrusting his head into the twilight of mother's room, he would mutter: "Still sitting on it," and then resume his restless promenade. . . .

I seem to have fallen asleep about then, and some time between one in the morning and breakfast mother of course rescued what remained of the *Pioneer Press* and provided a perfectly good substitute, but all the next day was a most dreadful day, for when cheerful, energetic, sparking grandmother appeared at breakfast, she was another creature—a changed woman. She scarcely spoke, sighed a great deal, and, listlessly protesting that she was perfectly well, left the table after having sipped a quarter of a cup of tea. From the garden, where she went to do a little weeding among the asters and dahlias, she, who had never in her life been tired, returned in less than half an hour in a state of complete exhaustion, and by noon she had thrown the household into an almost tearful panic by going upstairs and actually lying down. . . .

And then, at last, I heard her say rather tremulously: "Yes, something did happen—a dreadful thing. It was bound to come sooner or later—I've always know that, of course—but I didn't think it could come overnight. It has, though. Rebecca, I'm an old, old woman."

"But what utter nonsense!" mother protested. "People in perfect health simply don't get old right off like that. What in the world makes you imagine you have?"

"I don't exactly like to tell you," grandmother hesitated, "because you're far too young really to understand; but this morning while I was dressing, I remembered that when I was making my bustle yesterday, I noticed under 'Household Hints' a recipe for getting rid of mice in a pleasant, friendly way that they enjoy. Of course there aren't any mice, but you never can tell, and I meant to cut it out, and then, when I unfolded my bustle and began to look, it wasn't the *Pioneer Press* at all. It was last night's *Dispatch*.

"Yes, yes, but what of it?" mother urged her on.

"I knew you couldn't understand," grandmother sighed. "What happened was that I must have got up during the night, gone all the way downstairs, found the *Dispatch*, and made a new bustle; but the awful part of it is that I have no recollection of doing anything of the kind. From the time I went to bed, my mind was a perfect blank. I must have put the first bustle—the *Pioneer Press*—away somewhere, because I haven't been able to find it; but I can't remember even that. Rebecca, I am breaking up."

It was gay, I remembered, to see grandmother a moment or two later suddenly snap back from a self-imposed senility to a youthful middle age—not unlike being present when a locust leaves its shell on a fence, or a butterfly pops out of a cocoon. And I remembered, too, that the next day mother subscribed to the Butler, Pennsylvania, *Clarion Herald*, which nobody in the family ever by any chance wanted to read, and which grandmother wore undisturbed to the last. •

DECEMBER

Detail from Fools #1
© Dolan Cyr

The Invitation ● ETHNA MCKIERNAN

Sholom Nursing Home, for Kathy

Tonight she asks you to sleep
with her, both of you in the bed
with siderails, a plastic mattress pad
below. She is so happy
to have found you, her daughter
from the old house she loved.
And you are torn between her
and the world of things
you never finish, duty calling always.
Between you is the tunnel back
to childhood, where your 95-year-old mother
is young again, wanting nothing now
but to touch your cheek, stroke your hair,
claim you as her own.

DECEMBER 2014

S	M	T	W	T	F	S
	1	2	3	4	5	6
7	8	9	10	11	12	13
14	15	16	17	18	19	20
21	22	23	24	25	26	27
28	29	30	31			

A century ago, John E. Strauss, an ice skate maker from Saint Paul, invented the first closed toe blade. Made from one piece of steel, the skates were lighter and stronger.

MONDAY

1

TUESDAY

2

Richard Guindon, cartoonist best known for his gag panel *Guindon*, was born today in 1935.

WEDNESDAY

3

THURSDAY

4

Kenneth M. Wright, photographer, was born today in 1895.

FRIDAY

5

SATURDAY

6

SUNDAY

7

This Week's Events

Thursday
Bouquets: An Evening of Wine, Beer, and Food

Saint Paul Almanac Soul Sounds Open Mic

Friday
Saint Paul Ice Fishing and Winter Sports Show

Saturday
Downtown Saint Paul Winter Farmers' Market

Saint Paul Ice Fishing and Winter Sports Show

Holiday Flower Show

Grand Meander

Hill House Holidays

Sunday
Saint Paul Ice Fishing and Winter Sports Show

Holiday Flower Show

Hill House Holidays

> "Writing is something warm and dependable.... It's a little secret that you carry with you in public—the knowledge that you alone have the ability to escape to a wonderland where you can make anything happen."
>
> JUDY DELTON, *children's book writer*

Our Lady of Guadalupe ● LISA ANN PIERCE

Our Lady of Guadalupe,
leaning in the mercado window,
make intercession for the West Side.
Mystical rose of yellow, red, and blue,
protect those who journey through
the corners of George, State, and Chavez streets—
New Tepeyac, District del Sol.
We are the least of your children,
a thousand blessed Juan Diegos
from the mountains of Southeast Asia and Central America,
the deserts of Mexico and Somalia,
the far-off foreign districts of Lebanon, Chicago, and the suburbs.
Our faith shines bright as apparitions
on our winter cloaks,
a testament to the possibilities
that lie in the shadow of your love.

O Virgin of Guadalupe, Mother of the Americas,
smile on your children who toil at the clinic across the street
to heal the broken and the broken system.
Show pity to the neighbors in back,
who teach citizenship and keep the food shelf stocked.
Bless the smell of roasting corn
and the rhythm of Aztec dancers.
Watch over the homeless and the drunken
sleeping in Parque Castillo.
Grant comfort to your children
eating soul food at Cora's.
Remember especially the women in hijab and winter coats,
making their way to Al Salam Halal Market.
Touch the hearts of those who venture through for good food
and those who speak two languages to accommodate them.

Dear Lady of Guadalupe,
ringing in the bells of the parish that bears your name,
we proclaim you and the miracle of your appearance,
mystical rose of yellow, red, and blue,
leaning in the mercado window on the West Side.
Nowhere are we without you,
not even in the dead of winter in Saint Paul.
Amen.

Photo courtesy Minnesota Historical Society

Feast Day at Our Lady of Guadalupe Church, Saint Paul, 1971

DECEMBER 2014

S	M	T	W	T	F	S
	1	2	3	4	5	6
7	8	9	10	11	12	13
14	15	16	17	18	19	20
21	22	23	24	25	26	27
28	29	30	31			

"You're not born into a race. You're assigned a race by law."

MAHMOUD EL-KATI, *African American activist and educator*

MONDAY

8

TUESDAY

9

Dr. Mario Garcia, medical equipment inventor and active in Saint Paul's Filipino community, was born today in 1936.

WEDNESDAY

International Human Rights Day

10

THURSDAY

11

FRIDAY

12

Catherine Clark Kroeger—New Testament scholar, author, and a leading figure in the Biblical egalitarian movement—was born today in 1925.

SATURDAY

13

SUNDAY

Christmas Bird Count Begins

14

This Week's Events

Monday
Holiday Flower Show

Tuesday
Holiday Flower Show

Wednesday
Holiday Flower Show

Thursday
Holiday Flower Show
Saint Paul Almanac Soul Sounds
Open Mic

Friday
Holiday Flower Show

Saturday
Downtown Saint Paul
Winter Farmers' Market
Holiday Flower Show
Hill House Holidays

Sunday
Holiday Flower Show
Hill House Holidays

On December 11, 1883, the McQuillan Brothers Company issued their first bill of sale to a Mr. Hoyt for a day and a quarter of plumbing and the cost of two pounds of solder.

© Patrick McCutchan/PatrickMcCutchan.com

Saint Paul residents came out to see the newly rennovated and functioning Union Depot station, December 8, 2012.

Letter to the Lady Who Fell ● SHAUNTÉ DOUGLAS

Dear Lady Who Fell:

I'm sorry you fell Tuesday night, a little after 8 p.m. I hope you're okay. Your husband looked mighty upset when you fell. I would've been upset too, after spending all that money to live on property that allows ice to freeze in front of the entrance. If I were you, I would complain, and sue, if necessary.

I'm writing to you because I don't know if you recognized what happened that night. A brother and I watched you walk out that door, slip, scream, and land flat. We heard your exasperated cry in pain. We rushed to you, and I grabbed your hand. We listened to you tell us that your tailbone and head hurt. The caring brother pleaded with you to not rise right away. And you listened. You sat there for a few moments to regroup. You held my left hand gently during those moments. I watched you take breath after breath, and you grimaced with each one. Before we assisted you up from the brown ice beneath you, I ensured that you were ready to stand. Then, I released your hand and told you to take care of yourself, and we bid you good night.

Fifty years ago, I wouldn't have shown compassion to you because your race and my own would've judged me harshly. Just fifty years ago, you would've rejected my hand to help you up. You wouldn't have held my hand. Instead, you would've blamed me for making you fall and I wouldn't have been able to state my defense because my skin color would've convicted me. Hatred would've led you to spit on my sympathy and curse my concern. Fear would've made your husband push that brother away to protect you. Fifty years ago, I wouldn't have attended an ethnically diverse meeting concerning the community of Saint Paul. When I left that meeting, I witnessed your fall.

Since I don't know your name, I will refer to you as the lady who fell. Notice I don't use an adjective before "lady," describing color. That night when I held my hand out to you, I wasn't gesturing for a tip. Now, I'm not seeking a reward for helping you. I'm just recognizing that in fifty years race relations have changed so much. Today, I'm not afraid to reach out to you, not worried about what others will think if I react quickly to help you.

Thank you for not pulling away from that brother and me. Thank you for not repeating the vicious cycle that has hardened my people even more than the ice that made you slip and fall that night. Thank you for holding my hand.

Sincerely,
The Girl Who Helped You Up ●

© Leann E. Johnson/lea-way.com

DECEMBER 2014

S	M	T	W	T	F	S
	1	2	3	4	5	6
7	8	9	10	11	12	13
14	15	16	17	18	19	20
21	22	23	24	25	26	27
28	29	30	31			

▶ "As Asians we are taught to be modest . . . humble . . . not to brag, and I try to adhere to this philosophy."

KA VANG, *Saint Paul Hmong poet*

MONDAY

15

William West, early law book publisher, was born today in 1858.

TUESDAY

16

WEDNESDAY

Hanukah Begins

17

THURSDAY

18

FRIDAY

19

SATURDAY

20

Claudia Jennings, actress and model, was born today in 1949.

SUNDAY

Winter Solstice

21

Thomas F. Ellerbe, creator of the largest architectural practice in Minnesota, was born today in 1892.

This Week's Events

Monday
Holiday Flower Show

Tuesday
Holiday Flower Show

Wednesday
Holiday Flower Show

Thursday
Holiday Flower Show
Saint Paul Almanac Soul Sounds
Open Mic

Friday
Holiday Flower Show

Saturday
Downtown Saint Paul Winter
Farmers' Market
Holiday Flower Show
Hill House Holidays

Sunday
Holiday Flower Show
Hill House Holidays

Reflections

every day in the mirror i see
a girl who isn't me

Kaya Solheid

Downtown Saint Paul

Dancing at the Crossroads • SAED KAKISH

Saint Paul is my chosen home, the place where I feel most deeply that I belong. Now. It has not always been so.

In many ways my story is similar to countless Americans'; we are, as President Kennedy wrote, "a nation of immigrants." But when I arrived in Minnesota—my nine-year-old head swimming with tales of American opportunity, green cards already waiting—I felt extremely disoriented, almost as if I'd been kidnapped. My father, a dry grocer and merchant in Mafraq, Jordan, had come over two years earlier, working two jobs until he could bring the rest of us. Mafraq is a Bedouin town near the Syrian border; its name means crossroads, an apt description of its centrality on the road between Damascus and Amman. I had arrived, against my will, at an entirely different kind of crossroads.

We'd landed at O'Hare, my mother and the seven of us, and all the way to the Twin Cities, our earthly belongings strapped to the roof of my dad's Dodge Colt, I felt everything I knew falling away in a swirl: not just familiar desert architecture and landscapes, the palm trees and camels, but all the tastes, smells, colors, and sounds of my young life, all slipping away as we headed northwest across the alien prairie. In the suburb that became my first American home, we were the only family of color for as far as my legs could walk me in any direction. It was a difficult experience for a long time, breathing in and slowly taking up a new culture and home.

But when I went back to the Jordan I'd so ached for eleven years later, I found I was now a tourist in my country of origin, soaking up sites I'd never seen as a child. I couldn't get enough—visiting Petra; splashing, wading, and bobbing in the Dead Sea; a day at the ancient Roman-ruin amphitheater in Jarash—but even then villagers called me "the American," pointing out subtle differences in my dress and manner that marked me, even if I was unaware of them.

Innumerable nuances of culture and circumstance have carried me to this place where Minnesota's crossroads city, its capital, feels so thoroughly my home. Saint Paul is urban while being historically interesting, with its distinctive buildings and neighborhoods, its growing diverse cultures living together while retaining important features of their countries of origin. I created my coffee shop where people who trace their ancestries back to Minnesota territorial days mingle and feel at home with those recently arriving from other places and histories. All contribute to my sense of belonging here. Now.

I've always done traditional Middle-Eastern dances at family celebrations, but an experience I had more than a decade ago, the first time I performed on stage, helped me recognize I'd been reborn in this new place. The performance began with six of us dancer-actors, each from a different homeland, lying flat on the stage, hidden under a large sheet of white fabric. After slow, rhythmic stirrings, each of us emerged to tell his or her own story in that darkened auditorium. Something about that narrative-dance, a blend of traditional Arabic dance and my own invention, that movement from private act to public dialogue with a random audience, made me understand how much at home I was here in this new crossroads; how so many things had come together to make me belong.

Toward the end of our performance we sat under a tree on stage and drank coffee together, always a sign of community in Jordan; we ended with a joyous dance. My life in Saint Paul is not a joyous dance; no one's is. But this crossroads is where I now belong. ●

Saed Kakish performing Sabeel at the University of St. Thomas

DECEMBER 2014

S	M	T	W	T	F	S
	1	2	3	4	5	6
7	8	9	10	11	12	13
14	15	16	17	18	19	20
21	22	23	24	25	26	27
28	29	30	31			

The final broadcast of the "Lunch With Casey" show, a popular Saint Paul television program for children, was held on December 23, 1972.

MONDAY

22

TUESDAY

23

Willes B. Combs, researcher who developed Saint Paul's blue cheese industry in the West Side caves, was born today in 1892.

WEDNESDAY

Christmas Eve

24

THURSDAY

Christmas Day

25

FRIDAY

Kwanzaa Begins

26

SATURDAY

27

SUNDAY

28

Carol Ryrie Brink, children's book writer, was born today in 1895.

This Week's Events

Monday
Holiday Flower Show

Tuesday
Holiday Flower Show

Wednesday
Holiday Flower Show

Thursday
Holiday Flower Show

Friday
Holiday Flower Show

Saturday
Downtown Saint Paul
Winter Farmers' Market
Holiday Flower Show
Kwanzaa Family Celebration

Sunday
Holiday Flower Show

Kemps, an ice cream and dairy products company, head-quartered today in Saint Paul, started out in southeastern Minnesota a century ago.

© Tom Reynen/tom-reynen.artistwebsites.com

Holiday Cheer ● HENRY L. BUSHNELL

Song is an important part of Saint Paul in December. It is impossible to escape holiday music, especially on local radio stations. Cities 97 plays the standards. Classical KSJN 99.5 plays Handel's *Messiah*, and even The Current plays some old funky versions of popular tunes. Every store you visit has a familiar carol playing in the background as you shop for gifts or groceries. The atmosphere is comforting, familiar, and ordinary.

In early winter, a group of musical students from Central High School joined forces. Not only did we want to go caroling, but we also wanted to warm the heart of an unsuspecting stranger. Not just ordinary caroling, either—we were determined to sound amazing! Facebook groups were set up, sheet music was hunted down and handed out, and afterschool rehearsals were coordinated. It was an extensive production, but boy, did it pay off.

The weekend before Christmas, twenty of us gathered at a house on Summit Hill. We were a strange mix between an a cappella group and an arctic exploration. Bundled in scarves, gloves, earmuffs, and whatever else we could find, we did a quick vocal warm-up. You could feel the excitement in the room as we anxiously awaited the chance to show off our work. We were ready.

The eclectic group took to the streets, and after a few minutes of deciding which direction to go, we set off. We stopped at the first house, packed ourselves together on the steps, and of course nudged a girl forward to ring the doorbell. A face appeared at the door window, and a student in our group blew his pitch pipe. We looked around at each other, took one mutual inhale, and burst into spirited four-part harmony. "Hark the Herald Angels Sing" rang out with astounding force and resonance. The rest of the family came to the doorway. They huddled close together and listened. Some smiled while others held their mouths wide open. We were not what they were expecting. In that moment there was warmth, love, nostalgia, and euphoria. We caroled around the neighborhood that night, but the first house was special. On a December night in Saint Paul, we shared music with strangers, and in return we found joy. ●

A Mozart Mass with Orchestra
in the Cathedral ● MARYANN CORBETT

(first published in *Atlanta Review*)

In the beginning is the chaos.
Singers and instruments crowded into an organ loft,
the score of a second-row soprano flapping against my head,
the bow of the principal violin jabbing within inches of my face.

Yet somehow the spirit hovers over the waters:
we bring the unfallen world into being
by that acrobatic feat where sixty people hang on a pair of hands,
voice following voice in the fugue like evening and morning,

so that breath turns to music in the folds of the throat,
and the little clown of self
stops and is still,

down to the last note of the Agnus Dei,
that trapeze artist pushing off from the diaphragm
to sail over the nave and hang from the great baroque dome,
its triads shimmering,

its last trick, *peace*,
setting us down again in the lapsed world,
where instruments packed in cases are lugged
    down five flights,

and where, as I head for my bus stop,
the panhandler who is, as promised,
    always with us
uncurls himself from the rectory steps,
and asks, in the voice of God,
for my spare change.

*Detail from the Saint Paul Cathedral's cast reproduction of Michelangelo's
Pietà, depicting the Virgin Mary holding the body of Jesus Christ after his death.*
© Amber Michel/AAphotographyinMN.com

Earl Wolf and his wife put finishing touches on the sixteen-foot-high Paul Bunyan snow sculpture they made for the Saint Paul Winter Carnival on January 2, 1962.

MONDAY

29

Emory Parnell, Saint Paul–born vaudevillian and actor who appeared in over 250 films, was born today in 1892.

TUESDAY

30

WEDNESDAY

New Year's Eve

31

THURSDAY

JANUARY

New Year's Day

1

FRIDAY

JANUARY

2

SATURDAY

JANUARY

3

SUNDAY

JANUARY

4

This Week's Events

Monday
Holiday Flower Show

Tuesday
Holiday Flower Show

Wednesday
Holiday Flower Show
Noon Year's Party

Thursday
Holiday Flower Show
Noon Year's Party

Friday
Holiday Flower Show

Saturday
Downtown Saint Paul
Winter Farmers' Market
Holiday Flower Show

Sunday
Holiday Flower Show

Wilder Baths and Pool, designed to meet the needs of the Saint Paul residents without adequate bathing facilities, was opened a century ago. It boasted eighty-five shower baths and a swimming pool.

© Tom McGregor/mcgregorart.com

Vento at Daybreak

Christmas Unplugged ● SHERRY ROBERTS

Jenna already has her lights up, of course. I would have mine up, too, except ever since Sam fell into the Grand Canyon, I have been a little behind on things. I told my husband, leaning over the edge like that, that there wasn't anything down at the bottom of the Grand Canyon but river. Well, he proved me wrong. Men dance on the edge of the abyss, not even thinking about the mess they'll leave behind.

From the moment Sam hit that rocky bottom, my world changed. It didn't help that the stock market went splat, just like Sam, shortly thereafter. I have held on to my 1940s Saint Paul bungalow by judicious spending, prodigious coupon clipping, and lowering the thermostat. It's not so bad. Zoey the cat and I burrow under the down blankets and listen to the snowplows at night.

My one worry is the Christmas lights. Electricity is expensive, and I simply MUST have at least 5,459 lights. That is the number smothering Jenna's house, trees, and that tacky plastic North Pole diorama. She's been bragging all over the neighborhood about this year's display. If I can't produce one light more, she will win.

"You and Jenna have been competing with each other since the cradle," Sam always said.

It was true. When we were four and I took the crown at the Beautiful Babes Contest, Jenna threw a tantrum, ripping out all her pink hair bows. But she came back swinging at the State Fair when we were sixteen, becoming one of the beloved dairy princesses. As I fumed, my mother said, "Now be Minnesota nice, Abigail. Besides it's cold sitting in that freezer getting your likeness carved in real butter." I wanted to knock that tiara off Jenna's butter head with a hotdish.

And that's the way we've gone on for fifty years: frenemies. Neither will be the first to let our hair turn gray or admit our true age. She even moved in right across the street from me. Her house is bigger than mine, and newer, but mine is an original Craftsman, not one of those knockoffs.

I tear my gaze away from Jenna's house and stroke the cat sleeping on a nest of bills. I pluck the electric bill from the pile. "Zoey, where can we get a hundred dollars for my lights?"

"You could skip the lights this year," Sam would say.

"Not on your life," I tell Zoey.

Outside, Jimmy, the boy from down the street, is doing Sam's old job. He is my new light man. He lifts and untangles and hammers and strings. It will take him two days, and I just hope he knows his way around a roof.

While Jimmy works on the lights, I walk to the hair salon. This time of year, I always take a route that passes the Groveland Tap because it offers one heck of a Christmas display. As I'm taking in the decorations, I peek through the diner windows and see Bennie Nordgaard, Jenna's husband, in a booth, giggling and patting the hand of a woman who is at least twenty years younger. He glances in my direction and jerks back his hand. I raise an eyebrow. He looks away.

That night I can't sleep. Zoey is hogging all the covers. She is fifteen pounds of Maine Coon dead weight. I look like crap the next morning when Jimmy knocks on the door. He spends another day untangling and hammering, finishing about four o'clock. He has tested his work and swears that every one of my 5,460 bulbs is working. Five thousand four hundred and sixty—I make Jimmy count them twice.

That evening I bundle up and go outside to stand in the street and bask in the glow of my Yuletide extravaganza. Before long, Jenna joins me. As she stands beside me, the smell of her Chanel reaches across to me in the cold. We both stare at my house. I cross my arms. She crosses hers.

"How many?" she asks.

This is when I do the victory dance in the packed snow. I have the numbers and the money to keep them lit. But for some reason, I don't jump to respond. I find myself thinking of the blonde in the booth at the Groveland Tap.

Before I know it, I lie: "5,458."

Jenna stands a little taller, a satisfied smile on her face. "Too bad. 5,459."

"Well, there's always next year," I say.

"Yup, next year."

As Jenna minces her way across the icy walk back to her house, I return to mine. Zoey greets me at the door. I bend to stroke her, then whip off my hat and shake out my hair. I examine my gray roots in the mirror. Sam had been pushing me to go au naturel for years.

A dye job at the salon costs about a hundred bucks.

"Merry Christmas, Sam," I whisper. ●

A Family Tradition ● SHERONDA ORRIDGE

We have a family holiday tradition of an older member teaching a younger member how to cook. My grandmother passed the tradition down to my family. When she was a child, every Sunday after church her grandmother would have the grandchildren over for dinner. Immediately after church, my grandmother and her four sisters would run to their grandmother's house, wash their hands, and then rush into the kitchen to help her bake a cake.

After they put the cake into the oven, she would give them the bowl and the spoon to share the leftover cake batter. That experience was priceless. Spending time with her grandmother helped to mold my grandmother into a wonderful role model. Later, she passed this ritual down not only to her children, but to her grandchildren as well.

As a five-year-old girl, while spending time with my grandmother on the holidays, I learned how to bake cakes and pies. She would always save some of the batter so I could make my very own cake or pie, using my Easy Bake Oven pans. She bought me a mixer when I was ten, and pretty soon I began to help cook holiday meals.

Eighteen years ago, I was blessed with a daughter. I passed the

© KaBangi Ras Portraits Bob Marley Jr.

Sheronda with her daughter Akeeylah L. Watkins

tradition down to her, and to my nieces and nephews. When my daughter was ten, my grandmother bought her a mixer. One of the first things my daughter prepared was a turtle cheesecake.

Now, with great pleasure, I pass our tradition down to you. ●

Turtle Cheesecake

Ingredients
1 can (14 ounces) Eagle Brand sweetened condensed milk
Chocolate graham crackers
4 (8-ounce) packages cream cheese, softened at room temperature for 1 hour
1½ cups granulated sugar
¾ cup milk
4 eggs
1 cup sour cream
1 tablespoon vanilla extract
¼ cup all-purpose flour
¾ cup pecans

Directions
Place the unopened can of sweetened condensed milk into a medium pot full of water. Turn the flame on medium and let the can boil for 1½ hours on one side. Then flip the can onto the other side, add more water, and boil the can for 1½ hours on that side. Remove the can from the hot water and let cool.

While the can of condensed milk is cooling, preheat oven to 350 degrees. Spray a 9-by-13-inch pan with cooking spray and line the bottom and sides of the pan with crushed chocolate graham crackers.

In a large bowl, mix the cream cheese with the sugar until smooth. Blend the milk into the cream cheese mixture and then add the eggs, mixing them into the batter one at a time. Next, add the sour cream, vanilla, and flour, mixing the batter until smooth. Pour the batter into the prepared crust.

Bake in the preheated oven for 1 hour. Take the cake out of the oven and let it cool for 15 minutes. Next, open the can of condensed milk that has turned into caramel and pour it over the cheesecake. Sprinkle pecans over the top and wrap the cake loosely in foil. Chill for 8 hours.

Ma–Ka–To ● LISA J. YANKTON

A while ago in Minnesota
Time before children and adult responsibility
An elder said to me
We are going to Mankato for a pipe ceremony for the 38

We arrived in Ma-Ka-To
And went to a park
We climbed a snowy hill
Knee deep in snow
We stood in a circle on the sloped hill
There were fewer than a handful of us
Sage was lit and a sacred song was sung
The elder filled the sacred pipe and prayed
I was the only female
Too young to realize the significance of the event
However, my spirit knew and understood
The sacred pipe was smoked
An eagle arrived and circled overhead

This was a while ago
Before the park was renamed
Today, it is called the "Land of Memories Park"
Today there is a run starting Christmas Day midnight from
    Ft. Snelling to Ma-Ka-To
Today there is a horse ride from South Dakota to Ma-Ka-To
Today there is a movie about the ride
But a while ago there was only a handful who stood on a snowy
    sloped hill

Mending the Sacred Hoop
© Sarah Penman/sarahpenman.net

Saint Paul, MN ● CONNIE WANEK

Always, there was more than one Saint Paul.
Many fell off horses, many were saved,
many lost to the Flood as water climbed
the garden wall, as waves surged
over the threshold. A Paul and Pauline
came aboard the Ark and took
their muddy sandals off at the door
like good Minnesotans. "Lord I believe,
forgive me my unbelief."

My cousin Paul (born in Minneapolis) was no saint.
His twin, Peter, inherited the family conscience.
Strangers couldn't tell them apart
until one of them apologized.
The old streets tumble downhill toward the poor
brown Mississippi, a hard-working river,
a heavy drinker. It's moving south
as many do, only to return as summer rain.

Watch the water from afar—don't fall
under its spell. Then turn around:
there's the Capitol the crown,
the golden noggin. And within,
the same bickering that began in Eden.

Illustration © Shelley Rohlf
www.mnartists.org
/Shelley_S._Rohlf

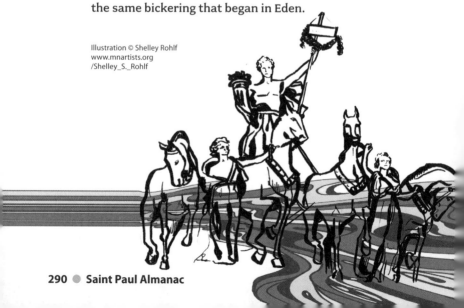

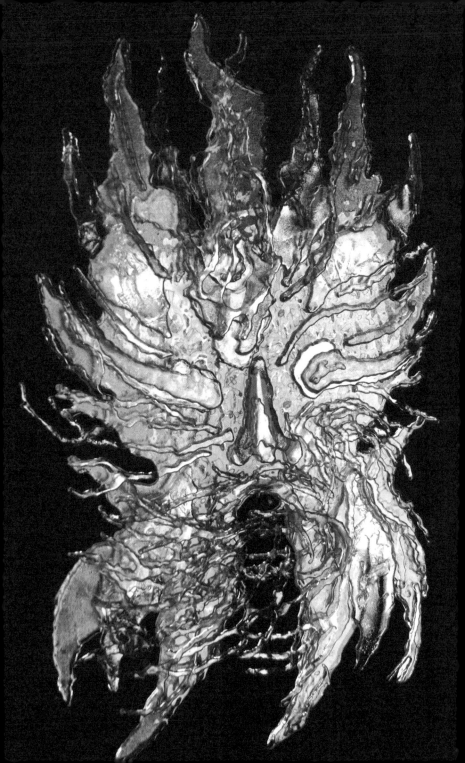

St. Paul Listings

Lisa Mathieson's luminescient glass sculpture of King Boreas, King of the Saint Paul Winter Carnival

© Amber Michel/AAphotographyinMN.com

Previous page: The sky and light dome above the City of Saint Paul, viewed from Cannon Falls. This time lapse photo is a combination of forty-seven images.

© Carlton McMillan/carlton.mcmillan@gmail.com

Events

JANUARY

Holiday Flower Show

Dec. 7, 2013—Jan. 5, 2014
Marjorie McNeely
   Conservatory, Como Park
651.487.8200
www.comozooconservatory.org
*Since 1925, the Holiday Flower
Show has been the most anticipated attraction of the year. It is a
visual sensation to behold, featuring hundreds of poinsettias.*

Downtown Saint Paul Winter Farmers' Market

Saturdays, 9 a.m.—1 p.m.
290 East Fifth St.
651.227.8101
www.stpaulfarmersmarket.com
*Local growers sell their fresh foods
directly to you.*

Winter Break K–12

Dec. 23, 2013—Jan. 1, 2014
Saint Paul Public Schools
www.spps.org

Land O' Lakes Kennel Club Dog Show

Jan. 3—5
Saint Paul RiverCentre
651.265.4800
www.rivercentre.org
*Come watch more than 2,000 dogs
strut their stuff.*

Broadway Songbook: George Gershwin

Jan. 3, 7:30 p.m.
Jan. 4, 2 p.m. and 7:30 p.m.
Jan. 5, 2 p.m. and 7:30 p.m.
Ordway Music Theater Stage
www.ordway.org

Minnesota Boychoir Concert

Sunday, Jan. 5
1 and 3:30 p.m.
Landmark Center
www.landmarkcenter.org

Music Under Glass

Jan. 5, 12, 19, 4:30—6:30 p.m.
Marjorie McNeely
   Conservatory, Como Park
651.487.8200
www.comozooconservatory.org
*Escape the winter chill in the
gardens of the Marjorie McNeely
Conservatory for a concert series
featuring a perfect blend of music
in a variety of genres. This FREE
music series allows guests to enjoy
live music by local musicians in the
Conservatory. Wine and beer are
available for purchase.*

Cocktails with Culture
Thursday, Jan. 9
5–7 p.m.
Landmark Center
www.landmarkcenter.org
*Free concerts featuring some of
the best Twin Cities talent. Drinks
available for purchase.*

Saint Paul Almanac
Soul Sounds Open Mic
Jan. 9, 16, 23, 30
6–8 p.m.
Golden Thyme Cafe
www.saintpaulalmanac.org
*First Thursday writing workshop,
5–6 p.m.*

**MN Sportsmen's, Boat,
Camping, and Vacation Show**
Jan. 9–12
Saint Paul RiverCentre
651.265.4800
www.rivercentre.org

**The Saint Paul
Chamber Orchestra**
Pekka Kuusisto Plays Vasks
Jan. 11, 8 p.m.
Ordway Center
www.thespco.org

Winter Flower Show
Jan. 11–Mar. 16
Marjorie McNeely Conservatory, Como Park
651.487.8200
www.comozooconservatory.org

**The Saint Paul
Chamber Orchestra**
Mendelssohn's Italian Symphony
Jan. 17, 10:30 a.m. and 8 p.m.
Jan. 18, 8 p.m.
Ordway Center
www.thespco.org

Urban Expedition: Spain
Sunday, Jan. 19
1 p.m.
Landmark Center
www.landmarkcenter.org

Saint Paul Almanac
Lowertown Reading Jam
Jan. 22, Guante/Kyle Myhre
7:30–8:30 p.m.
The Black Dog Café
308 Prince St.
www.saintpaulalmanac.org
*Selected writers curate readings
around a theme they have chosen
and invite other writers and artists
to perform with them.*

Fireside Reading Series
Jan. 22 and 29
Hamline Midway Library
1558 W. Minnehaha Ave.
www.thefriends.org
651.222.3242
*Visit www.thefriends.org for details
and updates.*

Saint Paul Winter Carnival
Jan. 23—Feb. 2
Downtown Saint Paul
651.223.4700
www.winter-carnival.com
*Lots of winter events: parades, ice
skating, ice sculpture, coronation,
medallion hunt.*

Fourth Friday at the Movies
Jan. 24
Golden Thyme Cafe
651.645.1340
*Social hour at 6:30 p.m. and film
at 7 p.m.*

**The Saint Paul
Chamber Orchestra**
Chamber Music Series #3
Jan. 24, 8 p.m.
Jan. 26, 2 p.m.
SPCO Center
www.thespco.org

**Minnesota Division 1 Men's
Hockey Tournament (MN Cup)**
Jan. 24—25
Xcel Energy Center
763.560.2262

**The Saint Paul
Chamber Orchestra**
xplorchestra! Musical X-periences!
Jan. 25, 9:30 a.m. and 11 a.m.
SPCO Center
www.thespco.org

Minnesota RollerGirls
Jan. 25
Roy Wilkins Auditorium
651.265.4800
www.mnrollergirls.com

Minnesota Opera
Macbeth
Jan. 25, 28, 30
Feb. 1, 2
mnopera.org

Saintly City Cat Show
Jan. 25—26
Wilkins Exhibit Halls
Saint Paul RiverCentre
651.265.4800
www.rivercentre.org

**Orchid Society of Minnesota
Winter Carnival Orchid Show**
Jan. 25—26
Marjorie McNeely
    Conservatory, Como Park
651.487.8200
www.comozooconservatory.org
*Hundreds of orchid plants owned
by individual and commercial
orchid growers transform the Marjorie McNeely Conservatory into a
tropical wonderland where instead
of King Boreas, orchids rule.*

World's Toughest Rodeo
Jan. 31—Feb. 1
Xcel Energy Center
763.560.2262

FEBRUARY

Saint Paul Winter Carnival
Jan. 23—Feb. 2
Downtown Saint Paul
651.223.4700
www.winter-carnival.com
Lots of winter events: parades, ice skating, ice sculpture, coronation, medallion hunt.

Saint Paul Almanac
Soul Sounds Open Mic
Feb. 6, 13, 20, 27
6—8 p.m.
Golden Thyme Cafe
www.saintpaulalmanac.org
First Thursday writing workshop, 5—6 p.m.

Downtown Saint Paul
Winter Farmers' Market
Saturdays, 9 a.m.—1 p.m.
290 East Fifth St.
651.227.8101
www.stpaulfarmersmarket.com
Local growers sell their fresh foods directly to you.

Winter Flower Show
Jan. 11—Mar. 16
Marjorie McNeely
   Conservatory, Como Park
651.487.8200
www.comozooconservatory.org

World's Toughest Rodeo
Jan. 31—Feb. 1
Xcel Energy Center
763.560.2262

Music Under Glass
Feb. 2, 9, 16
4:30—6:30 p.m.
Marjorie McNeely
   Conservatory, Como Park
651.487.8200
www.comozooconservatory.org
Escape the winter chill in the gardens of the Marjorie McNeely Conservatory for a concert series featuring a perfect blend of music in a variety of genres. This FREE music series allows guests to enjoy live music by local musicians in the Conservatory. Wine and beer are available for purchase.

© Julia Singer/WriteWorks.net

**The Saint Paul
Chamber Orchestra**
*Shostakovich's Fourteenth
Symphony*
Feb. 1, 8 p.m.
900 Summit Ave.
www.thespco.org

Fireside Reading Series
Feb. 5, 12, 19, 26
Hamline Midway Library
1558 W. Minnehaha Ave.
651.222.3242
www.thefriends.org
*Visit www.thefriends.org for details
and updates.*

**The Saint Paul
Chamber Orchestra**
Chamber Music Series #4
Feb. 7, 8 p.m.
Feb. 9, 2 p.m.
SPCO Center
www.thespco.org

Rennie Harris Puremovement
Feb. 7, 7:30 p.m.
Ordway Music Theater
TARGET® Dance Series
www.ordway.org
*RHPM's work encompasses rich and
diverse African American traditions of the past while simultaneously presenting the voice of a new
generation and sharing young
dancers' enthusiasm for hip-hop
dance theatre.*

Urban Expedition: Finland
Feb. 9, 1 p.m.
Landmark Center
www.landmarkcenter.org

Ladysmith Black Mambazo
Feb. 9, 7:30 p.m.
Ordway Music Theater
TARGET® World Music Series
www.ordway.org

Cocktails with Culture
Feb. 13, 5–7 p.m.
Landmark Center
www.landmarkcenter.org
*Free concerts featuring some of
the best Twin Cities talent. Drinks
available for purchase.*

**Minnesota Home
and Patio Show**
Feb. 13–16
Saint Paul RiverCentre
651.265.4800
www.rivercentre.org

**The Saint Paul
Chamber Orchestra**
Beethoven's Eighth Symphony
Feb. 14, 10:30 a.m. and 8 p.m.
Feb. 15, 8 p.m.
Ordway Center
www.thespco.org

Scottish Ramble
Feb. 16, 12–5 p.m.
Landmark Center
www.landmarkcenter.org

Maria de Barros
Feb. 19, 7:30 p.m.
Ordway Music Theater
TARGET® World Music Series
www.ordway.org

**MSHSL Girls Hockey
Tournament**
Feb. 19—22
Xcel Energy Center
763.560.2262
www.mshsl.org

**The Saint Paul
Chamber Orchestra**
Mozart and Hindemith
Feb. 21 10:30 a.m. and 8 p.m.
Feb. 22, 8 p.m.
Ordway Center
www.thespco.org

***Saint Paul Almanac*
Lowertown Reading Jam**
Feb. 26, Chay Douangphouxay
7:30—8:30 p.m.
The Black Dog Café
308 Prince St.
www.saintpaulalmanac.org

MSHSL Wrestling Tournament
Feb. 27—March 1
Xcel Energy Center
763.560.2262
www.mshsl.org

Fourth Friday at the Movies
Feb. 28
Golden Thyme Cafe
651.645.1340
*Social hour at 6:30 p.m. and film
at 7 p.m.*

MARCH

**Downtown Saint Paul
Winter Farmers' Market**
Saturdays, 9 a.m.—1 p.m.
290 East Fifth St.
651.227.8101
www.stpaulfarmersmarket.com
*Local growers sell their fresh foods
directly to you.*

Audience at one of the Saint Paul Almanac's *Lowertown Reading Jams*

Winter Flower Show
January 11—Mar. 16
Marjorie McNeely
    Conservatory, Como Park
651.487.8200
www.comozooconservatory.org

Minnesota Opera
The Dream of Valentino
Mar. 1, 4, 6, 8, 9
www.mnopera.org

The Saint Paul Chamber Orchestra
Vivaldi's Four Seasons
Mar. 1, 8 p.m.
900 Summit Ave.
www.thespco.org

Urban Expedition: Cambodia
Mar. 2, 1 p.m.
Landmark Center
www.landmarkcenter.org

MSHSL Boys Hockey Tournament
Mar. 5—8
Xcel Energy Center
763.560.2262
www.mshsl.org

***Saint Paul Almanac*
Soul Sounds Open Mic**
Mar. 6, 13, 20, 27
6—8 p.m.
Golden Thyme Cafe
www.saintpaulalmanac.org
*First Thursday writing workshop,
5—6 p.m.*

Let's Play Hockey Expo
Mar. 7—8
Saint Paul RiverCentre
651.265.4800
www.rivercentre.org

Minnesota RollerGirls
Mar. 8
Roy Wilkins Auditorium
651.265.4800
www.mnrollergirls.com

The Saint Paul Chamber Orchestra
Tchaikovsky's Serenade for Strings
Mar. 8, 8 p.m.
900 Summit Ave.
www.thespco.org

Seniors in Mind
Mar. 11
Minnesota History Center
345 West Kellogg Blvd.
651.259.3000
www.mnhs.org
Free programs of music, photography, and lectures on Minnesota history and culture for people 55+.

The Saint Paul Chamber Orchestra
Beethoven's Second Piano Concerto
Mar. 13, 7:30 p.m.
Mar. 14, 10:30 a.m. and 8 p.m.
Mar. 15, 8 p.m.
Ordway Center
www.thespco.org

Saint Patrick's Day Parade
Mar. 15
Downtown Saint Paul
www.stpatsassoc.org

Irish Day Dance
Mar. 16, 11 a.m.—5 p.m.
Landmark Center
www.landmarkcenter.org

Irish Celebration
St. Patrick's Day
Mar. 17, 10 a.m.—5 p.m.
Landmark Center
www.landmarkcenter.org

Big Ten Hockey Championship
Mar. 20—22
Xcel Energy Center
763.560.2262

AXIS Dance Company
Mar. 21, 7:30 p.m.
Ordway Music Theater
TARGET® Dance Series
www.ordway.org

The Saint Paul
Chamber Orchestra
Timo Andres: Work Songs
Mar. 21 and 22, 8 p.m.
SPCO Center
www.thespco.org

Spring Flower Show
Mar. 22—Apr. 27
Marjorie McNeely
   Conservatory, Como Park
651.487.8200
www.comozooconservatory.org
Fling into spring with the Spring Flower Show and springtime favorite flowers.

Como flower show

The Gershwins' *Porgy and Bess*
Mar. 25—28, 7:30 p.m.
Mar. 29—30, 2 p.m.
    and 7:30 p.m.
Ordway Music Theater
www.ordway.org

Saint Paul Almanac
Lowertown Reading Jam
Mar. 26, Ifra Mansour
7:30—8:30 p.m.
The Black Dog Café
308 Prince St.
www.saintpaulalmanac.org

Fourth Friday at the Movies
Mar. 28
Golden Thyme Cafe
651.645.1340
Social hour at 6:30 p.m. and film at 7 p.m.

**The Saint Paul
Chamber Orchestra**
Chamber Music Series #5
Mar. 28, 8 p.m.
Mar. 30, 2 p.m.
SPCO Center
www.thespco.org

Donnie Smith Bike Show
Mar. 28—30
Saint Paul RiverCentre
651.265.4800
www.rivercentre.org

**2014 NCAA Men's Ice Hockey
West Regional**
Mar. 29—30
Xcel Energy Center
763.560.2262
www.xcelenergycenter.com

Spring Break K–12
Mar. 31—Apr. 4
www.spps.org

APRIL

Spring Break K–12
Mar. 31—Apr. 4
www.spps.org

Spring Flower Show
Mar. 22—Apr. 27
Marjorie McNeely
    Conservatory, Como Park
651.487.8200
www.comozooconservatory.org
Fling into spring with the Spring Flower Show and springtime favorite flowers.

**Downtown Saint Paul
Farmers' Market**
Apr.—Nov. 23
Saturdays, 6 a.m.—1 p.m.
Sundays, 8 a.m.—1 p.m.
290 East Fifth St.
651.227.8101
www.stpaulfarmersmarket.com
Local growers sell their fresh produce directly to you.

Saint Paul Almanac
Soul Sounds Open Mic
Apr. 3, 10, 17, 24
6—8 p.m.
Golden Thyme Cafe
www.saintpaulalmanac.org
First Thursday writing workshop,
5—6 p.m.

The Saint Paul
Chamber Orchestra
SPCO with the Miró Quartet
Apr. 3, 7:30 p.m.
Apr. 4, 10:30 a.m.
Apr. 5, 8 p.m.
Ordway Center
www.thespco.org

Minnesota RollerGirls
Apr. 5
Roy Wilkins Auditorium
651.265.4800
www.mnrollergirls.com

27th Minnesota Book Awards
Apr. 5
651.222.3242
www.thefriends.org
Visit www.thefriends.org for details
and updates.

Cocktails with Culture
Thursday, Apr. 10
5—7 p.m.
Landmark Center
www.landmarkcenter.org
Free concerts featuring some of
the best Twin Cities talent. Drinks
available for purchase.

American Craft Council Saint Paul Show

Apr. 11—14
Saint Paul RiverCentre
651.265.4800
www.rivercentre.org

Asian Pacific Heritage Day

Apr. 12
Minnesota History Center
345 West Kellogg Blvd.
651.259.3000
www.mnhs.org

The Saint Paul Chamber Orchestra

Copland's Appalachian Spring
Apr. 12, 8 p.m.
900 Summit Ave.
www.thespco.org

Minnesota Opera

The Magic Flute
Apr. 12, 13, 15, 17, 19
www.mnopera.org

Urban Expedition: Senegal

Apr. 13, 1 p.m.
Landmark Center
www.landmarkcenter.org

Minnesota RollerGirls

Apr. 19
Roy Wilkins Auditorium
651.265.4800
www.mnrollergirls.com

Saint Paul Almanac Lowertown Reading Jam

Apr. 23, Mankwe Ndosi
7:30—8:30 p.m.
The Black Dog Café
308 Prince St.
www.saintpaulalmanac.org

The Saint Paul Chamber Orchestra

Haydn, Stravinsky, and Kernis
Apr. 24, 7:30 p.m.
Apr. 25, 10:30 a.m.
Apr. 26, 8 p.m.
Ordway Center
www.thespco.org

Fourth Friday at the Movies

Apr. 25
Golden Thyme Cafe
651.645.1340
Social hour at 6:30 p.m. and film at 7 p.m.

Saint Paul Art Crawl

Apr. 25—27
Downtown Saint Paul
651.292.4373
www.artcrawl.org
More than 200 artists open their studios to the public.

Rose Ensemble Concert

Sunday Apr. 27, 1 p.m.
Landmark Center
www.landmarkcenter.org

Blue Man Group
Apr. 29, 7:30 p.m.
Apr. 30, 7:30 p.m.
Ordway Music Theater
www.ordway.org

MAY

**Downtown Saint Paul
Farmers' Market**
Apr.—Nov. 23
Saturdays, 6 a.m.—1 p.m.
Sundays, 8 a.m.—1 p.m.
290 East Fifth St.
651.227.8101
www.stpaulfarmersmarket.com
*Local growers sell their fresh
produce directly to you.*

Blue Man Group
May 1—2, 7:30 p.m.
May 3—4, 2 p.m. and 7:30 p.m.
Ordway Music Theater
www.ordway.org

Saint Paul Almanac
Soul Sounds Open Mic
May 1, 8, 15, 22, 29
6—8 p.m.
Golden Thyme Cafe
www.saintpaulalmanac.org
*First Thursday writing workshop,
5—6 p.m.*

**20th Annual
Great River Gathering**
May 8
5—8:30 p.m.
Saint Paul RiverCentre
www.riverfrontcorporation.com
*The Great River Gathering brings
together citizens, artists, policy
makers, corporate leaders, entre-
preneurs, environmentalists, elected
officials, and philanthropists from
all walks of life to celebrate the best
of Saint Paul.*

© Tony Ernst/gamelaner on Flickr

Cinco de Mayo dancer

Cinco de Mayo Festival

May 2–4
District del Sol
651.222.6347
www.districtdelsol.com
Celebrate with live music, food, children's area, community wellness village, parade, and vendors.

Festival of Nations

May 2–4
Saint Paul RiverCentre
651.265.4800
www.rivercentre.org

The Saint Paul Chamber Orchestra

Beethoven's Violin Concerto
May 3, 8 p.m.
900 Summit Ave.
www.thespco.org

Summer Flower Show

May 3–Oct. 5
Marjorie McNeely
    Conservatory, Como Park
651.487.8200
www.comozooconservatory.org
The Summer Flower Show offers the greatest plant diversity as well as the longest season of all five flower shows.

Summit Avenue Walking Tours

May 3, 10, 17, 24, 31, 11 a.m. and
    2 p.m.
May 4, 11, 18, 25, 2 p.m.
www.mnhs.org
Take a 1.5-mile, 90-minute tour of the Summit Avenue neighborhood, named one of America's "Great Streets" in 2008. Check www.mnhs.org for times and fees. Reservations recommended.

The Saint Paul Chamber Orchestra

Liquid Music
Daniel Bjarnason and Nadia Sirota
May 6, 7:30 p.m.
Amsterdam Bar and Hall
www.thespco.org

The Saint Paul Chamber Orchestra

Chamber Music Series #6
May 9, 8 p.m.
May 11, 2 p.m.
SPCO Center
www.thespco.org

The Saint Paul Chamber Orchestra

Family Music
Start the Music! Pounding Percussion: Meet the Percussion Family
May 10 and 24
10:15 a.m. and 11:15 a.m.
SPCO Center
www.thespco.org

TU Dance

May 10, 7:30 p.m.
Ordway Music Theater
TARGET® Dance Series
www.ordway.org

Mother's Day Bonsai Show
May 10 and 11
Marjorie McNeely
    Conservatory, Como Park
651.487.8200
www.comozooconservatory.org
The Minnesota Bonsai Society Mother's Day Weekend Bonsai Show is a unique opportunity to see privately owned bonsai. Bonsai are "trees in pots" and are an ancient Japanese art form that blends artistic vision and horticultural expertise. Each bonsai represents nature in miniature and creates appreciation for the aesthetic of great age and rugged form as represented by the trees.

Saint Paul Civic Symphony Mother's Day Concert
May 11, 1 p.m.
Landmark Center
www.landmarkcenter.org

Bring It On: The Musical
May 13–16, 7:30 p.m.
May 17–18, 2 p.m.
    and 7:30 p.m.
Ordway Music Theater
www.ordway.org

Seniors in Mind
May 13
Minnesota History Center
345 West Kellogg Blvd.
651.259.3000
www.mnhs.org
Free programs of music, photography, and lectures on Minnesota history and culture for people 55+.

© Tony Ernst/gamelaner on Flickr

The Cinco De Mayo festival in West Saint Paul

RetroRama
May 16
Minnesota History Center
345 West Kellogg Blvd.
651.259.3000
www.mnhs.org

**The Saint Paul
Chamber Orchestra**
*Britten, Mendelssohn, and
Shostakovich*
May 17, 8 p.m.
900 Summit Ave.
www.thespco.org

Urban Expedition: Brazil
May 18, 1 p.m.
Landmark Center
www.landmarkcenter.org

Fourth Friday at the Movies
May 23
Golden Thyme Cafe
651.645.1340
*Social hour at 6:30 p.m. and film
at 7 p.m.*

**The Saint Paul
Chamber Orchestra**
The Turn of the Screw
May 23 and 24, 8 p.m.
Ordway Center
www.thespco.org

Saint Paul Almanac
Lowertown Reading Jam
May 28, Katie Hae Leo
7:30—8:30 p.m.
The Black Dog Café
308 Prince St.
www.saintpaulalmanac.org

JUNE

**Downtown Saint Paul
Farmers' Market**
Apr.—Nov. 23
Saturdays, 6 a.m.—1 p.m.
Sundays, 8 a.m.—1 p.m.
290 East Fifth St.
651.227.8101
www.stpaulfarmersmarket.com
*Local growers sell their fresh
produce directly to you.*

**Saint Paul (Seventh Place)
Farmers' Market**
June—Sept.
Tuesdays and Thursdays
10—1:30 p.m., Seventh Place
651.227.8101
www.stpaulfarmersmarket.com
*Local growers sell their fresh
produce directly to you.*

Summer Flower Show
May 3—Oct. 5
Marjorie McNeely
    Conservatory, Como Park
651.487.8200
www.comozooconservatory.org
*The Summer Flower Show offers the
greatest plant diversity as well as
the longest season of all five flower
shows.*

Grand Old Day
June 1
Grand Avenue
www.grandave.com

Summit Avenue Walking Tours

June 7, 14, 21, 28, 11 a.m.
and 2 p.m.
June 1, 8, 15, 22, 29, 2 p.m.
www.mnhs.org
Take a 1.5-mile, 90-minute tour of the Summit Avenue neighborhood, named one of America's "Great Streets" in 2008. Check www.mnhs.org for times and fees. Reservations recommended.

Saint Paul Almanac
Soul Sounds Open Mic

June 5, 12, 19, 26
6–8 p.m.
Golden Thyme Cafe
www.saintpaulalmanac.org
First Thursday writing workshop, 5–6 p.m.

Nooks and Crannies Tours

June 3, 10, 17, 24
240 Summit Ave.
651.297.2555
www.mnhs.org

History Pub Crawl

June 4, 11, 18, 25
Minnesota History Center
345 West Kellogg Blvd.
651.259.3000
www.mnhs.org

Music in Mears

Mears Park
June 5, 12, 19, 26
www.musicinmears.com

Last Day of School K–12

June 6
www.spps.org

Cajon drum workshop hosted by EmpoweredPercussion.com at the all-night Northern Spark Festival in Lowertown

The Saint Paul Chamber Orchestra
Schubert's Unfinished Symphony
June 6—8, 8 p.m.
Ordway Center
www.thespco.org

Hamline-Midway Heartland Festival
June 7, 11 a.m.—5 p.m.
Newell Park
651.494.7683
www.hamlinemidway.org

Saint Anthony Park Arts Festival
June 7, 10 a.m.—5 p.m.
2245 Como Ave.
www.stanthonyparkarts
    festival.org

Broadway Songbook: Comden and Green
June 13, 7:30 p.m.
June 14—15, 2 p.m. and
    7:30 p.m.
Ordway Music Theater Stage
www.ordway.org

Summer History HiJinx Craft Activity
June 17—Aug. 15 (Tuesdays—
    Fridays)
Minnesota History Center
345 West Kellogg Blvd.
651.259.3000
www.mnhs.org
*Families and children can create
a make-it take-it craft (included
with museum admission).*

Saint Paul Almanac
Lowertown Reading Jam
June 25, TBD
7:30—8:30 p.m.
The Black Dog Café
308 Prince St.
www.saintpaulalmanac.org

Fourth Friday at the Movies
June 27
Golden Thyme Cafe
651.645.1340
*Social hour at 6:30 p.m. and film
at 7 p.m.*

JULY

Downtown Saint Paul Farmers' Market
Apr.—Nov. 23
Saturdays, 6 a.m.—1 p.m.
Sundays, 8 a.m.—1 p.m.
290 East Fifth St.
651.227.8101
www.stpaulfarmersmarket.com
*Local growers sell their fresh pro-
duce directly to you.*

Saint Paul (Seventh Place) Farmers' Market
June—Sept.
Tuesdays and Thursdays
10 a.m.—1:30 p.m.
Seventh Place
651.227.8101
www.stpaulfarmersmarket.com
*Local growers sell their fresh
produce directly to you.*

Summer Flower Show

May 3–Oct. 5
Marjorie McNeely
    Conservatory, Como Park
651.487.8200
www.comozooconservatory.org
The Summer Flower Show offers the greatest plant diversity as well as the longest season of all five flower shows.

Nooks and Crannies Tours

July 1, 8, 15, 22, 29
240 Summit Ave.
651.297.2555
www.mnhs.org

Music in Mears

Mears Park
July 3, 10, 17, 24, 31
www.musicinmears.com

Saint Paul Almanac
Soul Sounds Open Mic

July 3, 10, 17, 24, 31
6–8 p.m.
Golden Thyme Cafe
First Thursday writing workshop
5–6 p.m.

Summit Avenue Walking Tours

July 5, 12, 19, 26, 11 a.m.
    and 2 p.m.
July 6, 13, 20, 27, 2 p.m.
www.mnhs.org
Take a 1.5-mile, 90-minute tour of the Summit Avenue neighborhood, named one of America's "Great Streets" in 2008. Check www.mnhs.org for times and fees. Reservations recommended.

Dancers at the Irish Fair

Summer History HiJinx Craft Activity

June 17–Aug. 15 (Tuesdays–
    Fridays)
Minnesota History Center
345 West Kellogg Blvd.
651.259.3000
www.mnhs.org
*Families and children can create
a make-it take-it craft (included
with museum admission).*

Nine Nights of Music Outdoor Concert Series

July 1, 8, 15, 22, 29
Minnesota History Center
345 West Kellogg Blvd.
651.259.3000
www.mnhs.org

Saint Anthony Park Parade

July 4, 11 a.m.
www.sapcc.org
*Children's bikes, trikes, wagons,
etc., assemble at Park Station.
Bands, vehicles, and marching
units assemble on Luther Place.
Get your free American Flag!*

Hmong international Sports Tournament and Freedom Festival

July 6–7
651.221.0069
www.laofamily.org

Seniors in Mind

July 8
Minnesota History Center
345 West Kellogg Blvd.
651.259.3000
www.mnhs.org
*Free programs of music, photog-
raphy, and lectures on Minnesota
history and culture for people 55+.*

History Pub Crawl

July 9, 16, 23, 30
Minnesota History Center
345 West Kellogg Blvd.
651.259.3000
www.mnhs.org

Summer Movies

July 11, 18, 25
Saint Paul Central Library
651.222.3242
www.thefriends.org
*Shows begin at dusk (about 9:30
p.m.). Visit www.thefriends.org for
details and updates.*

Dragon Festival and Boat Races

July 12 and 13
Lake Phalen
www.dragonfestival.org

Sunset Affair Gala
July 17
Marjorie McNeely
   Conservatory, Como Park
651.487.8200
www.comozooconservatory.org
Sunset Affair is an elegant event that draws community leaders together to support Como Park Zoo and Conservatory, a free zoo and botanical garden. As the highlight of Como Park Zoo and Conservatory's social calendar, Sunset Affair is Como's largest fundraiser, featuring dinner, entertainment, and auction.

Highland Fest
July 18—20
Friday, 2—10:30 p.m.
Saturday, 10 a.m.—10:30 p.m.
Sunday, 11 a.m.—5 p.m.
Highland Village
651.699.9042
www.highlandfest.com

Home Expo and Art Fair
July 18—20
Friday, 2—8 p.m.
Saturday, 10 a.m.—8 p.m.,
Sunday, 11 a.m.—5 p.m.

Rondo Days
July 19
651.315.7676
www.rondoavenueinc.org
Rondo Days are a central gathering time for celebrating the unique heritage of Saint Paul's historic Black community.

Saint Paul Almanac Lowertown Reading Jam
July 23, TBD
7:30—8:30 p.m.
The Black Dog Café
308 Prince St.
www.saintpaulalmanac.org

Fourth Friday at the Movies
July 25
Golden Thyme Cafe
651.645.1340
Social hour at 6:30 p.m. and film at 7 p.m.

Circus Juventas Summer Show
July 30—Aug. 17
www.circusjuventas.org

AUGUST

Downtown Saint Paul Farmers' Market

Apr.—Nov. 23
Saturdays, 6 a.m.—1 p.m.
Sundays, 8 a.m.—1 p.m.
290 East Fifth St.
651.227.8101
www.stpaulfarmersmarket.com
Local growers sell their fresh produce directly to you.

Summer Flower Show

May 3—Oct. 5
Marjorie McNeely
   Conservatory, Como Park
651.487.8200
www.comozooconservatory.org
The Summer Flower Show offers the greatest plant diversity as well as the longest season of all five flower shows.

Saint Paul (Seventh Place) Farmers' Market

June—Sept.
Tuesdays and Thursdays
10 a.m.—1:30 p.m.
Seventh Place
651.227.8101
www.stpaulfarmersmarket.com
Local growers sell their fresh produce directly to you.

Summer History HiJinx Craft Activity

June 17—Aug. 15 (Tuesdays—
   Fridays)
Minnesota History Center
345 West Kellogg Blvd.
651.259.3000
www.mnhs.org
Families and children can create a make-it take-it craft (included with museum admission).

Circus Juventas Summer Show

July 30—Aug. 17
www.circusjuventas.org

Summer Movies

Aug. 1
St. Paul Central Library
651.222.3242
www.thefriends.org
Shows begin at dusk (about 9:30 p.m.). Visit www.thefriends.org for details and updates.

Summit Avenue Walking Tours

Aug. 2, 9, 16, 23, 30, 11 a.m.
   and 2 p.m.
Aug. 3, 10, 17, 24, 31, 2 p.m.
www.mnhs.org
Take a 1.5-mile, 90-minute tour of the Summit Avenue neighborhood, named one of America's "Great Streets" in 2008. Check www.mnhs. org for times and fees. Reservations recommended.

Paws on Grand

Aug. 3
www.grandave.com
Enjoy the Paws on Grand dog wash, rescue a pet, get a doggie phototaken, and even watch your pooch walk down the aisle and into wedded bliss!

**Nine Nights of Music
Outdoor Concert**
Aug. 5, 12, 19, 26
Minnesota History Center
345 West Kellogg Blvd.
651.259.3000
www.mnhs.org

Nooks and Crannies Tours
Aug. 5, 12, 19, 26
240 Summit Ave.
651.297.2555

History Pub Crawl
Aug. 6, 13, 20, 27
Minnesota History Center
345 West Kellogg Blvd.
651.259.3000
www.mnhs.org

Music in Mears
Mears Park
Aug. 7, 14, 21, 28
www.musicinmears.com

Irish Fair
Aug. 8–10
Harriet Island
www.Irishfair.com

Saint Paul Almanac
Soul Sounds Open Mic
Aug. 7, 14, 21, 28, 6–8 p.m.
Golden Thyme Cafe
www.saintpaulalmanac.org
*First Thursday writing workshop,
5–6 p.m.*

**Japanese Lantern
Lighting Festival**
Aug. 17
Marjorie McNeely
    Conservatory, Como Park
651.487.8200
www.comozooconservatory.org
This family-friendly event, reminiscent of Japan's Obon holiday, features Bonsai, martial arts, singing, dancing, drumming, and delicious food.

Minnesota State Fair
Aug. 21–Sept. 1
State Fairgrounds
www.mnstatefair.org

Minnesota State Fair

Fourth Friday at the Movies
Aug. 22
Golden Thyme Cafe
651.645.1340
*Social hour at 6:30 p.m. and film
at 7 p.m.*

SEPTEMBER

**Downtown Saint Paul
Farmers' Market**
Apr.—Nov. 23
Saturdays, 6 a.m.—1 p.m.
Sundays, 8 a.m.—1 p.m.
290 East Fifth St.
651.227.8101
www.stpaulfarmersmarket.com
*Local growers sell their fresh
produce directly to you.*

**Saint Paul (Seventh Place)
Farmers' Market**
June—Sept.
Tuesdays and Thursdays
10 a.m.—1:30 p.m.
Seventh Place
651.227.8101
www.stpaulfarmersmarket.com
*Local growers sell their fresh
produce directly to you.*

Summer Flower Show
May 3—Oct. 5
Marjorie McNeely Conserva-
    tory, Como Park
651.487.8200
www.comozooconservatory.org
*The Summer Flower Show offers the
greatest plant diversity as well as
the longest season of all five flower
shows.*

Minnesota State Fair
Aug. 21—Sep 1
State Fairgrounds
www.mnstatefair.org

Saint Paul Almanac
Soul Sounds Open Mic
Sept. 4, 11, 18, 25, 6—8 p.m.
Golden Thyme Cafe
www.saintpaulalmanac.org
*First Thursday writing workshop,
5—6 p.m.*

Summit Avenue Walking Tours
Sept. 6, 13, 20, 27, 11 a.m.
    and 2 p.m.
Sept. 7, 14, 21, 28, 2 p.m.
www.mnhs.org
*Take a 1.5-mile, 90-minute tour of
the Summit Avenue neighborhood,
named one of America's "Great
Streets" in 2008. Check www.mnhs.
org for times and fees. Reservations
recommended.*

Seniors in Mind
Sept. 9
Minnesota History Center
345 West Kellogg Blvd.
651.259.3000
www.mnhs.org
*Free programs of music, photog-
raphy, and lectures on Minnesota
history and culture for people 55+.*

Saint Paul Almanac
Book Release Party
Thurs., Sept. 11
Black Dog Cafe
651.785.6268
www.saintpaulalmanac.org
Book release party for the 2015
Saint Paul Almanac. Enjoy the party!

Golden Thyme Jazz Festival
Sep. 14
Golden Thyme Cafe
651.645.1340

F. Scott Fitzgerald Walking Tour
Sept. 20 and 21
240 Summit Ave.
651.297.2555
www.mnhs.org

Fourth Friday at the Movies
Sept. 26
Golden Thyme Cafe
651.645.1340
Social hour at 6:30 p.m. and film
at 7 p.m.

Oktoberfest
(now in September)
Dates to be announced
651.253.5261
www.saintpauloktoberfest.org

OCTOBER

Downtown Saint Paul
Farmers' Market
Apr.—Nov. 23
Saturdays, 6 a.m.—1 p.m.
Sundays, 8 a.m.—1 p.m.
290 East Fifth St.
651.227.8101
www.stpaulfarmersmarket.com
Local growers sell their fresh pro-
duce directly to you.

Summer Flower Show
May 3—Oct. 5
Marjorie McNeely Conservatory,
     Como Park
651.487.8200
www.comozooconservatory.org
The Summer Flower Show offers the
greatest plant diversity as well as the
longest season of all five flower shows.

© LMNOP/www.goo.gl/E7b17

Lillies at Como Conservatory

Saint Paul Almanac
Soul Sounds Open Mic
Oct. 2, 9, 16, 23, 30
6—8 p.m.
Golden Thyme Cafe
www.saintpaulalmanac.org
First Thursday writing workshop,
5—6 p.m.

Medtronic Twin Cities Marathon Health and Fitness Expo
Oct. 3—4
Saint Paul RiverCentre
651.265.4800
www.rivercentre.org

Saint Paul Art Crawl
Oct. 10—12
Downtown Saint Paul
651.292.4373
www.artcrawl.org
More than 200 artists open their
studios to the public.

Fall Flower Show
Oct. 11—Nov. 30
Marjorie McNeely
   Conservatory, Como Park
651.487.8200
www.comozooconservatory.org
Featuring warm autumn colors,
this flower show is sure to keep you
cozy on those brisk fall days.

ZooBoo
Oct. 18, 19, 24—26
Marjorie McNeely
   Conservatory, Como Park
651.487.8200
www.comozooconservatory.org
A non-scary Halloween festival
for families and young children.
For this unique fall fundraiser, the
grounds of Como Zoo transform
into a world of fairytales and fun.
Over 200 live costumed characters
interact and entertain children.
This magical event offers families
a safe trick-or-treating alternative
with many Halloween surprises.

Victorian Ghost Stories
Oct. 19 and 26
240 Summit Ave.
651.297.2555

Saint Paul Almanac
Lowertown Reading Jam
Oct. 23, David Mura
7:30—8:30 p.m.
Black Dog Cafe
308 Prince St.
651.785.6268
www.saintpaulalmanac.org

Fourth Friday at the Movies
Oct. 24
Golden Thyme Cafe
651.645.1340
Social hour at 6:30 p.m. and film
at 7 p.m.

Dia de los Muertos Family Day
Oct. 25
Minnesota History Center
345 West Kellogg Blvd.
651.259.3000
www.mnhs.org

Boo Bash
Date to be announced
www.grandave.com
Celebrate Halloween with Grand Avenue's Boo Bash.

NOVEMBER

Downtown Saint Paul Farmers' Market
Apr.—Nov. 23
Saturdays, 6 a.m.—1 p.m.
Sundays, 8 a.m.—1 p.m.
290 East Fifth St.
651.227.8101
www.stpaulfarmersmarket.com
Local growers sell their fresh produce directly to you.

Fall Flower Show
Oct. 11—Nov. 30
Marjorie McNeely
    Conservatory, Como Park
651.487.8200
www.comozooconservatory.org
Featuring warm autumn colors, this flower show is sure to keep you cozy on those brisk fall days.

Capital City Lights
Mid-Nov.—Mar.
Downtown Saint Paul
651.291.5600
www.capitalcitypartnership.com
Come downtown and enjoy the holiday lights in winter.

MSHSL Volleyball Tournament
Nov. 6—8
Xcel Energy Center
763.560.2262

Saint Paul Almanac
Soul Sounds Open Mic
Nov. 6, 13, 20, 6—8 p.m.
Golden Thyme Cafe
www.saintpaulalmanac.org
First Thursday writing workshop, 5—6 p.m.

Seniors in Mind
Nov. 11
Minnesota History Center
345 West Kellogg Blvd.
651.259.3000
www.mnhs.org
Free programs of music, photography, and lectures on Minnesota history and culture for people 55+.

Hmong New Year
Nov. 26–30
Saint Paul RiverCentre
651.265.4800
www.rivercentre.org

Fourth Friday at the Movies
Nov. 28
Golden Thyme Cafe
651.645.1340
Social hour at 6:30 p.m. and film at 7 p.m.

DECEMBER

Downtown Saint Paul Winter Farmers' Market
Saturdays, 9 a.m.–1 p.m.
290 East Fifth St.
651.227.8101
www.stpaulfarmersmarket.com
Local growers sell their fresh foods directly to you.

Bouquets: An Evening of Wine, Beer, and Food
December 4
Marjorie McNeely
    Conservatory, Como Park
651.487.8200
www.comozooconservatory.org
Escape the chilly temperatures and enjoy a night out sampling more than 80 fine wines, locally brewed beer, and tidbits from area restaurants in the most beautiful winter setting in Minnesota: the Marjorie McNeely Conservatory. Plus get a special preview of the Holiday Flower Show.

Saint Paul Almanac Soul Sounds Open Mic
Dec. 4, 11, 18, 6–8 p.m.
Golden Thyme Cafe
www.saintpaulalmanac.org
First Thursday writing workshop, 5–6 p.m.

Saint Paul Ice Fishing and Winter Sports Show
December 5–7
Saint Paul RiverCentre
651.265.4800
www.rivercentre.org

Holiday Flower Show
Dec. 6, 2014–Jan. 4, 2015
Marjorie McNeely
    Conservatory, Como Park
651.487.8200
www.comozooconservatory.org
Since 1925, the Holiday Flower Show has been the most anticipated attraction of the year. It is a visual sensation to behold, featuring hundreds of poinsettias.

Grand Meander

Dec. 6
Grand Ave., Dale to Fairview
407.521.6335
www.grandave.com

Hill House Holidays

Dec. 6, 7, 13, 14, 20, and 21
   (Saturdays and Sundays)
James J. Hill House
240 Summit Ave.
651.297.2555

Kwanzaa Family Celebration

Dec. 27
Minnesota History Center
345 West Kellogg Blvd.
651.259.3000
www.mnhs.org

Noon Year's Party

Dec. 31 and Jan. 1,
   11 a.m.—1 p.m.
Marjorie McNeely
   Conservatory, Como Park
651.487.8200
www.comozooconservatory.org
*A family event so popular, we're
doing it twice! Ring in the "Zoo"
year during a special Noon Year's
Celebration. The Noon Year's Party
features noise-maker making, a
scavenger hunt, special animal
enrichments, and a countdown to
noon with a beach ball drop.*

Lowertown SantaCon celebrates its seventh annual event in December 2014.

Health and Fitness Events

Compiled by Teri J. Dwyer

Opportunities abound for outdoor recreation enthusiasts in Saint Paul, offering all of the conveniences of an urban setting plus many hidden (and not-so-hidden) treasures. Paved paths run along the river; bike lanes line major roads, parks, and lakes. Sidewalks, paths, and trails throughout the city provide wonderful places to enjoy many different outdoor recreational activities. Through snow, ice, rain, heat, and humidity, Saint Paul's most active residents participate in a number of events throughout the year.

Here's a month-by-month look at some of the health and fitness events that make this city a great place to live, work, and work out.

JANUARY

Saint Paul Winter Carnival's Half Marathon and 5K
Jan. 25
Downtown Saint Paul
www.winter-carnival.com
Saint Paul heartily embraces winter by throwing a Winter Carnival each year. One of its many events is The Coolest Race on Earth, which begins and ends downtown, with a portion of each course following the Mississippi River.

Saint Paul Winter Carnival's "King Boreas" Ski Race and Family Outdoors Events
Jan. 25
Lake Phalen Park
www.winter-carnival.com
A family-friendly event with something for everyone. 15K skate race, 7.5K tour, kids' races, ice bike racing, skijorging, snowshoeing, and more.

Saint Paul Winter Carnival's "King Boreas" Skijor Race
Jan. 25
Lake Phalen Park
www.winter-carnival.com
The race has a single class for a 7.5K loop around the Phalen course.

Saint Paul Winter Carnival's Winter Carnival Disk Festival
Jan. 25—26
Como Park
www.winter-carnival.com
This two-day disc golf tournament can be played one or both days.

Saint Paul Winter Carnival Geocaching
Jan. 23—Feb. 2
www.winter-carnival.com
Family-friendly geocaching throughout the run of the Winter Carnival (various locations throughout Saint Paul).

Twin Cities Bicycling Club (TCBC)
Frequent group rides year round.
Various Saint Paul locations.
www.biketcbc.org
Join them for their Winter Warm-up, Think Spring, We Don't Need No Stinkin' Winter, Fridays on the Bike, and other events. They meet in various locations throughout the year.

FEBRUARY

Valentine's Day Hearts 'r' Running 5K and 1.5-Mile Family and Friends Fun Walk
Feb. 8
Como Lake
www.charitieschallenge.org
One in a series of holiday-themed races around Como Lake.

Saint Paul Winter Carnival Geocaching
Jan. 23—Feb. 2
www.winter-carnival.com
Family-friendly geocaching throughout run of Winter Carnival (various locations throughout Saint Paul).

Twin Cities Bicycling Club (TCBC)
www.biketcbc.org
See January for description.

MARCH

St. Pat's Irish Traditions 5K
Mar. 16
Como Lake
www.charitieschallenge.org
One in a series of holiday-themed races around Como Lake.

© David Johnson

Kiss & Run—a sketch of a runner receiving a kiss before he sets off

Irish Run Saint Paul

Mar. 23

Summit Ave./Ramsey Jr. High

www.tslevents.com

For more than three decades, runners and walkers in the region have equated the St. Patrick's Day race running and walking events with the start of the spring racing season in Saint Paul. The event offers an 8K run, a 5K run/walk, and youth runs.

APRIL

Challenge Obesity 5K

Apr. 12

Como Lake

www.charitieschallenge.org

One in a series of events together called Life Challenge 5K Events, which also include 1.5-mile and half-mile courses for families and children.

Easter Sunday Rise 'n' Shine 5K

Apr. 20

Como Lake

www.charitieschallenge.org

Part of a series of holiday-themed races around Como Lake.

Challenge Happiness 5K

Apr. 23

Como Lake

www.charitieschallenge.org

One in a series of events together called Life Challenge 5K Events, which also include 1.5-mile and half-mile courses for families and children.

Saint Paul Saints Running of the Pigs

Apr. 26

Midway Stadium

www.andersonraces.com

The Running of the Pigs, brought to you by the Saint Paul Saints, isn't "just a 5K," since the Saints aren't "just a baseball team." As you have heard us say, FUN is Good! Check out the all-new ZeroK Zone, the ultimate race for non-racers.

Next Steps 5K

Apr. 26

Upper Landing/Shepard Road

www.andersonraces.com

The Next Steps 5K is all about helping homeless people reach for a healthier lifestyle through fitness.

Annual Spring Parks Clean-Up

A Saturday in April

www.stpaul.gov/parks

Each year, Saint Paul Parks and Recreation hosts this event for families, groups, and individuals to help clean up the trash in Saint Paul's parks and recreation centers.

MAY

Run or Dye 5K

May 3

Harriet Island

www.andersonraces.com

The world's most colorful 5K: the color-blasted fun run that's taking the Twin Cities by storm.

Menudo 5K

May 3

Saint Paul's West Side

www.cincodemayosaintpaul
.com/5k-race.html

The West Side, with its large Hispanic population, hosts a Cinco de Mayo celebration each spring on the weekend closest to May 5. The Menudo 5K takes place on the Saturday of this celebratory weekend.

7th Annual Joe Plant Memorial Living the Dream 5K Run and Walk

May 3

Lake Phalen

www.runningventures.com

A race in memory of Joe Plant, an avid runner who died unexpectedly at age 24 of an undiagnosed, likely congenital, heart condition.

The Nova Classic 2K, 5K, 10K

May 3

Shepard Road

www.novaclassical.org/run

Serious Fun—in the classical tradition! All race proceeds benefit the students of Nova Classical Academy.

Northern Voices Walk for Talk

May 4

Como Park, Midway Pavilion

www.andersonraces.com

Northern Voices is the only nonprofit school in Minnesota that teaches children with hearing loss how to listen and talk. The goal of the event is to raise funds to enable all students to reach their full potential regardless of their family's income level.

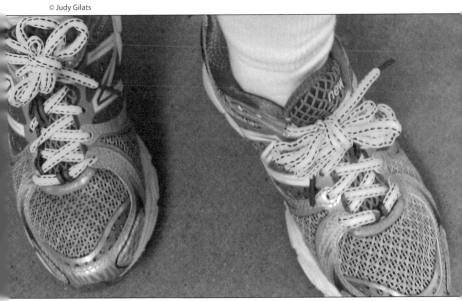

Walk for Animals

May 4

Como Park

www.animalhumanesociety.org

Hosted by the Humane Society, this event kicks off the national Be Kind to Animals Week at Como Park.

8th Annual Cinco de Mayo 5K Run/Walk

May 4

Highland Park

www.friendsoftheorphans.org

Help fight global poverty . . . one kilometer at a time!

Mother's Day 5K

May 11

Como Lake

www.charitieschallenge.org

One in a series of holiday-themed races around Como Lake.

Challenge Hearts and Minds 5K

May 26

Como Lake

www.charitieschallenge.org

One in a series of events together called Life Challenge 5K Events, which also include 1.5-mile and half-mile courses for families and children. (Also part of Charities Challenge's holiday-themed races around Como Lake.)

Mississippi 10 Miler

May 26

Summit Ave. at East Mississippi River Blvd.

www.runmdra.org

This long-standing event is sponsored by MDRA (Minnesota Distance Running Association). The course is out and back along the Saint Paul side of the Mississippi River.

Electric Run

May 30

Minnesota State Fairgrounds, Falcon Heights

www.andersonraces.com

Electric Run is a 5K run/walk at night with amazing lighting elements and sound spread throughout the course.

JUNE

American Lung Association Lung Walk and 5K Run

June 1

Como Park

www.lungusa.org/associations /states/minnesota

Proceeds benefit the American Lung Association.

Walk Like MADD and MADD Dash 5K

June 7

Lake Phalen

www.andersonraces.com

This annual event is a fun, family-friendly 5K run/walk to support Mothers Against Drunk Driving (MADD) of Minnesota.

Lederhosenlauf 5K Run and 1-Mile Fitness Walk

June 7

Summit Ave.

www.gai-mn.org

Part of the Deutsche Tage Weekend Festival at the Germanic-American Institute on Summit Avenue. This race course takes runners on a loop around the Saint Paul Cathedral.

Walk on the Wild Side

June 8

Como Lake

www.dakotacommunities.org

A 5K run/walk benefiting Dakota Communities, an organization providing a variety of services to people with disabilities.

Nature Valley Bicycle Festival

June 11

Downtown Saint Paul

www.naturevalleybicycle
    festival.com

This multi-day Minnesota festival comes to downtown Saint Paul for one day with the Saint Paul Downtown Criterium. Proceeds benefit Children's Hospitals and Clinics of Minnesota.

Father's Day 5K

June 15

Como Lake

www.charitieschallenge.org

One in a series of holiday-themed races around Como Lake.

© Katrina Hannemann/stulagu2.com

The Nice Ride program offers subscription bicycle rental at niceridemn.org.

Time to Fly 10K and 5K
June 21
Harriet Island
www.childrenscancer.org
Children's Cancer Research Fund hosts the 10K and 5K races, plus a 2K and 1K kids' run.

TC Pride Rainbow Run
June 22
Como Park, Midway Pavilion
www.andersonraces.com
Experience a different side of Pride and take part in the Twin Cities Pride Rainbow Run.

Challenge Diabetes 5K
June 28
Como Lake
www.charitieschallenge.org
One in a series of events together called Life Challenge 5K Events, which also include 1.5-mile and half-mile courses for families and children.

CrossFit Saint Paul Outdoor Bootcamp
Mid-June through late July (6 weeks)
M, W, F at 6 a.m.
Macalester College Track (Snelling Ave. and St. Clair Ave.)
www.crossfitstpaul.com
CFSP bootcamp is for people looking for fast results in a 6-week program. Workouts are short, intense, and fun, and can be scaled to any individual's physical abilities.

JULY

Langford Park Races
July 4
St. Anthony Park
These very-low-key races (runners choose a 2- or 4-mile option) have had an entry fee of 50 cents since they began in 1974. The course is a 2-mile loop on the streets of Saint Paul's picturesque St. Anthony Park. Races begin and end at Langford Park.

Free to Run 4 Miles
July 4
Harriet Island
www.charitieschallenge.org
One in a series of holiday-themed races (this one at Harriet Island).

Richard A. Hoska Midsummer Mile
July 9
Minnesota State Fairgrounds, Falcon Heights
www.runningventures.com
This race has a new name, location, and date since 2013. Don't miss this opportunity to run one of the shortest road races offered in Saint Paul.

The 9th Annual
MOST Amazing Race
July 19

Saint Paul and Minneapolis

www.andersonraces.com

The annual MOST Amazing Race is an official event of the Minneapolis Aquatennial. Patterned after the CBS show The Amazing Race, this scavenger-hunt-like-race leads qualifying teams of two on a large-scale race around Minneapolis and Saint Paul. This fundraising event benefits The Salvation Army's Bed and Bread Club.

Highland Fest 5K Run/Walk
July 20

Highland Park

www.andersonraces.com

This year will mark the 30th anniversary of this neighborhood festival. Celebrate summer with food, drink, music, art and this 5K race!

Challenge Cancer 5K
July 26

Como Lake

www.charitieschallenge.org

One in a series of events together called Life Challenge 5K Events, which also include 1.5-mile and half-mile courses for families and children.

SkirtChaser 5K
July 26

Como Lake

www.skirtsports.com
    /skirtchaser5k/stpaul

Women start first at 5 p.m. Three minutes later, the Chaser wave follows. Part of a national series of races.

© Ken Friberg/RatRaceStudios.com

Kids race at the Nature Valley Bicycle Festival, which raises money for the Children's Lighthouse of Minnesota hospice project.

CrossFit Saint Paul Outdoor Bootcamp

Mid-June through late July (6 weeks)

M, W, F at 6 a.m.

Macalester College Track (Snelling Ave. and St. Clair Ave.)

www.crossfitstpaul.com

CFSP bootcamp is for people looking for fast results in a 6-week program. Workouts are short, intense, and fun, and can be scaled to any individual's physical abilities.

AUGUST

Minnesota Half Marathon and 5K

Aug. 2

Downtown Saint Paul

www.minnesotahalfmarathon.com

In-line skaters and runners can all enjoy a course along the beautiful Mississippi River in Saint Paul. The half marathon is for skaters and runners; the 5K is for runners and walkers. The race ends in downtown Saint Paul at Mears Park.

MDRA Cross-Country Runs

Aug. 6, 13, 20, 27

Como Park

www.runmdra.org

Since 1974, MDRA has sponsored this series of cross-country races every Wednesday evening in August at Como Park in Saint Paul. The races are open to all ages and abilities.

Dream Mile 5K & 10K

Aug. 9

Saint Paul

www.andersonraces.com

The Dream Mile is the flagship event in Vibha's continued efforts to increase awareness about the struggles battled by underprivileged children.

Miles for Melanoma 5K Run

Aug. 9

Como Park, Midway Pavilion

www.andersonraces.com

As part of this event, dermatologists will offer skin cancer screenings in accordance with the American Academy of Dermatology.

Challenge Addiction 5K

Aug. 10

Como Lake

www.charitieschallenge.org

One in a series of events together called Life Challenge 5K Events, which also include 1.5-mile and half-mile courses for families and children.

Saint Paul Triathlon

Aug. 17

Lake Phalen

www.frontrunnerusa.com /event/st-paul-triathlon

Participants choose the Sprint (half-mile swim, 20K bike, 5K run) or International (1-mile swim, 40K bike, 10K run).

Challenge Arthritis 5K

Aug. 23
Como Lake
www.charitieschallenge.org
One in a series of events together called Life Challenge 5K Events, which also include 1.5-mile and half-mile courses for families and children.

Minnesota State Fair Milk Run 5K

Aug. 24
Minnesota State Fairgrounds
www.mnstatefair.org
Participants receive an admission ticket to the fair and a coupon for a free malt.

SEPTEMBER

Saint Paul Classic Bike Tour

Sept. 7
Throughout Saint Paul
www.bikeclassic.org
This event offers a rare opportunity to bicycle around and through the city of Saint Paul on streets free of car traffic. This family-friendly event offers a 15-mile tour of Saint Paul or a 30-mile ride.

Challenge Aging 5K

Sept. 21
Como Lake
www.charitieschallenge.org
One in a series of events together called Life Challenge 5K Events, which also include 1.5-mile and half-mile courses for families and children.

Milk Run at the State Fair

KEY TO RACE DISTANCES

1K (0.62 miles)
2K (1.24 miles)
4K (2.5 miles)
5K (3.1 miles)
6K (3.75 miles)
8K (4.97 miles)
10K (6.2 miles)
Half Marathon (13.1 miles)
Marathon (26.2 miles)

Race for Research
Sept. 28
Lake Phalen
www.themmrf.org
5K walk/run benefits the Multiple Myeloma Research Foundation.

OCTOBER

Twin Cities in Motion 10K, 5K, and Family Events
Oct. 4
Summit Ave.
www.twincitiesmarathon.org
The Twin Cities Marathon, a Twin Cities tradition for more than 30 years, traverses the Mississippi River. On the Saturday before Sunday's big marathon, TCM hosts running events exclusively in Saint Paul. The races, starting and finishing near the Capitol, offer something for all ages and abilities.

Twin Cities Marathon and TC 10 Mile
Oct. 5
Summit Ave.
www.twincitiesmarathon.org
Traditionally called "the most beautiful urban marathon in America," TCM and the companion TC 10 Mile begin in downtown Minneapolis, winding through a chain of Minneapolis parks, but the final six miles are run in Saint Paul, with a finish right in front of the State Capitol on the edge of downtown.

2013 ALS Super Hero 5K–10K Dash/Walk
Oct. 11
Lake Phalen
www.andersonraces.com
Participants are encouraged to dress up as a favorite superhero. This event benefits The ALS Association, MN/ND/SD Chapter.

CNHS Boo Run Run Run
Oct. 18
Harriet Island
www.andersonraces.com
Run wearing a costume and you will automatically get entered in the costume contest.

Halloween Fearless 5K and 1.5-Mile Fun Run
Oct. 25
Como Lake
www.charitieschallenge.org
One in a series of holiday-themed races around Como Lake.

NOVEMBER

Rocky's Run
Nov. 2
Les Bolstad University Golf Course
www.tslevents.com
This cross-country race offers the public a rare opportunity to run on the same course as the University of Minnesota men's and women's cross-country teams, at the Les Bolstad University Golf Course. The 8K and 5K races benefit a scholarship in Rocky Racette's name for the women's track-and-field and cross-country teams at the U of M.

Veterans Day 5K
Nov. 9
Como Lake
www.charitieschallenge.org
One in a series of holiday-themed races around Como Lake.

Turkey Run
Nov. 23
Como Lake
www.tslevents.com
A tradition for the Sunday before Thanksgiving each year, this family-friendly fun run encircles Como Lake, beginning and ending at warm indoor headquarters at Como Elementary School.

Giving Thanks 5K
Nov. 27
Como Lake
www.charitieschallenge.org
One in a series of holiday-themed races around Como Lake.

TCBC events
www.biketcbc.org
See January for description.

DECEMBER

JCC Dreidel Dash
Dec. 7
Jewish Community Center
www.andersonraces.com
Fundraiser for Saint Paul Jewish Community Center.

Fifth Annual Joyful 5K
Christmas Day
Dec. 25
Como Lake
www.charitieschallenge.org
One in a series of holiday-themed races around Como Lake.

New Year's Eve Day Hopeful 5K
Dec. 31
Como Lake
charitieschallenge.org
One in a series of holiday-themed races around Como Lake.

TCBC events
www.biketcbc.org
See January for description.

Crime-fighter runners in the Super Hero Dash/Walk

Year-round Saint Paul Activities

The Saint Paul Hiking Club

www.stpaulhike.org

This group meets regularly at various locations throughout Saint Paul. Anyone is welcome. Check your local newspaper's recreation/events calendar for current hike locations and contact information.

Meetup.com

www.meetup.com

Check out meetup.com for outdoor groups and events year-round in Saint Paul—hiking, volleyball, bird-watching, etc. Meetup is a great resource for connecting with people and groups who have interests similar to yours. Search for "outdoor fitness" and enter "Saint Paul, MN" or your zip code.

SEASONAL ACTIVITIES

Rowing

www.boatclub.org

The Minnesota Boat Club—rowing in Saint Paul since 1870. Promoting health and fitness through the sport of rowing. Located on the shores of Raspberry Island, directly across from downtown Saint Paul. From novice to competitor, rowers of all ages and abilities can take part in classes, camps, and events of this well-established Mississippi River tradition.

Star Swim Team

www.starswimteam.net

Programs for swimmers of all ages and abilities. Outdoors in summer at Highland Park pool.

WINTER ACTIVITIES

Cross-Country Skiing

www.stpaul.gov/parks

Saint Paul grooms trails at three sites each winter: Como Golf Course, Phalen Golf Course, and the Highland 9-Hole Golf Course. Lessons in classic and skate skiing are available through Saint Paul Parks and Recreation.

Ice Skating Rinks

There is a variety of outdoor ice-skating rinks located throughout the city. Amenities, including availability of rental skates, vary by location.

www.stpaul.gov/parks

www.capitalcitypartnership.com

Ai Hues Bakery and Deli

432B University Ave.

651.602.0231

Serving coffee and meals on the avenue during light rail construction.

American Joe

344 Wabasha St. N.

651.602.9999

Coffee drinks and ice cream near the Victory Ramp.

Amore Coffee

879 Smith Ave. S.

651.330.0570

www.amorecoffee.com

Featuring award-winning coffee and authentic Italian gelato.

Bars Bakery

612 Selby Ave.

651.224.8300

www.barsbakery.com

Espresso, pour over, and brewed coffees along with made-from-scratch baked goods featuring local organic ingredients.

Black Bear Crossings on the Lake

1360 N. Lexington Pkwy.

651.488.4920

www.blackbearcrossings.com

Located in the historic Como Lakeside Pavilion, offering a gourmet café open year round, free summer concerts, and paddle boat rentals on Lake Como. Its mission: to celebrate positive American Indian identity, provide a venue for multicultural sharing, and to promote community.

Black Dog Coffee & Wine Bar

308 Prince St.

651.228.9274

www.blackdogstpaul.com

Locally roasted coffees, creative wines and beers, and tasty daily specials for breakfast, lunch, and dinner.

Bravo! Café & Bakery

1106 Grand Avenue

651.287.9118

www.bravobakery.net

A full-service bakery well known for its signature products—Cream Puff and Mango Cakes—plus a wide selection of baked goods, including some dairy-free products.

Bread and Chocolate

867 Grand Ave.

651.228.1017

www.cafelatte.com/bread
_chocolate.html

Coffee, sandwiches, and baked goods, including their famous brownies.

Cahoots Coffee Bar

1562 Selby Ave.

651.644.6778

Bohemian atmosphere, great coffee, and Middle Eastern—inspired foods.

Claddagh Coffee

459 Seventh St. W.
651.600.3400
www.claddaghcoffeecafe.com
Welcoming "yogis, bikers, runners, and all cool people everywhere."

Coffee Bené

53 Cleveland Ave. S.
651.698.2266
www.coffeebene.com
Organic beans from master roasters and yummy goods from the bakery.

The Coffee Grounds

1579 Hamline Ave. N.
651.644.9959
www.thecoffeegrounds.net
A friendly gathering place with a bridge club and creative beading group; ongoing open mic the first and third Sundays.

Coffee 'n Tea

895 Randolph Avenue
855.999.4TEA
www.booksandtea.net
A new coffee shop in the West Seventh neighborhood. Open 6 a.m. Monday through Friday.

Dr. Chocolate's Chocolate Chateau

579 Selby Ave.
651.379.3676
www.drchocolate.com
Located just minutes from Cathedral Hill in the heart of the historic downtown district. Specialty chocolate shop, wine, craft beer, hot chocolate, gift shop, and intimate banquet spaces for public and private events.

Dunn Bros on Grand

1569 Grand Ave.
651.698.0618
www.dunnbrosgrand.com
The original Dunn Bros Coffee features live music daily.

Espresso Royale

475 Fairview Ave. S.
651.699.1117
www.espressoroyale.com
A coffee shop plus extras: soups, sandwiches, frappés, and ice cream.

Fresh Grounds

1362 Seventh St. W.
651.224.2348
www.freshgroundscoffee.com
A nonprofit shop offering coffee and light meals, music, art, and job training for youth.

Ginkgo Coffeehouse

721 Snelling Ave. N.
651.645.2647
www.ginkgocoffee.com
Serves tea and fruit smoothies in addition to coffee, and local seasonal foods.

Golden's Deli

275 Fourth St. E.
651.224.8888
www.goldensdeli.us
Homemade soups, sandwiches, and baked goods served for breakfast and lunch with a healthy side of green practices.

Golden Thyme Coffee Café

921 Selby Ave.

651.645.1340

www.goldenthymecoffeecafe

A community hub offering drinks named after jazz legends (and a really great gumbo); meeting room available. Omelets and crêpes too.

Grand Central

1672 Grand Ave.

651.964.1012

An elegant new café-style restaurant from the owners of nearby Shish restaurant. Artisan sandwiches and salads, decadent pastries, and a wide array of coffee drinks and sodas.

Groundswell Coffee

1342 Thomas Ave.

651.645.6466

www.groundswellcoffee.wordpress

This neighborhood spot serving pizza and salads as well as coffee is operated by a community nonprofit.

Grumpy Steve's Coffee

215 Wabasha St. S.

651.224.1191

www.wabashastreetcaves.com

"Come start your morning with a snarl. Or put a little grouchy in your lunch" at the Wabasha Caves.

J & S Bean Factory

1518 Randolph Ave.

651.699.7788

www.jsbeanfactory.com

Full-service roaster features the Obama blend; occasional live music.

Java Train Café

1341 Pascal St. N.

651.646.9179

www.javatraincafe.com

Family-friendly table service with Izzy's ice cream and a play area for children.

Scooters outside Claddagh Coffee

Jerabek's New Bohemian Coffeehouse and Bakery

63 Winifred St. W.
651.228.1245
www.jerabeks.com
A relaxed and casual coffeehouse serving flaky pastry specialties.

Kopplin's Coffee

2038 Marshall Ave.
651.698.0457
www.kopplinscoffee.com
The local micro-culture for brewing connoisseurs offering seasonal beverage creations.

Lady Elegant's Tea Room

2230 Carter Ave.
651.645.6676
www.ladyelegantstea.com
Tea in the British tradition with three-, four-, and six-course events.

Lowertown Daily Perk

180 Fifth St. E., Ste. 266
651.228.9820
www.lowertowndailyperk.com
A skyway workday staple; formerly Executive Coffee and Tea.

Lucy Coffee Cafe

540 Fairview Ave.
651.260.0625
www.lucycoffeecafe.com
Pastries, sandwiches, and salads in the Griggs Midway Building.

Mad Hatter Coffee Cafe and Teahouse

943 Seventh St. W.
651.227.2511
www.justcomm.org/pax-salon
Social justice salons and acoustic music with the St. Paul Gallery of Art adjoined.

Mojo Monkey Donuts

1169 Seventh St. W.
651.224.0142
www.mojomonkey.biz
Coffee and fresh donuts from real recipes made by real people daily.

Nina's Coffee Café

165 Western Ave. N.
651.292.9816
This art-friendly corner of Cathedral Hill hosts frequent art and literary events.

Polly's Coffee Cove

1382 Payne Ave.
651.771.5531
Comfortable kitsch and convenient boxed lunches; Polly is the bird.

Quixotic Coffee

769 Cleveland Ave. S.
651.699.5448
www.quixoticcoffee.com
Emphasizing both quality coffee and a supportive relationship with coffee farmers.

Saint Paul Classic Cookie
2386 Territorial Rd.
651.288.3807
www.saintpaulclassiccookie
    .blogspot
Check out their cookie apparel, mugs, and accessories.

Saint Paul Coffee
101 Fifth St. E.
651.221.9859
The sunniest corner in the skyway; formerly Steep & Brew.

Seventh Heaven Coffee & Antiques
327 Seventh St. W.
651.222.0122
www.masterbuilder.org
Family owned and staffed. A St. Paul original.

St. Paul Corner Drug
240 Snelling Ave. S.
651.698.8859
www.stpaulcornerdrug.com
A neighborhood pharmacy with five-cent coffee at the old-fashioned soda fountain.

SugaRush
712 University Ave. W.
651.797.3354
Donuts too. Near the Cycles for Change.

Swede Hollow Bakery and Cafe
725 Seventh St. E.
651.776.8810
www.swedehollowcafe.com
An expansive breakfast menu features daily quiche and oven-baked French toast.

The Tea Garden
1692 Grand Ave.
651.690.3495
www.teagardeninc.com
Bubble tea delights with chewy tapioca.

TeaSource
752 Cleveland Ave. S.
651.690.9822
www.teasource.com
Extraordinary teas and Tuesday free samples; check the website for classes.

Trotter's Cafe and Bakery
232 Cleveland Ave. N.
651.645.8950
www.trotterscafe.com
Neighborhood café and bakery using high-quality local and organic ingredients to make products "from scratch" every day. Now serving wine and beer, with new dinner hours.

More than thirty-five tap beers are available at the Groveland Tap.
© Jeremy Downie/JeremyDownie.com

The text on the floor of Jerabek's New Bohemian Coffeehouse and Bakery is Henry Wadsworth Longfellow's famous line "the forget-me-nots of the angels" from his poem Evangeline: A Tale of Acadie.
© Tony Ernst/gamelaner on Flickr

Opposite: Nina's Coffee Café on the ground floor of the Blair Arcade, or Blair Flats, built in 1887 and in the National Register of Historic Buildings. The Blair Flats originally housed the Angus Hotel (see page 157).
© Marianne McNamara

Restaurants

128 Café
128 Cleveland Ave. N.
651.645.4128
www.128cafe.net
*Upscale dining with a chang-
ing menu of fresh and seasonal
ingredients. $$*

American Burger Bar
354 Wabasha St. N.
651.222.2123
www.americanburgerbar.com
*The ultimate handcrafted burger
den. $$*

Amsterdam Bar & Hall
6 Sixth St. W.
612.285.3112
www.amsterdambarandhall.com
*Music every night at this bar and
restaurant on Wabasha. The mus-
sels are large, fresh, and garlicky. $$*

Aroma's Pizza
350 St. Peter St.
651.293.9040
www.aromascafe.com
*Build your own pizza for dine-in or
take-out. $*

Babani's Kurdish Restaurant
544 St. Peter St.
651.602.9964
www.babanis.com
*Authentic menu offers
a Kurdish take on cuisine. $*

Bangkok Cuisine
432 University Ave. W.
651.414.0058
www.bangkok-cuisine.com
*Balancing the five fundamental
tastes: spicy, sour, sweet, salty, and
sharp. Try their spicy green curry. $*

Bangkok Thai Deli
333 University Ave. W.
651.224.4300
*Superior green curry. One of the
publisher's favorite restaurants. $*

Barbary Fig
720 Grand Ave.
651.290.2085
www.thebarbaryfig.com
*Grand Avenue location with
inspired Mediterranean cuisine. $$*

Barrio Tequila Bar
235 Sixth St. E.
651.222.3250
www.barriotequila.com
*Meet across from Mears Park for
happy hour: tacos, enchiladas, sea-
food, chicken, ribs, or steak. $$*

Bennett's Chop & Rail House
1305 Seventh St. W.
651.228.1408
www.bennettschopand
    railhouse.com
*A casual steakhouse atmosphere
with nightly specials for top-of-the-
line cuts. $$*

Big Daddy's BBQ
625 University Ave.
651.222.2516
www.bigdaddysbbq-stpaul.com
Old-fashioned BBQ across from the Rondo Library, in the heart of Frogtown. $

Bin
400 Sibley St., Ste. 150
651.224.9463
www.binwinebar.com
Wine and light fare, exposed brick and timbers, and an antique bar. $$

Black Bear Crossings on the Lake
1360 Lexington Pkwy. N.
651.488.4920
www.blackbearcrossings.com
Serving breakfast, lunch, and dinner all year round in the historic Lake Como pavilion. $

Black Sea
737 Snelling Ave. N.
651.917.8832
www.blacksearestaurant.com
Offering fine Turkish cuisine from Ali's hometown of Akçaabat, Trabzon Province. $

Black Sheep Pizza
512 Robert St. N.
651.227.4337
www.blacksheeppizza.com
Coal-fired ovens and exceptional ingredients create an American "pizza pioneer" experience. $

The Blue Door Pub
1811 Selby Ave.
651.493.1865
www.thebdp.com
Fun Americana décor and a menu featuring the Juicy Blucy (bleu cheese–stuffed burgers). $

Boca Chica Restaurante Mexicano & Cantina
11 Cesar Chavez St.
651.222.8499
www.bocachicarestaurant.com
Minutes from downtown in the District Del Sol of Saint Paul's West Side; patio dining and mariachi music. $ (lunch) $$ (dinner)

Boca Chica's Taco House
407 Wabasha S.
651.222.8226
www.bocachicatacohouse.com
The fast food version of Boca Chica with the same great taste. $

Bonfire Wood Fire Cooking
850 Grand Ave.
651.312.1299
www.axelsbonfire.com
American and Southwestern cuisine with creative bar service and live music. $$

Bonnie's Café
2160 University Ave. W.
651.644.3393
Grab breakfast before the train at this favorite "stop-and-eat" at the edge of Saint Paul. $

Bon Vie Bistro and
A Piece of Cake Bakery
485 Selby Ave.
651.846.0016
www.apieceofcakebakery.net
*Breakfast and lunch café that
serves up "the good life" with a
changing monthly menu.* $

Brasa Premium Rotisserie
777 Grand Ave.
651.224.1302
www.brasa.us
*Featuring local, slow-cooked rotis-
serie meats for dine-in or take-out.* $

The Bulldog
Lowertown
237 Sixth St. E.
651.221.0750
www.thebulldoglowertown.com
*Stop for lunch, after work, or on
weekends for pub grub like Tater
Tot Hotdish.* $

Burger Moe's
242 Seventh St. W.
651.222.3100
www.burgermoes.com

*A relaxed outdoor patio and more
than 60 beers from around the
world.* $

The Buttered Tin
237 Seventh St. E.
651.224.2300
www.thebutteredtin.com
*Located in Lowertown, The
Buttered Tin is a warm and welcoming corner café and bakery, offering real food that's simple, fresh,
local, and delicious.* $

Cafe Latté
850 Grand Ave.
651.224.5687
www.cafelatte.com
*Cafeteria, bakery, and pizza wine
bar; this Victoria Crossing landmark is three restaurants in one.* $

Café Minnesota
Minnesota History Center
345 Kellogg Blvd. W.
651.259.3000
www.mnhs.org/historycenter
　/cafemn
*Cafeteria-style service, weekly Min-
nesota menus, free Wi-Fi.* $

Caffe Biaggio
2356 University Ave. W.
651.917.7997
www.caffebiaggio.com
*Country favorites and family reci-
pes from all over Italy.* $ *(lunch)* $$
(dinner)

Capital View Café
637 Smith St. S.
651.290.0218
www.capitalviewcafe.com
*Mexican and American home cook-
ing for breakfast and lunch.* $

*Carlos stretching the dough
at Black Sheep Pizza*

Cecil's Delicatessen, Bakery, and Restaurant

651 Cleveland Ave. S.

651.698.6276

www.cecilsdeli.com

Committed to quality delicatessen fare for three generations; delivery available. $

Chatterbox Pub

800 Cleveland Ave. S.

651.699.1154

www.chatterboxpub.net

A full-service neighborhood menu with old-school video games to "bring out the '80s kid in everyone." $

Cheeky Monkey Deli

525 Selby Ave.

651.224.6066

www.cheekymonkeydeli.com

This "deli by day and bistro by night" offers full table service after 5 p.m. $

Cheng Heng

448 University Ave. W.

651.222.5577

A photo-album menu of authentic Cambodian cuisine for those who are weary of Americanized Asian. $

Cherokee Tavern

886 Smith Ave. S.

651.457.2729

www.cherokeetavern.com

Traditional steaks, seafood, and spirits; open every day. $$

Christos

Union Depot Place

214 Fourth St. E.

651.224.6000

www.christos.com

Formal Greek dining or a weekday lunch buffet in a breathtaking Union Depot setting. $

Colossal Cafe

2315 Como Ave.

651.797.4027

www.colossalcafe.com

Food made from scratch: seasonal menus, weekly specials, and catering. $

Cossetta Italian Market

211 Seventh St. W.

651.222.3476

www.cossettas.com

Cafeteria-style classic Italian food and a gourmet grocery shop. Check out the new rooftop restaurant. $

Costello's Bar & Grill

393 Selby Ave.

651.291.1015

www.costellosbar.com

A traditional Cathedral Hill restaurant with a friendly environment. $

Dari-ette Drive In
1440 Minnehaha Ave. E.
651.776.3470
Italian, American, and ice cream!
Family-owned and operated
from March to October for over
50 years. Love the banana malt
shakes. $

Dar's Double Scoop
1046 Rice St.
651.489.2422
Over 40 tasty flavors of deluxe ice
cream from dairies in Minnesota
and Wisconsin, as well as sand-
wiches and pizza. $

Day by Day Café
477 Seventh St. W.
651.227.0654
www.daybyday.com
Breakfast is their specialty all day
long; linger over coffee and
conversation. Beautiful back patio. $

DeGidio's
425 Seventh St. W.
651.291.7105
www.degidios.com
Famous for pasta and a red sauce
made daily with ingredients
imported from Italy. $

Destiny Café at Sunrise Market
995 University Ave. W.
651.209.3392
1151 Clarence St, Ste. 101
651.771.1409
Hmong deli and sit-down
restaurant. $$

Saint Paul offers a diverse range of cuisines from around the world.
University Avenue is a hub for Asian restaurants.

Dixie's on Grand
695 Grand Ave.
651.222.7345
www.dixiesongrand.com
Casual dining and Southern comfort; live jazz and soul throughout the week. $$

Downtowner Woodfire Grill
253 Seventh St. W.
651.228.9500
www.downtownerwoodfire.com
A comfortable retreat with classic cuts grilled over an oak fire. $$

Eagle Street Grille
174 Seventh St. W.
651.225.1382
www.eaglestreetgrille.net
Pre-event sports bar with a full menu and great views of downtown Saint Paul. $$

Eastside Thai
879 Payne Ave.
651.776.6599
www.thaicuisine.com
Delicious Thai food in satisfying portions. $

Eden Pizza
629 Aldine St.
651.646.7616
www.edenpizza.com
Create your specialty pizza with a gluten-free crust: dine-in, take-out, or delivery. $

Egg & I East
2550 University Ave. W.
651.647.1292
www.eggandimn.com
Open daily 'til 2 p.m. serving quality breakfast for over 20 years. $

El Amanecer
194 Cesar Chavez St.
651.291.0758
Authentic Mexican, El Amanecer is located right in the heart of Saint Paul's District del Sol, at the intersection of Cesar Chavez and State Streets. $

El Burrito Mercado
175 Cesar Chavez St.
651.227.2192
www.elburritomercado.com
Shop and eat at this authentic Mexican taquería in the West Side Supermercado. $

Everest on Grand
1278 Grand Ave.
651.696.1666
www.everestongrand.com
A mix of tastes, from spicy North Indian curries to Tibetan dumplings and noodles. $$

Fabulous Fern's
400 Selby Ave.
651.225.9414
www.fabulousferns.com
Classic entrées, salads, pastas, and sandwiches; kids' menu and weekly features. $$

FACES Mears Park

380 Jackson St.
651.209.7776
www.facesmearspark.com
*American cuisine mixing modern
and old-world artistry, includes a
wine bar, bottle shop, and bakery.
$$*

Falafel King
1199 Seventh St. W.
651.207.5777
*Features a neighborhood Greek
and Italian menu. $*

Fasika
510 Snelling Ave. N.
651.646.4747
www.fasika.com
*Ethiopian fare with a variety
of stewed, curried, and char-
broiled meats (vegetarian entrées
available). $*

Finnish Bistro
2264 Como Ave.
651.645.9181
www.finnishbistro.com
*Finnish and European specialties in
charming St. Anthony Park. $*

Flamingo
490 Syndicate St. N.
651.917.9332
www.flamingorestaurantmn.com
*Savory East African—Eritrean
menu with specialty lamb and goat
dishes. $*

Forepaugh's
276 Exchange St. S.
651.224.5606
www.forepaughs.com
*New American Cuisine and 19th-
century manners in a historic
architectural setting. $$*

The Four Inns
101 Fifth St. E. (Skyway level)
651.291.7939
www.thefourinns.com
*In the heart of downtown for over
25 years. Open Sundays. $*

Foxy Falafel
791 Raymond Ave.
651.888.2255
www.foxyfalafel.com
*Inspired Middle Eastern flavors in a
great Saint Paul location. $*

The French Hen
518 Selby Ave.
*European bistro serving breakfast
and lunch. $*

French Meadow
Bakery and Cafe
1662 Grand Ave.
www.frenchmeadowcafe.com
*Promoting sustainable agricul-
ture, making and serving slow
foods, and generally providing a
tasty little oasis of thoughtful and
healthy living, they produce pure,
organic and artfully crafted, yeast-
free breads. $*

Fuji Ya

465 Wabasha St. N.

651.310.0111

www.fujiyasushi.com

A Japanese food experience for lunch or dinner with an extensive happy-hour menu. $$

Glockenspiel

605 Seventh St. W.

651.292.9421

www.Glockenspielrestaurant.com

Great chef specials and an exhaustive beer list at Saint Paul's German restaurant. $

Golden's Deli

275 Fourth St. E.

651.224.8888

www.goldensdeli.us

Homemade soups, sandwiches, and baked goods served for breakfast and lunch with a healthy side of green practices; now serving wine and beer. $

Grand Ole Creamery

750 Grand Ave.

651.293.1655

www.grandolecreamery.com

A classic ice cream parlor and pizzeria. $

Grandview Grill

1818 Grand Ave.

651.698.2346

www.newgrandviewgrill.com

In pursuit of the perfect breakfast and lunch for more than 20 years. $

Great Waters Brewing Company

426 St. Peter St.

651.224.2739

www.greatwatersbc.com

Award-winning brewpub and restaurant with a year-round patio. $ (lunch) $$ (dinner)

Happy Gnome

498 Selby Ave.

651.287.2018

www.thehappygnome.com

Craft beers and culinary adventure. $$

Heartland Restaurant & Farm Direct Market

289 Fifth St. E.

651.699.3536

www.heartlandrestaurant.com

Fresh farm-direct fare for gourmet lunch, dinner, and weekend brunch. $$$

Highland Grill

771 Cleveland Ave. S.

651.690.1173

www.highlandgrill.com

Trendy comfort food prepared with flair. $

Ho Ho Gourmet Restaurant

1985 Old Hudson Rd.

651.731.0316

www.hohomn.com

Chinese buffet and à la carte items; memorable chicken wings and roast duck. $

Homi Restaurant Mexicano

864 University Ave. W.

651.222.0655

www.homirestaurant.com

Chilaquiles, enchiladas, moles, empanadas, tamales, and caldos made from scratch. $

Hunan Garden

380 Cedar St.

651.224.7588

www.hunangardenstpaulmn.com

Lunch, dinner, and take-out menus, and enhanced karaoke weekly with Ray Evangelista. $

Italian Pie Shoppe & Winery

1670 Grand Ave.

651.221.0093

www.italianpieshoppe.com

Award-winning pizzas and pasta since 1976 with online and dine-in specials. $

Izzy's Ice Cream Café

2034 Marshall Ave.

651.603.1458

www.izzysicecream.com

Artisan ice cream with inspired, quirky flavors. $

Joan's in the Park

631 Snelling Ave. S.

651.690.3297

www.joansinthepark.com

A modern-meets-classic restaurant and wine bar in Highland Park. $$

Keys Café & Bakery

767 Raymond Ave.

651.646.5756

504 Robert St. N.

651.222.4083

www.keyscafe.com

The made-from-scratch recipes "you grew up with" from a family restaurant favorite since 1973. $

© Bianca Pettis

Khyber Pass Cafe

1571 Grand Ave.

651.690.0505

www.khyberpasscafe.com

Authentic Afghan menu, which combines the best of several Asian cuisines, with special attention to chutneys. Lunch buffet. $ (lunch) $$ (dinner)

Kincaid's Fish, Chop & Steakhouse

380 St. Peter St., #125

651.602.9000

www.kincaids.com

Classic American dining; every restaurant is uniquely local. $$$

Kolap Restaurant

601 Dale St. N.

651.222.2488

True Thai food in a warm and friendly space that is perfect for large groups. $

La Cucaracha

36 Dale St. S.

651.221.9682

www.lacucacharestaurante.com

Established Mexican restaurant with an ambitious list of tequilas. $$

La Grolla

452 Selby Ave.

651.221.1061

www.lagrollastpaul.com

Romance and garlic on Cathedral Hill; dine inside or on the patio. $ (lunch) $$ (dinner)

Lao-Thai Family Restaurant

501 University Ave.

651.224.5026

Traditional Lao-Thai cuisine includes raw beef laab, yummy pad thai, and chicken wings. $

Lee's & Dee's Barbeque Express

161 North Victoria St.

651.225.9454

Ribs and catfish served up right by this welcoming husband-wife team. $

The Lexington

1096 Grand Ave.

651.222.5878

www.thelexongrand.com

A timeless Saint Paul landmark featuring steaks, seafood, and nostalgia. $$

The Liffey

175 Seventh St. W.

651.556.1420

www.theliffey.com

Irish hospitality and an urban patio view of beautiful downtown. $ (lunch) $$ (dinner)

The Little Oven

1786 Minnehaha Ave. E.

651.735.4944

www.thelittleoven.com

Reasonably priced Italian fare with monthly coupons and specials that are easy on the wallet. $

Little Szechuan

422 University Ave. W.
651.222.1333
www.littleszechuan.com
Adventurous, eclectic Chinese dishes alongside traditional favorites. $

Luci Ancora

2060 Randolph Ave.
651.698.6889
www.ristoranteluci.com
Fresh and local gourmet Italian food prepared by traditional chefs. $$

Lucio's Grill

433 Robert St. S.
651.414.9060
Philly cheese steak sandwiches and Chicago dogs. $

The M St. Café

Saint Paul Hotel
350 Market St.
651.228.3855
www.mstcafe.com
Sophisticated yet casual with à la carte menu items or Euro-style sideboard servings; Sunday brunch. $$

Magnolias Restaurant

1081 Payne Ave.
651.774.3333
www.magnolias-stpaul.com
Quality family dining with home-cooked comfort food. $

Mai Village

394 University Ave. W.
651.290.2585
www.maivillage.net
Enjoy steaming meals and a full-service bar near the koi pond or outdoor rose patio. $$

© Lisa Steinmann

Mickey's Diner, 24/7/365

Mama's Pizza

961 Rice St.

651.489.2005

www.mamaspizzaparlor.com

Italian and American eatery for lunch, dinner, and take-out. $

Mancini's Char House & Lounge

531 Seventh St. W.

651.224.7345

www.mancinis.com

Serving charbroiled steak and lobster with a lounge as classic as the day it was built. $$$

Mango Thai Restaurant

610 Selby Ave.

651.291.1414

www.mangothaimn.com

Mango spring rolls and pan-grilled tuna salad in a hip, visual setting. BYOB. $$

Meritage

410 St. Peter St.

651.222.5670

www.meritage-stpaul.com

Sustainable and seasonal New American cuisine that tends toward the French with a Crepe Stand weekdays from 11 a.m. to 2 p.m. $$$

Mickey's Dining Car

36 Seventh St. W.

651.222.5633

www.mickeysdiningcar.com

Their amusing Art Deco dining car is on the National Register of Historic Places; open every day, 24 hours. $

Minnesota Music Café

499 Payne Ave.

651.776.4699

www.minnesotamusiccafe.com

"Where the food's great and the music's cooking." $

Mirror of Korea

761 Snelling Ave. N.

651.647.9004

www.mirrorofkorea.com

Second-generation, family-owned restaurant with summer and winter menus. $

Moscow on the Hill

371 Selby Ave.

651.291.1236

www.moscowonthehill.com

Post-perestroika Russian dining and the essential vodka bar. $$

Muddy Pig

162 Dale St. N.

651.254.1030

www.muddypig.com

Neighborhood bistro with an extensive beer list and "better than pub fare." $

Muffuletta

Milton Square
2260 Como Ave.
651.644.9116
www.muffuletta.com
An imaginative daily menu of seasonal ingredients, and a wine list tended by a sommelier. $ (lunch) $$ (dinner)

The Neighborhood Cafe

1570 Selby Ave.
651.644.8887
www.theneighborhoodcafemn.com
Open for dinner Tuesdays—Saturdays, with six beers on tap, full wine list, and a great Happy Hour! $

Ngon Vietnamese Bistro

799 University Ave. W.
651.222.3301
www.ngonbistro.com
Contemporary Vietnamese cuisine that holds true to the flavors of traditional dishes. $

The Nook

492 Hamline Ave. S.
651.698.4347
www.crnook.com
After a fire gutted the place, the Nook is up and running, and cooking your favorite hamburger and scrumptious fries. $

Obb's Sports Bar & Grill

1347 Burns Ave.
651.776.7010
www.obbsbar.com
Watch your favorite sports while enjoying a wide selection of draft and bottled beer, or wine. $

On's Kitchen

1613 University Ave. W.
651.644.1444
www.onskitchen.com
Options from spring rolls to curry, including a few specialty dishes you can't find anywhere else. $

Padelford Packet Boat Co.

Harriet Island
651.227.1100
www.riverrides.com
A variety of meal cruises including a sunset dinner cruise, "Lunch and Lock," Sunday lunch, and special occasions. $$

Pad Thai Grand Café

1681 Grand Ave.
651.690.1393
www.padthaiongrand.com
Homemade Thai food, exposed brick and timbers, and service with a smile. $$

Pappy's Chicago Style Eatery
1783 Maryland Ave. E.
651.771.4500
Philly cheese steaks, Italian beef, and the ubiquitous Chicago dog; stand in line to order and get your drink (it's worth the wait). $

Patrick McGovern's Pub
225 Seventh St. W.
651.224.5821
www.patmcgoverns.com
Pub food and drinks in a historic brick building with a three-tiered outdoor dining patio. $

Pazzaluna
360 St. Peter St.
651.223.7000
www.pazzaluna.com
Acclaimed Italian cuisine in a stylish downtown location; offers complimentary valet parking. $$

Peking Garden
1488 University Ave.
651.644.0888
www.pekinggardenmn.com
Serving quality homeland Cantonese dishes. $

Pizza Luce
1183 Selby Ave.
651.288.0186
www.pizzaluce.com
Creative, artistic pizzas with vegan and gluten-free options for dine-in, take-out, or delivery. $

Punch Neapolitan Pizza
704 Cleveland Ave.
651.696.1066
769 Grand Ave.
651.602.6068
www.punchpizza.com
Gourmet pizzas cooked fresh in a wood-burning oven for a smoky crust flavor. $

Que Nha Vietnamese Restaurant
849 University Ave. W.
651.290.8552
Unassuming décor belies noteworthy dishes like goat curry and rice porridge. $

Red's Savoy Inn and Pizza
421 Seventh St. E.
651.227.1437
520 White Bear Ave. N.
651.731.1068
Countless topping combinations on that famous red sauce. $

Restaurante La Laguna
433 Robert St. S.
651.683.2286
www.lalagunasaintpaul.com
Menu includes traditional antojitos, specialty entrées, delicious desserts, and refreshing drinks. $

The Happy Gnome looks cozy and welcoming on a cold winter's night.

The Happy Gnome

Ristorante Luci

470 Cleveland Ave. S.

651.699.8258

www.ristoranteluci.com

Romantic, classical Italian cuisine with a multi-course tasting menu. $$

Ruam Mit Thai Cafe

475 St. Peter St.

651.222.7871

www.ruam-mit-thai.net

Convenient downtown location; family-friendly lunch buffet. $

Russian Tea House

1758 University Ave. W.

651.646.4144

Serving borscht, piroshki, cabbage rolls, and real Russian tea; Tuesday through Friday. $

Rusty Taco

508 Lexington Pkwy.

651.698.2777

www.rustytacomn.com

Breakfast tacos, Mex tacos, beer, and coffee at the corner of Lexington and Randolph. $

Saigon Restaurant

704 University Ave. W.

651.225.8751

Familiar Vietnamese favorites with pho, broken rice dishes, banh mi sandwiches, and more. (Closed Mondays.) $

St. Clair Broiler

1580 St. Clair Ave.

651.698.7055

www.stclairbroiler.com

Burgers, sandwiches, and buttermilk fried chicken in a classic American diner. $

St. Paul Cheese Shop

1573 Grand Ave.

651.698.3391

www.france44cheeseshop.com

An rBGH-free cheese list, cured-meat sandwiches, and delicious accompaniments. $

St. Paul Grill

The Saint Paul Hotel

350 Market St.

651.224.7455

www.stpaulgrill.com

Impeccable service and classic American entrées; Scotch, whiskey, and cognac for connoisseurs. $$$

Saji-Ya

695 Grand Ave.

651.292.0444

www.sajiya.com

Japanese sauté cooking with a bar and teppanyaki grill. $$

Sakura

Carriage Hill Plaza

350 St. Peter St.

651.224.0185

www.sakurastpaul.com

Timeless Japanese food and drink; begin an evening downtown at the full-length bar. $$

Salut Bar Américain
917 Grand Ave.
651.917.2345
www.salutbaramericain.com
French-inspired cuisine in an ooh-la-la venue. $$

Scusi
1806 St. Clair Ave.
651.789.7007
www.scusistpaul.com
A shared-plate approach to Italian dining. $

Señor Wong
111 Kellogg Blvd. E.
651.224.2019
www.senorwong.com
A convincing combination of Asian and Hispanic foods gives a unique twist to the menu. $ (lunch) $$ (dinner)

Serlin's Café
1124 Payne Ave.
651.776.9003
Find homey goodness and old-fashioned comfort food at this step-back-in-time all-American café. $

Shamrocks
995 Seventh St. W.
651.228.9925
www.crshamrocks.com
A real Irish pub with live entertainment serving famous Nook food. $

Shish
1668 Grand Ave.
651.690.2212
www.shishcafe.net
Serves winning Mediterranean and American cuisine for breakfast, lunch, and dinner. $

Skinners Pub & Eatery
919 Randolph Ave.
651.291.0146
www.skinnersmn.com
Fun for the whole family with Thursday bingo, Saturday night tacos, and specials every day of the week. $

The Strip Club
378 Maria Ave.
651.793.6247
www.domeats.com
Playful, sophisticated atmosphere for meat and fish dinners on Dayton's Bluff. $$

Supatra's Thai Cuisine
967 Seventh St. W.
651.222.5859
www.supatra.com
Chef and owner Supatra Johnson is the author of Crying Tiger: Thai Recipes from the Heart. *$*

Swede Hollow Bakery and Cafe
725 Seventh St. E.
651.776.8810
www.swedehollowcafe.com
Menu items made from scratch for breakfast and lunch on Dayton's Bluff. $

Tanpopo Noodle Shop
308 Prince St., #140
651.209.6527
www.tanpoporestaurant.com
Simple, elegant, and affordable Japanese food. $

Taste of Thailand
1671 Selby Ave.
651.644.3997
www.tasteofthailandmn.com
Order with as much or as little spice as you want, but remember that hot means HOT. $

Tavern on Grand
656 Grand Ave.
651.228.9030
www.tavernongrand.com
Go for the fried walleye and log cabin décor. $$

Tavern on the Avenue
825 Jefferson Ave.
651.227.6315
www.tavontheavenue.com
No-frills neighborhood bar that offers food made from scratch. $

Tay Ho Restaurant
302 University Ave. W.
651.228.7216
Small dining space with big flavors in traditional and old-world Asian fare. $

The Tea House
1676 Suburban Ave.
651.771.1790
www.ourteahouse.com
A Szechuan gem on the East Side. $

Thai Cafe
371 University Ave. W.
651.225.8231
www.thaicafemn.com
Chef Yuwadee Poophakumpanart, born and raised in Thailand, brings her vision of Thai food to Saint Paul. $

Tin Cup's
1220 Rice St.
651.487.7967
The North End burger bar. $

Tom Reid's Hockey City Pub
258 Seventh St. W.
651.292.9916
www.tomreidshockeycitypub.com
Generous portions for lunch, dinner, and after the game; serves late at night. $

Trattoria da Vinci
400 Sibley St.
651.222.4050
www.trattoriadavinci.com
Fine Italian food amid antique stone fountains and architectural elegance. $$

Trieu Chau Restaurant
500 University Ave. W.
651.222.6148
Busy shop with outstanding soups and tasty banh mi sandwiches. $

Trotter's Cafe & Bakery

232 Cleveland Ave. N.
651.645.8950
www.trotterscafe.com
Find local and organic food at this charming café in Merriam Park. $

Trung Nam French Vietnamese

739 University Ave. W.
651.229.0887
Bakery and restaurant specializing in Vietnamese sandwiches and croissants. $

Twisted Fork Grille

1342 Grand Ave.
651.690.5901
www.twistedforkgrille.com
American-inspired recipes with seasonal foods for breakfast, lunch, and dinner. $

University Buffet

225 University Ave. W.
651.366.6858
www.universitybuffetmn.com
Lunch and dinner buffets Monday through Saturday; sushi, seafood, and a variety of Asian cuisines. $

W. A. Frost & Company

Dacotah Building
374 Selby Ave.
651.224.5715
www.wafrost.com
Incomparable ambience and an old-world wine cellar to complement romantic artisanal cuisine. $$$

Ward 6

858 Payne Ave.
651.348.8181
www.ward6stpaul.com
A new restaurant and bar on the East Side of St. Paul serves hot breakfast and great coffee and espresso, and great food and drink all day long, with local beer and a full bar. $

Yarusso Bros.

635 Payne Ave.
651.776.4848
www.yarussos.com
Family-owned Italian classic since 1933; famous for Francesco's sauce and Bocce Ball. $

Zamboni's Pizza

184 Seventh St. W.
651.225.2999
www.zambonipizza.com
A new café pizza pub for Wild home games. $

Street Food

Food truck caravans roam our city streets with popular mobile locations at Rice Park, Mears Park, Kellogg Boulevard, and the Capitol.

128 Café Mobile
www.128cafe.net
Traditional and progressive American fare.

The Cave Cafe
www.cavecafeandcatering.com
Afro-Italiano fusion.

Chef Shack
www.chefshack.org
A seasonal, organic menu that's always changing.

A Cupcake Social
www.acupcakesocial.com
Uniquely crafted flavors and visual presentations.

Cupcakes on the Go
www.roaminghunger.com
   /cupcake-on-the-go
From-scratch cupcakes spreading sweetness.

Fork in the Road
www.forkintheroadtruck.com
The big orange truck with fresh and familiar foods.

Gastrotruck
www.gastrotruck.mobi
Creative culinary offerings with zero waste.

Home Street Home
www.homestreethometruck.com
Globally inspired comfort food.

I Heart MN Coffee
www.iheartmncoffee.com
Local partners. Outstanding quality.

Joe's Hot Dogs
www.facebook.com/Joes-Hot-Dogs
Three convenient locations: Mears and Rice Parks and the Ramsey Courthouse.

Leprechaun's Dreamcycle
www.leprechaunsdreamcycle.com
"A roving courier of happiness with a magical tricycle."

Messy Guiseppe
www.messyg.com
Italian sandwiches, salads, and sweet treats.

Neato's
www.neatosburgers.com
Serving drive-in burgers and duck-fat fries.

Ngon Vietnamese Bistro
www.ngonbistro.com
Authentic Vietnamese dishes using local and sustainable ingredients.

Potters Pasties and Pies

www.potterspasties.com

Perfecting the balance of durability and flakiness.

R.A. MacSammy's

www.ramacsammys.com

Gourmet comfort food with a rotating variety of Mac and Cheese dishes.

Romocky Cheddar Bratz

www.romockycheddarbratz
　.blogspot.com

Open during St. Paul Farmer's Market hours on Saturdays and Sundays.

Sassy Spoon

www.sassyspoontruck.com

Wholesome food with attitude.

Simply Steve's

www.simplystevesfoodtruck.com

Breakfast served all day. Hot sandwiches for lunch.

West Indies Soul Food

www.westindiessoulfood.com

Authentic Caribbean dishes and southern soul food cooking.

© Bob Muschewske/370SummitStPaul.com

Restaurants by Genre

Breakfasts and Diners
Black Bear Crossings on the Lake, Black Dog Coffee & Wine Bar, Bon Vie, Bonnie's Café, The Buttered Tin, Café Minnesota, Capital View Café, Chatterbox Pub, Colossal Cafe, Day by Day Café, Egg & I, Finnish Bistro, The Four Inns, The French Hen, Golden's Deli, Grandview Grill, Keys Café & Bakery, Mickey's Dining Car, Mojo Monkey Donuts, The Neighborhood Café, Patrick McGovern's Pub, Serlin's Café, Shish, Swede Hollow Bakery and Cafe, Twisted Fork Grille, Wabasha Deli & Cafe.

Classic Saint Paul Eating Establishments
Bennett's Chop & Rail House, Big Daddy's BBQ, The Blue Door Pub, BYO Burger, Cafe Latté, Cecil's Delicatessen, Bakery, and Restaurant, Cherokee Tavern, Cossetta Italian Market & Pizza, Dixie's on Grand, Downtowner Woodfire Grill, Fabulous Fern's, Forepaugh's, Grand Ole Creamery, Grandview Grill, Hunan Garden, Lee's & Dee's Barbeque Express, The Lexington, Mai Village, Mancini's Char House, Mickey's Dining Car, Minnesota Music Café, Moscow on the Hill, The Nook, Padelford Packet Boat Co., Patrick McGovern's Pub, Russian Tea House, St. Clair Broiler, St. Paul Grill, Serlin's Café, Tavern on Grand, Tin Cup's, W. A. Frost, Yarusso Bros.

European & Mediterranean
Black Sea, Caffe Biaggio, Christos, DeGidio's, Falafel King, Finnish Bistro, Foxy Falafel, Glockenspiel, La Grolla, Luci Ancora, Meritage, Moscow on the Hill, Pazzaluna, Ristorante Luci, Russian Tea House, Salut Bar Américain, Scusi, Shish, Trattoria da Vinci.

Ice Cream Parlors and Candy
American Joe, Candyland, Conny's Creamy Cone, Chocolat Celeste, Dari-ette Drive In, Dar's Double Scoop, Dr. Chocolate's Chocolate Chateau, Grand Ole Creamery, Izzy's Ice Cream Café, Lynden's Soda Fountain, Regina's Fine Candies, Snuffy's Malt Shop, St. Paul Corner Drug.

Indian & South Asian
Everest on Grand, Khyber Pass Cafe.

Mexican, Latin & Caribbean

Barrio Tequila Bar, Boca Chica Restaurante Mexicano & Cantina, Boca Chica's Taco House, Brasa Premium Rotisserie, El Amanecer, El Burrito Mercado, Homi Restaurant Mexicano, La Cucaracha, La Hacienda, Mañana Restaurant y Pupuseria, Restaurante La Laguna, Rusty Taco, Señor Wong.

Middle Eastern & African

Babani's Kurdish Restaurant, Barbary Fig, Black Sea, Damera Ethiopian Bar & Restaurant, Fasika, Flamingo, Foxy Falafel, Khyber Pass.

Pizza & Italian

Aroma's Pizza, Black Sheep Pizza, Caffe Biaggio, Cossetta Italian Market & Pizza, Dar's Double Scoop, DeGidio's, Eden Pizza, Grand Ole Creamery, Italian Pie Shoppe & Winery, La Grolla, The Little Oven, Luci Ancora, Lucio's Grill, Mama's Pizza, Palace's Pizza, Pazzaluna, Pizza Luce, Punch Neapolitan Pizza, Red's Savoy Inn and Pizza, Ristorante Luci, Scusi, Trattoria da Vinci, Yarusso Bros., Zamboni's Pizza.

Waffle cones at Izzy's Ice Cream Café

Southeast Asian

Bangkok Cuisine, Bangkok Thai Deli, Cheng Heng, Eastside Thai, Fuji Ya, Ho Ho Gourmet Restaurant, Kolap Restaurant, Lao-Thai Family Restaurant, Little Szechuan, Mai Village, Mango Thai Restaurant, Mirror of Korea, Ngon Vietnamese Bistro, On's Kitchen, Pad Thai Grand Café, Palace's Pizza, Peking Garden, Que Nha Vietnamese Restaurant, Ruam Mit Thai Café, Saigon Restaurant, Saji-Ya, Sakura, Señor Wong, Supatra's Thai Cuisine, Tanpopo Noodle Shop, Taste of Thailand, Tay Ho Restaurant, Thai Cafe, The Tea House, Trung Nam French Vietnamese, Trieu Chau Restaurant, University Buffet.

Sports Bars & Brew Pubs

Billy's on Grand, The Bulldog Lowertown, Burger Moe's, Cherry Pit Bar & Grill, Cork's Irish Pub, Costello's Bar & Grill, Eagle Street Grille, Glockenspiel, Great Waters Brewing Company, Half Time Rec, Happy Gnome, The Liffey, Muddy Pig, Obb's Sports Bar & Grill, O'Gara's Bar & Grill, Patrick McGovern's Pub, Skinners' Pub & Eatery, Sweeney's Saloon, Tavern on the Avenue, Tin Cup's, Tom Reid's Hockey City Pub, Wild Onion, Wild Tymes Sports Bar and Grill, Zamboni's Pizza.

Kelly's Depot Bar, next to the reopened Union Depot in Lowertown

Actors Theater of Minnesota

350 Saint Peter St., Ste. 254
651.290.2290
www.actorsmn.org
Resident theater company offering annual (and extended!) seasons at the Lowry Lab and other venues.

Anodyne Theatre

825 Carleton St.
651.642.1684
www.anodyneart.org
A visual and performing arts center especially for artists with disabilities.

The Bach Society of Minnesota

1043 Grand Avenue
651.602.9507
www.bachsocietymn.org
Building a community to perform and promote the music of J.S. Bach.

Ballet Minnesota

249 E. Fourth St.
651.222.7919
www.balletminnesota.org
Creating and sharing dance artistry "that enriches the human spirit."

Bedlam Theatre

213 Fourth St. E.
651.209.0597
www.bedlamtheatre.org
The Bedlam Universe includes a wide range of theater, performance, cabaret, community and creative collaboration.

Blank Slate Theatre

499 Wacouta St.
612.481.2234
www.blankslatetheatre.com
Collaborating with young artists to produce and perform dramatic works.

Camp Cabaret

490 Robert St. N.
651.292.1844
www.camp-bar.net
With 5,000 square feet and a back mezzanine lounge, distinctive performance stage, and dance floor.

Canvas

1610 Hubbard Ave.
651.298.4393
www.canvas651.com
Workshops and events, materials and support for young writers, dancers, visual artists, and performers.

Center for Hmong Arts and Talent (CHAT)

995 University Ave W., Ste. 220
651.603.6971
www.aboutchat.org
CHAT empowers the local Hmong American community through the arts.

Circus Juventas

1270 Montreal Ave.
651.699.8229
www.circusjuventas.org
Offering circus arts training and performance opportunities for children and youth ages 3 to 21.

Previous page (left): Dancer Abbie Schmitt from the Cities Classical Ensemble during a shoot at the Twin Cities Photography Studios on University Avenue
© Cary Rothschild/CaryRothschild.com

Previous page (right): Balinese dancer Duwita F. Wahjoe at a performance with the Sumunar Gamelan and Dance Ensembles in Como Lake Pavilion, Saint Paul
© Tony Ernst/gamelaner on Flickr

Commedia Beauregard
1043 Grand Ave., No. 358
651.214.2905
www.cbtheatre.org
Making classic and modern works from around the world accessible to modern audiences.

Dreamland Arts
677 Hamline Ave. N.
651.645.5506
www.dreamlandarts.com
A gathering place for creative expression through art that builds healthy community.

Fitzgerald Theater
10 Exchange St. E.
651.290.1200
fitzgeraldtheater.publicradio.org
The city's oldest theater and home to A Prairie Home Companion.

The Gonzo Group Theatre
111 Kellogg Blvd. E.
651.330.2404
www.gonzogroup.org
Weird, different, and even dangerous.

Gremlin Theatre
2400 University Ave. W.
651.228.7008
www.gremlin-theatre.org
Intimate space for a "relevant, entertaining, and enjoyable theatrical experience."

Hamm Brewery
707 Minnehaha Ave. E.
651.776.0550
www.swedehollow.org
An East Side performance space for artists and art lovers alike.

The Historic Mounds Theatre
1029 Hudson Rd.
651.772.2253
www.moundstheatre.org
An Art Deco landmark on Dayton's Bluff that benefits Portage for Youth.

History Theatre
30 E. Tenth St.
651.292.4323
www.historytheatre.com
Producing new works based on Minnesota's past and the American experience; Sample Night Live offered the first Wednesday of the month.

Jewel Theatre
250 Seventh St. E.
612.823.1118
www.theatreoffools.com
Vaudeville for the 21st Century.

Lehr Theater
16 Fifth Street
651.290.2225
www.spcpa.org/conservatory
/lehr-theatre
*Providing a place for students to
experience the artistic process
firsthand.*

Lex-Ham Community Theater
1184 Portland Ave.
651.644.3366
www.lexhamarts.org
*Quality theater activities by and
for the residents of the Lexington-
Hamline and surrounding neighborhoods.*

**Lowry Lab /
Theater Space Project**
350 Saint Peter St.
651.222.0149
www.theaterspaceproject.org
*Offering affordable, convenient
performance space in downtown
Saint Paul.*

**Minnesota Jewish
Theatre Company**
1978 Ford Pkwy.
651.647.4315
www.mnjewishtheatre.org
*Performances at Hillcrest Center.
"Igniting your mind by touching your heart (even if you're not
Jewish!)."*

Nautilus Music-Theater
308 Prince St., Ste. 250
651.298.9913
www.nautilusmusictheater.org
*Dedicated to new operas and inno-
vative productions of existing works.*

**Ordway Center
for Performing Arts**
345 Washington St.
651.224.4222
www.ordway.org
*Broadway-style shows, music, and
dance.*

O'Shaughnessy Auditorium
St. Catherine University
2004 Randolph Ave.
651.690.6700
oshaughnessy.stkate.edu
*An arts presenter and rental hall
for every type of performance.*

Padelford Packet Boat Company
Harriet Island
651.227.1100
www.riverrides.com
*Come aboard the Showboat for
stand-up comedy and live theater.*

Park Square Theatre
20 West Seventh Place
651.291.7005
www.parksquaretheatre.org
*Exceptional downtown theater
staging favorite classics and fresh
new stories.*

Penumbra Theatre Company
270 Kent St. N.
651.224.3180
www.penumbratheatre.org
*Illuminating "the human condition
through the prism of the African
American experience."*

Prospero Theatre Company

Twin Cities Friends
    Meetinghouse
1725 Grand Ave.
651.705.6184
www.prosperotheatre.org
*A band of budding theatre artists
whose "revels are just beginning."*

Saint Paul City Ballet

1680 Grand Ave.
651.690.1588
www.spcballet.org
Classical training and extraordinary performances.

Saint Paul Civic Symphony

www.saintpaulcivicsymphony.org
*Free concerts featuring the music
of Masters past and present.*

Sendero Flamenco

153 E. 10th St.
612.203.6188
www.sendero-flamenco.com
*Traditional flamenco dance and
acoustic guitar.*

Skylark Opera

Landmark Center, Ste. 414
75 W. Fifth St.
651.292.4309
www.skylarkopera.org
*Familiar favorites and "off-the-
beaten-path adventures" at the E.
M. Pearson Theatre of Concordia
University.*

SteppingStone Theatre

55 Victoria St. N.
651.225.9265
www.steppingstonetheatre.org
*Youth-centered theater art for
family entertainment that feeds
the mind.*

Sundin Music Hall

1531 Hewitt Avenue
651.523.2459
www.hamline.edu/sundin
*Home of Hamline University's
music ensembles and resident
music series.*

Teatro del Pueblo

209 Page St. W., Ste. 208
651.224.8806
www.teatrodelpueblo.org
*Serving communities across the
state with educational residencies
and touring shows.*

TU Dance

2121 University Ave. W.
www.tudance.org
Celebrating diversity with the connective power of dance.

*The Fitzgerald is Saint Paul's oldest theater and home to Garrison Keillor's
radio show,* A Prairie Home Companion, *broadcasting for its fortieth year
in 2014.*

Music Venues

Whether you prefer a jazz-drenched late night tormented by crying saxophones in the formerly smoky basement of the Artists' Quarter, or an early classical evening listening to America's premier chamber orchestra in the crisp and beautiful SPCO hall, Saint Paul is the place to be. Our city offers something for every musical taste, including death metal bands on any given night at Lowertown's Station 4.

Amsterdam Bar & Hall
6 Sixth St. W.
612.285.3112
www.amsterdambarandhall.com
*Keeps Wabasha hopping with
nightly entertainment.*

Arnellia's
1183 University Ave. W.
651.642.5975
www.arnellias.net
*The "Legendary Club Apollo"
of Minnesota.*

Artists' Quarter
408 St. Peter St.
651.292.1359
www.artistsquarter.com
*Located downstairs in the historic
Hamm Building with a subterra-
nean classic jazz vibe.*

The Baroque Room
275 Fourth St. E., Ste. 280
651.705.6772
www.thebaroqueroom.com
*An inviting downtown performance
venue for classical chamber music.*

Black Dog Coffee & Wine Bar
308 Prince St.
651.228.9274
www.blackdogstpaul.com
*A Lowertown meeting place for
music, ideas, and good food.*

Camp Bar
490 Robert St. N.
651.292.1844
www.camp-bar.net
*With 5,000 square feet and a back
mezzanine lounge, distinctive performance stage, and dance floor.*

The Coffee Grounds
1579 Hamline Ave.
651.644.9959
www.thecoffeegrounds.net
*Committed to remaining free and
open to all ages. No cover.*

Dubliner Pub
2162 University Ave. W.
651.646.5551
www.thedublinerpub.com
*No-frills Irish bar: whiskey, scotch,
beer, and an up-to-the-minute
music calendar.*

Dunn Bros on Grand

1569 Grand Ave.

651.698.0618

www.dunnbrosgrand.com

*The original Dunn Bros Coffee
features live music daily.*

Ginkgo Coffeehouse

721 Snelling Ave. N.

651.645.2647

www.ginkgocoffee.com

*Corner café serving coffee and
seasonal foods with a diverse mix
of music and clientele. Folk music
is a specialty.*

Half Time Rec

1013 Front St.

651.488.8245

www.halftimerec.com

*A neighborhood nightclub with a
variety of music and the only indoor
bocce ball courts in Saint Paul.*

Hat Trick Lounge

134 Fifth St. E.

651.228.1347

www.hat_trick_lounge.htm

*Classic saloon offering rock and
roll, blues, country, folk, jazz,
and pop.*

The Lexington

1096 Grand Ave.

651.222.5878

www.thelexongrand.com/jazz

*Jazz at the Lex on Thursdays and
Saturdays.*

Mancini's Char House & Lounge

531 Seventh St. W.

651.224.7345

www.mancinis.com

*Live music every Wednesday
through Saturday.*

Minnesota Music Café

499 Payne Ave.

651.776.4699

www.minnesotamusiccafe.com

*"Where the food's great and the
music's cooking!"*

Music in Mears

221 Fifth St. E.

651.248.0857

www.musicinmears.com

*Thursday evening outdoor concerts
from 6 to 9 p.m., June through
August.*

O'Gara's Bar & Grill

164 Snelling Ave. N.

651.644.3333

www.ogaras.com

*Neighborhood pub with music,
grill food, and the free Shamrock
Shuttle to sports events, including
the Wild and Minnesota RollerGirls.*

Shamrocks

995 Seventh St. W.

651.228.9925

www.crnook.com

A loyal customer following for bands: Soul Tree, Mouldy Figs, Loose Cannon, and more.

SPCO Music Room / Saint Paul Chamber Orchestra

Historic Hamm Building

408 St. Peter St., 3rd floor

651.291.1144

www.thespco.org

The intimate performance space of the only full-time professional chamber orchestra in the nation.

Station 4

201 Fourth St. E.

651.224.6372

www.station-4.com

This vintage downtown club puts a variety of cult artists onstage.

Studio Z / Zeitgeist

275 Fourth St. E.

651.755.1600

www.zeitgeistnewmusic.org

A small ensemble of percussion, piano, and woodwinds performing a diverse range of new music.

Sundin Music Hall

1531 Hewitt Avenue

651.523.2459

www.hamline.edu/sundin

Home of Hamline University's music ensembles and resident music series.

Tavern on the Avenue

825 Jefferson Ave.

651.227.6315

www.tavontheavenue.com

Cozy venue with classic rock and roll, rhythm, blues, and soul.

 ## Turf Club

1601 University Ave. W.

651.647.0486

www.turfclub.net

The newest music performed in a gritty relic of old-school Saint Paul: "The best remnant of the '40s."

Wilebski's Blues Saloon

1638 Rice St.

651.331.0929

www.wilebskiblues.com

Hardwood floors and out-of-this-world blues.

Wild Tymes Palace Stage

33 Seventh Place W.

651.224.8181

www.wildtymes.net/shows

Never a cover. All shows 18+.

French avant-garde cellist Didier Petit at the Black Dog Coffee & Wine Bar, known for its extensive jazz programming

© Tony Ernst/gamelaner on Flickr

Dance Venues

Celtic Junction
836 Prior Ave.
612.722.7000
www.thecelticjunction.com
Third Saturday family céilí with the Twin Cities Céilí Band.

Dubliner Pub
2162 University Ave. W.
651.646.5551
www.thedublinerpub.com
First Saturday afternoon céilí (under 12 free).

FACES Mears Park
380 Jackson St.
651.209.7776
www.facesmearspark.com
Live Salsa music at 9 p.m. Fridays. 18+ to party; 21+ to drink.

Half Time Rec
1013 Front St.
651.488.8245
www.halftimerec.com
The Half Time Rec bar in St. Paul has been going strong for decades. It is one of St. Paul's most popular Irish-themed bars.

Minnesota Music Café
499 Payne Ave.
651.776.4699
www.minnesotamusiccafe.com
"Where the food's great and the music's cooking!"

Oddfellows' Hall
2380 Hampden Ave.
651.222.5475
www.wildgoosechasecloggers.com
First Saturday night New England Contra dance.

Wabasha Street Caves
215 Wabasha St. S.
651.224.1191
www.wabashastreetcaves.com
Thursday night Swing dance.

Wilebski's Blues Saloon
1638 Rice St.
651.331.0929
www.wilebskiblues.com
Hardwood floors and out-of-this-world blues.

Art Galleries

*private (sell)

AAW Gallery of Wood Art
Landmark Center
75 Fifth St. W.
651.484.9094
www.galleryofwoodart.org
Sponsored by the American Association of Woodturners.

Artist Mercantile*
24 West Seventh Place
651.222.0053
www.artistmerc.com
An eclectic mix of art and gifts with a focus on Midwest artists.

AZ Gallery*
308 Prince St., No. 130
651.224.3757
www.theazgallery.org
A fine arts co-op in Lowertown.

Big Table Studio
375 Wabasha St. N.
651.222.6428
www.bigtablestudio.com
Hand-printed posters and custom-designed artwork; 12 shows a year.

Catherine G. Murphy Gallery
St. Catherine University
2004 Randolph Ave.
651.690.6644
www.stkate.edu/gallery
Visual arts that support the mission of the university.

AZ Gallery is host to the annual Saint Paul Almanac *book launch and art show.*

Concordia Arts Center
Concordia University
275 Syndicate St. N.
651.641.8230
www.csp.edu/art
*Showing local and national artists
as well as juried student and senior
exhibitions.*

Evoke Gallery*
275 Fourth St. E., Ste. 260
612.839.3079
www.evokegallery.com
*A mix of fair trade and eco-friendly
gifts, handmade jewelry, and fine
art.*

The FrameWorks Gallery*
2022A Ford Pkwy.
651.698.3372
www.frameworksmn.com
*Includes an ongoing exhibition of
works by local artists with a new
featured artist every six weeks.*

Goldstein Museum of Design
1985 Buford Ave.
612.624.7801
www.goldstein.design.umn.edu

The Grand Hand Gallery*
619 Grand Ave.
651.312.1122
www.thegrandhand.com
*Contemporary fine American crafts
in a variety of media; emphasis on
regional artists.*

Grand Hill Gallery
333 Grand Ave.
651.227.4783
*Open Tuesday through Saturday
or Sunday and Monday by appointment only.*

Gordon Parks Gallery
Metro State University
645 Seventh St. E.
651.793.1631
www.metrostate.edu/cas
    /cwa/gallery
*Supports the arts curriculum and
cultural activities of the university,
and preserves the legacy of 20th
century artist Gordon Parks.*

Hosko Gallery*
56 Sixth St. E., Ste. 305
651.222.4767
www.billhosko.com
*Architectural art and photography
that features Saint Paul.*

James J. Hill House
240 Summit Avenue
651.297.2555
www.mnhs.org/places/sites
  /jjhh/history
*Hill's red sandstone mansion from
the gilded age was considered a
model of a modern gallery when
the home was completed in 1891.
A 1,006-pipe mechanical-action
tracker organ is still played most
Saturdays and at many special
events. Guided 75-minute tours
Wednesday through Saturday.*

Johnson Gallery
Bethel University
Clauson Center, second floor
3900 Bethel Dr.
651.638.6400
www.bethel.edu/galleries
*Works by students along with local
and national artists.*

Larson Art Gallery
University of Minnesota
  Student Center, lower level
2017 Buford Ave.
612.625.7281
www.sua.umn.edu/events/arts
*Curated, designed, installed,
and promoted by the Visual Arts
Committee of the student union's
Program Board.*

Lift Kids at Global Village
Produce Exchange Building
153 10th St. E.
651.298.9200
www.liftkids.org
*Serving coffee, tea, and social
responsibility to increase peace and
justice for people of all ages.*

Macalester College Art Gallery
Janet Wallace Fine Arts Center
130 Macalester Street
651.696.6416
www.macalester.edu/gallery
*Emphasis on contemporary art
with exhibitions on a wide range of
historical and sociological topics.*

Minnesota History Center
345 W. Kellogg Blvd., St. Paul
651.259.3000
www.minnesotahistorycenter
  .org/exhibits
*Building is made of Minnesota
materials, including Rockville
granite and Winona limestone.
Breathtaking views of downtown
St. Paul and the State Capitol.*

Minnesota Museum of
American Art Project Space
The Pioneer Building
332 N. Robert St.
St. Paul, MN 55102
651.222.6080
www.mmaa.org
*Exhibitions devoted to American
artists and craftspeople of all types
and all ages.*

Nevermind Gallery
201 Seventh St. N.W.
651.292.1623
www.nevermindgallery.com
*Art prints, gig posters, original and
unique pieces.*

Raymond Avenue Gallery*
761 Raymond Ave.
651.644.9200
www.raymondavenuegallery
.blogspot.com
The works of recognized regional artists in media from pottery to fiber.

Soeffker Gallery
Hamline University, Drew Fine
Arts Center
1536 Hewitt Ave.
651.523.2800
www.hamline.edu/features
/tour/drew_fine_arts.html
Houses the permanent collection and hosts touring exhibitions.

Three Sisters Eclectic Arts
253 East Fourth St.
651.222.6052
www.threesisterseclecticarts.com
An art gallery, gift shop, and artistic experience located in the heart of Lowertown.

Twining River Arts
Northern Warehouse
308 Prince St.
651.292.0321
Exploring artistic connections to the natural world.

UST Department of Art History /Exhibitions
University of St. Thomas
2115 Summit Ave.
651.962.5560
www.stthomas.edu/arthistory
/exhibitions
Hosts three exhibitions a year featuring emerging and established artists working in a variety of media.

Water and Oil Art Gallery*
506 Kenny Rd.
651.774.2260
www.waterandoil.com
Bringing the art of Europe to the heart of Minnesota.

Western Sculpture Park
Marion and University Avenues
Saint Paul, MN 55101
651.290.0921
www.publicartstpaul.org
Check out Western Sculpture Park Festival each September.

Women's Art Resources of Minnesota (WARM)
550 Rice St.
651.567.9276
www.thewarm.org
Serves Midwest women artists through exhibits, mentoring, and networking.

A Tale of Two Documentarians: Patrick McCutchan's photo of Roberta Avidor sketching at the opening of the newly rennovated Union Depot station, December 8, 2012

Bookstores

Common Good Books

38 Snelling Ave. S.
651.225.8989
www.commongoodbooks.com
*A nice local store to buy a book
or two.*

Half Price Books

2041 Ford Pkwy.
651.699.1391
www.hpb.com
*Committed to promoting literacy
and kindness to the environment.*

Hmong ABC

Two locations: 217 Como Ave.
    and 1001 Johnson Pkwy.
651.293.0019
www.hmongabc.com
*Also sells handmade crafts, cloth-
ing, and jewelry.*

Micawber's Books

2238 Carter Ave.
651.646.5506
www.micawbers.com
Everyone's neighborhood bookstore.

*Double the smiles at Half Price
Books in Highland Park*
© Judy Hawkinson

Midway Books

1579 University Ave. W.
651.644.7605
www.midwaybook.com
*Rare, used, and out-of-print books
and comics, and a wide array of
memorabilia.*

Red Balloon Bookshop

891 Grand Ave.
651.224.8320
www.redballoonbookshop.com
*Independent children's bookseller
with a terrific selection of hand
puppets.*

Sixth Chamber Used Books

1332 Grand Ave.
651.690.9463
www.sixthchamber.com
*A searchable online inventory and
convenient on-street parking.*

Subtext

165 Western Ave. N.
651.493.3871
www.subtext.indiebound.com
*Saint Paul's newest bookstore.
Have coffee or tea while you
hang out.*

ALEXANDER RAMSEY
HOUSE

Alexander Ramsey House

265 Exchange St. S.

651.296.8760

www.mnhs.org/ramseyhouse

Near Irvine Park, the 19th-century Victorian home of Alexander Ramsey offers "a glimpse into family and servant life" with guided tours; closed January 2 to May 31.

American Museum of Asmat Art

University of St. Thomas

2115 Summit Ave.

651.962.5560

www.stthomas.edu/arthistroy
/asmat

On display in The Gallery at Anderson Student Center.

Assumption Church

51 Seventh St. W.

651.224.7536

www.assumptionsp.org

A Roman Catholic church built in 1871 with a self-guided tour brochure available online.

Cathedral of Saint Paul

239 Selby Ave.

651.228.1766

www.cathedralsaintpaul.org

One of the city's most recognizable buildings since it was completed in 1915; tours most weekdays at 1 p.m.

Germanic-American Institute

301 Summit Ave.

651.222.6295

www.gai-mn.org/about

Fosters understanding of the culture, language, arts, and ongoing history of the German-speaking peoples.

Gibbs Museum

2097 Larpenteur Ave. W.

651.646.8629

www.rchs.com

Summer day camps re-create the pioneer and Dakota life; closed mid-November to mid-April.

Goldstein Museum of Design

University of Minnesota,
McNeal Hall

1985 Buford Avenue

612.624.7801

www.goldstein.design.umn.edu

The only design museum in the Upper Midwest.

Governor's Residence
1006 Summit Ave.
651.297.2161
www.admin.state.mn.us/govres
Summer tours in June, July, and August; holiday tours in December.

Historic Fort Snelling
200 Tower Avenue
(Hwys 5 & 55)
612.726.1171
www.mnhs.org/fortsnelling
1820s military post and prison with costumed guides and demos; open Memorial Day Weekend through Labor Day.

Jackson Street Roundhouse
Minnesota Transportation
Museum
193 Pennsylvania Ave. E.
651.228.0263
www.mtmuseum.org
Kids of all ages enjoy the railroading experience at this former steam engine maintenance facility; open Wednesday and Saturday year round.

James J. Hill House
240 Summit Ave.
651.297.2555
www.mnhs.org/hillhouse
Hill's red sandstone mansion from the gilded age was completed in 1891; 75-minute guided tours Wednesday through Saturday.

Julian H. Sleeper House
66 St. Albans St. S.
651.225.1505
www.julianhsleeperhouse.com
Tour the dream home of this Saint Paul entrepreneur, real estate speculator, and theatrical promoter; nine decorative exhibition rooms (by appointment only).

Landmark Center
75 Fifth St.
651.292.3233
www.landmarkcenter.org
The downtown cultural center for music, dance, theater, exhibitions, public forums, and countless special events.

Minnesota Children's Museum
10 Seventh St. W.
651.225.6000
www.mcm.org
A hands-on teaching and learning environment for children age 6 months to 10 years; closed Monday.

Minnesota History Center
345 Kellogg Blvd. W.
651.259.3000
www.mnhs.org
An interactive museum with changing exhibits that inform and inspire; free admission on Tuesday from 5 to 8 p.m.

MINNESOTA HISTORY
CENTER

Minnesota Korean War Veterans' Memorial

State Capitol Grounds

www.mdva.state.mn.us
/memorials

Installed in 1998, the complex bronze statues and paving stones stand in memory of the war years from 1950 to 1955.

Minnesota Museum of American Art

The Pioneer Building
Fourth and Robert Streets
651.797.2571
www.mmaa.org
The new MMAA is open! Come visit.

Minnesota State Capitol

75 Rev. Dr. Martin Luther King Jr. Blvd.
651.296.2881
www.mnhs.org/statecapitol
Designed by architect Cass Gilbert and opened in 1905; plan ahead for a theme tour, or choose the 45-minute overview (free, on the hour).

Minnesota Vietnam Veterans' Memorial

State Capitol Grounds
www.mvvm.org
Dedicated in 1992, this granite memorial honors the 68,000 Minnesotans who served.

Old Muskego Church

Luther Seminary
2481 Como Ave.
651.641.3456
www2.luthersem.edu/tour
Built in Racine, Wisconsin, by Norwegian immigrants, the log church was moved to Luther in 1904; contact the information desk for tour information.

Pig's Eye Island Heron Rookery Scientific & Natural Area

Ramsey County Twp 28N Rng 22W Sec 14,15,22,23 (See web page for directions.)
651.259.5800
www.dnr.state.mn.us/snas
/detail.html?id=sna01009
This metropolitan site, named after its famous settler, is notable for being one of the largest nesting sites for colonial waterbirds within the state. Species that nest in the rookery include great blue heron, great egret, black-crowned nightheron, double-crested cormorants, and yellow-crowned night-heron.

Ramsey County Courthouse and Saint Paul City Hall

15 Kellogg Blvd. W.
651.266.8002
www.co.ramsey.mn.us
This 21-story art deco high-rise includes Carl Milles's imposing statue Vision of Peace; self-guided tours and by appointment during weekday work hours.

Raptor Center

University of Minnesota
1920 Fitch Ave.
612.624.4745
www.raptor.cvm.umn.edu

A learning center that's hospital and home to birds of prey; closed on Monday and University holidays.

Roy Wilkins Memorial

State Capitol Grounds

Designed by Curtis Patterson, this memorial was erected in 1995 to honor prominent civil rights activist Roy Wilkins.

Saint Paul Central Library

90 Fourth St. W.
651.266.7000
www.stpaul.lib.mn.us

Italian Renaissance revival building completed in 1917; guided tours available the first Sunday of the month at 1:30 p.m.

The Schubert Club Museum

Landmark Center
75 Fifth St. W.
651.292.3267
www.schubert.org

An interpretive guide to keyboards, the recital tradition, and an Ordway manuscript collection; Sunday through Friday, 12 to 4 p.m. (free).

© smm.org

Exploring the dinosaur fossil exhibit at the Science Museum of Minnesota

SCIENCE MUSEUM of MINNESOTA

"BIG BACK YARD"
GARDEN OF NATIVE PLANTS
(SCIENCE MUSEUM)

Science Museum of Minnesota
120 Kellogg Blvd. W.
651.221.9444
www.smm.org
Dynamic traveling exhibits, and science movie thrills at the Omnitheater.

Twin City
Model Railroad Museum
Bandana Square, Ste. 222
1021 East Bandana Blvd.
651.647.9628
www.tcmrm.org
State-of-the-art miniature railroads plus a toy train division; American Flyer, Lionel, K-Line, MTH, and other formats.

Union Depot
214 Fourth St. E.
www.uniondepot.org
651.202.2700
Transformed from a defunct rail station to an active transportation center in the heart of a thriving urban neighborhood, Union Depot is a historic gem that will be the terminus of the Twin Cities' newest LRT line, connecting the downtowns of Minneapolis and Saint Paul.

Wabasha Street Caves
215 Wabasha St. South
651.292.1220
www.wabashastreetcaves.com
Cave tours Thursday at 5 p.m., Saturday and Sunday at 11 a.m. Gangster tours Saturday at noon.

Delis, Grocers, and Food Co-ops

Aesop's Table
919 North Dale St.
651.488.6591
www.aesopstable.com
Friendly, family-owned business since 1986. Great home cooking and gourmet food. Come in and try the daily specials!

Al-Salam Halal Market
160 George St.
651.493.7807
Sample a variety of East African and even Indian specialties, along with fresh roasted coffee at the coffee bar.

Cecil's Delicatessen, Bakery, and Restaurant
651 Cleveland Ave. S.
651.698.6276
www.cecilsdeli.com
Committed to quality delicatessen fare for three generations; delivery available.

Coastal Seafoods
74 Snelling Ave. S.
651.698.4888
www.coastalseafoods.com
Serving and educating the community since 1993.

Cossetta Italian Market & Pizza
211 Seventh St. W.
651.222.3476
Cafeteria-style classic Italian food and a gourmet grocery shop.

Destiny Café at Sunrise Market
995 University Ave. W.
651.209.3392
1151 Clarence St, Ste. 101
651.771.1409
Hmong deli and sit-down restaurant. $$

El Burrito Mercado
175 Cesar Chavez St.
651.227.2192
www.elburritomercado.com
Shop and eat at this authentic Mexican taquería in the West Side Supermercado.

Golden Fig
790 Grand Ave.
651.602.0144
www.goldenfig.com
Specialty foods items blended and bottled in small batches on a weekly basis.

Hampden Park Food Co-op
928 Raymond Ave.
651.646.6686
www.hampdenparkcoop.com
Organic, unprocessed, bulk, fresh foods; member discounts and a common interest.

Heartland Restaurant & Farm Direct Market
289 E. Fifth St.
651.699.3536
www.heartlandrestaurant.com
Lunch, dinner, and weekend brunch with an attached gourmet market of meats, produce, and dairy.

J.P.'s Deli East

9th Floor, Human Services
  Building
444 Lafayette Rd. N
651.266.4089
www.wabashadeli.com
  /jps-deli.html
*Specializing in made-from-scratch
comfort food at this and other
locations. (See Landmark Deli and
Wabasha Deli)*

Landmark Deli

345 Saint Peter St., Suite 201
Landmark Towers (In the
  Skyway)
651.224.5573
www.wabashadeli.com
  /landmark-deli.html
*Specializing in made-from-scratch
comfort food at this and other
locations. (See J.P's Deli East and
Wabasha Deli)*

Lulu's Market & Deli

1626 Selby Ave.
651.645.2160
www.mylulus.com
*Under new ownership to provide all
your daily needs.*

Mississippi Market Food Co-op

1500 Seventh St. W.
651.690.0507
622 Selby Ave.
651.310.9499
www.msmarket.coop
*Mindful deli and sustainable shop-
ping with an emphasis on organic
and local foods.*

Morelli's Market

535 Tedesco Street (at Payne
  Ave.)
651.774.5961
www.morellismarket.com
*Since 1915, providing a wide selec-
tion of meats, wines, beers, and
Italian fare on St. Paul's East Side.*

Nelson Cheese & Deli

1562 Como Ave.
651.647.1288
www.nelsoncheese.net
*A full-service store for over 150
years with a complete selection
of cheeses direct from factories
throughout the Upper Midwest.*

Rivertown Market

437 Wabasha N.
651.224.4828
www.rivertownmarket.com
*Downtown's full-service grocery
store.*

St. Paul Cheese Shop

1573 Grand Ave.
651.698.3391
www.france44cheeseshop.com
*An rBGH-free cheese list, cured-
meat sandwiches, and delicious
accompaniments.*

Wabasha Deli & Cafe

32 East Fillmore Ave.
651.291.8868
www.wabashadeli.com
*Specializing in made-from-
scratch comfort food. Serving the historic West Side
and surrounding area.*

LOWERTOWN
BALLPARK

Sports and Competitions

Midway Baseball
1221 Marshall Ave.
651.659.1391
www.rteamsite.com/league
   /midwaybaseball
*Premier youth little league baseball
at historic Dunning Fields.*

Minnesota Boat Club
1 Wabasha S.
651.228.1602
www.boatclub.org
Learn to row on Raspberry Island.

Minnesota Men's Roller Derby
600 Cedar St.
www.tcterrors.com
*Destruction Workers, Skate Pauli
Boys, and TC Terrors at the Armory.*

Minnesota RollerGirls
175 Kellogg Blvd. W., Ste. 501
651.265.4899
www.mnrollergirls.com
*Fast-paced action at Roy Wilkins
Auditorium.*

Minnesota Swarm
317 Washington St.
888.MN.SWARM
www.mnswarm.com
Lacrosse for the whole family.

Minnesota Wild
317 Washington St.
651.222.WILD (box office)
www.wild.com
*The State of Hockey's NHL games at
the Civic Center.*

Hockey night at the Xcel Energy Center for the Minnesota Wild
© Kyle Hanson/RKH-images.com

Opposite: Artist renderings of the Lowertown Ballpark
Courtesy City of Saint Paul

Saint Paul Bicycle Racing Club

www.spbrc.org
Bringing all levels of cyclists together for fun and competition.

St. Paul Blackhawks Soccer Club

875 Orchard Ave.
651.894.2437
www.blackhawksoccer.org
A year-round soccer development and training center.

Saint Paul Curling Club

470 Selby Ave.
651.224.7408
www.stpaulcurlingclub.org
Pull up a chair at the viewing windows.

St. Paul Figure Skating Club

848 Pleasant Ave.
612.804.0328
www.stpaulfsc.org
Skate Saint Paul all year round.

St. Paul Hiking Club

1647 Brooks Ave. E., Maplewood
651.693.4412
www.stpaulhike.org
Happiness—one step at a time.

St. Paul Pioneers Football

Seafoam Stadium
1380 Concordia Ave.
612.804.2461
www.pioneersfootball.org
Semi-pro football is back in Saint Paul.

St. Paul Saints

1771 Energy Park Dr.
651.644.6659
www.saintsbaseball.com
Saint Paul's minor league baseball games at Midway Stadium.

Saints COMING TO LOWERTOWN

We wish they all could be Minnesotan Rollergirls.

Parks, Recreation, and Nature Reserves

The city of Saint Paul is home to one of the best park systems in the country and features well-kept hiking trails, sports facilities, woodlots, picnic areas, and fishing piers. Saint Paul holds so many parks that this publication was unable to include all of them. The following is a compilation of community and regional retreats that best represent the city—a list that offers something unique for sports and fitness fans, pet lovers, urban anglers, nature enthusiasts, and the child within all of us. For more information visit www.stpaul.gov/index.aspx?NID=245

Arlington/Arkwright Park (Community)
400 Arlington Ave. E.
651.632.5111
Known for a large off-leash dog area, this park includes wooded trails and a long, rounded slope that is perfect for play. It is tucked in a quiet neighborhood with a nearby baseball and soccer field. There is also a shelter for rainy picnic days.

Aurora/St. Anthony's Community Peace Sanctuary Garden
851 Aurora Avenue
www.aurorastanthony.org /partners.html
The garden exists to create a Social and Environmental Peace Sanctuary. Partners in this effort include Sabathani Community Center, St. Paul Area Public Schools Learning Center, Maxfield Elementary School, the St. Paul Police Department, and the Summit/University WEED/SEED program.

Battle Creek Recreation Center
75 South Winthrop Street
St. Paul, MN 55119
651.501.6347

Bruce Vento Nature Sanctuary (East of Downtown)
Commercial St. and Fourth St. E.
651.266.6400
www.nps.gov/miss/planyour visit /ventosanctuary.htm
This sanctuary, located along the north shore of the Mississippi River east of downtown Saint Paul, was/is a significant site for Native Americans. Activities include walking and bicycling the trails, birdwatching, photography, and nature observation.

Celeste's Dream Community Garden

1884 Randolph Ave.

www.csjstpaul.org
/celeste2010_garden.aspx

Celeste's Dream is a ministry of the Sisters of St. Joseph Carondelet & Consociates St. Paul Province. The goals of the garden are to learn organic growing methods, to enjoy healthy heirloom produce, to build community with the earth and other gardeners, to participate in a local food system, and to share the harvest!

Clarence W. Wigington Pavilion

200 Dr. Justus Ohage Blvd.

www.stpaul.gov/index
.aspx?NID=278

The Clarence W. Wigington Pavilion on Harriet Island is located at 200 Dr. Justus Ohage Blvd. across the Mississippi River from downtown Saint Paul. It is a beautiful 5,000-square-foot, year-round rental facility.

College Park (Community)

2223 Carter Ave.

www.ci.stpaul.mn.us/facilities
.aspx?search=1&CID=1&RID
=19&Page=detail

College Park is a bit of a hidden gem for tennis players. There's also a small playground for the kids and lots of green space.

Community Design Center– Dayton's Bluff Children's Garden

3rd St. and Maria

Since 1996 the Community Design Center has engaged youth from St. Paul's East Side in sustainable urban agriculture.

Como Park (Regional)

1199 Midway Pkwy.

651.632.5111

A Saint Paul jewel for over 100 years, Como Park plays a vital role in the social and recreational needs of the city. Both the shelter and pavilion provide electricity and seating for private events, and Como Lake, Como Zoo, and the Marjorie McNeely Conservatory are busy destinations year round.

Como Regional Park Pool

1151 Como Ave.

www.ci.stpaul.mn.us/index
.aspx?NID=2664

Como Regional Park Pool is located in the Como neighborhood of Saint Paul across from the Como Zoo and Conservatory. This facility features a main pool equipped with two basketball hoops, a 400-foot lazy river, and an aquatic zone. There is also a diving area well equipped with a one-meter diving board, two diving platforms, and an aquatic climbing wall.

Conway Recreation Center

2090 Conway Ave.

651.501.6343

www.stpaul.gov/facilities
.aspx?RID=115&Page=detail

Facility amenities: baseball field, basketball court, child play area, craft room, fitness room, general ice rink, kitchen, large gym, meeting room, multi-purpose room, softball fields, tennis courts, and warming room.

Crosby Farm Park (Regional)

2595 Crosby Farm Rd.

651.632.5111

In 1858 the park was the 160-acre farm of English immigrant Thomas Crosby. It now offers multiple trails for hiking and jogging, a sandy beach, and a picnic shelter.

Dayton's Bluff Recreation Center

800 Conway St.

651.793.3885

www.stpaul.gov/facilities.aspx?pa genum=3&RID=116&Page=detail

Facilities: auditorium/theater, baseball field, child play area, computer lab, craft room, dance studio, game room, kitchen, large gym, meeting rooms, 3 softball fields, 2 tennis courts, and warming room.

Gateway State Trail

Located on a converted rail-trail, the Gateway State Trail offers 18 miles of paved trail for non-motorized use. www.dnr.state.mn.us/state _trails/gateway/index.html

The trail begins in the city of St. Paul, travels northeast through the cities of Maplewood, North St. Paul, and Oakdale, through Washington County, and ends at Pine Point Regional Park, just 4 miles northwest of the city of Stillwater. It is generally level and wheelchair accessible.

Harriet Island Park (Regional)

200 Dr. Justus Ohage Blvd.

651.292.7010

Historic Harriet Island hosts festivals and books riverboat excursions all summer long. Just across the Mississippi from downtown, it features a newly renovated picnic area with a large shelter and easy parking.

Hidden Falls (Regional)

1415 Mississippi River Blvd. S.

651.632.5111

The scenic beauty of the waterfall is worth planning a visit. With spacious grounds, towering trees, a boat launch, and a picnic area, Hidden Falls offers a variety of summer activities.

Highland Park (Regional)

1200 Montreal Ave.

651.632.5111

Acquired in 1925, Highland Park now features an 18-hole golf course, aquatic center, pavilion, picnic shelters, and a Frisbee golf course.

Hillcrest Recreation Center

1978 Ford Pkwy.

651.695.3706

www.stpaul.gov/facilities.aspx?pa
   genum=5&RID=130&Page=detail

Home of the Jewish Theatre Company and other community events. Facilities: auditorium/theater, baseball field, child play area, computer lab, small craft room, dance studio, game room, kitchen, large gym, large meeting rooms, 3 softball fields, 2 tennis courts, and warming room.

Indian Mounds Park (Regional)

10 Mounds Blvd.

651.632.5111

An integral part of Minnesota's history, this park on the bluffs is home to native prairie flowers and a Native American Indian burial ground. Enjoy a stroll through the past with a view of downtown and the banks of the ancient River Warren.

Iris Park

1884 University Ave. W.

Saint Paul, MN 55104

651.632.5111

www.stpaul.gov/facilities.aspx?pa
   genum=22&RID=54&Page=detail

Quaint quiet park nestled along the light rail line.

Irvine Park (Neighborhood)

251 Walnut St.

651.632.5111

The beautifully ornate fountain is a central feature of this popular park for weddings. Nestled in a neighborhood just west of downtown, it offers shelter, seating, and electricity.

Kellogg Mall (Neighborhood)

62 Kellogg Blvd. E.

651.632.5111

An inspiring view of Mississippi commerce lies just beyond the wall, while two fountains and an arbor are reminders of work's rewards. The mall offers a view of fireworks on the Fourth of July and during the Winter Carnival.

Lilydale Park (Regional)

950 Lilydale Rd.

651.632.5111

Bring the whole family for a day enjoying the picnic shelters, athletic fields, riverboat cruises, and boating and fishing on Pickerel Lake.

Marydale Park (Community)
542 Maryland Ave. W.
651.632.5111
This park surrounds Loeb Lake and has a fishing pier where anglers cast for crappies, bluegills, bullheads, and (on a good day) bass. It is designated as a children's fishing pond by the Minnesota Department of Natural Resources.

Mears Park (Community)
221 E. Fifth St.
651.632.5111
Lowertown's gem has a bandstand for summer music and a garden stream running from corner to corner. It's surrounded by after-work hot spots like Barrio, the Bulldog, and Bin Wine Bar.

Newell Park (Community)
900 North Fairview Ave.
651.632.5111
One of the oldest green spaces in the city, with rolling hills and large oaks, this 10-acre plot is the place for Frisbee with friends or to sit and read a book. The pavilion is perfect for family get-togethers and has been standing since 1929.

Oxford Community Center
270 Lexington Pkwy. N.
651.642.0650
www.stpaul.gov/index
   .aspx?nid=1743
Located in the heart of the historic Rondo neighborhood of Saint Paul and reconstructed from the Oxford/ Jimmy Lee Recreation Center built in the 1960s, the new Jimmy Lee Recreation Center & Great River Water Park continues to play a vital role in the community. This comprehensive community center combines water park features and state-of-the-art recreation and fitness amenities.

Delfeayo Marsalis Octet performing in Mears Park

Phalen Park (Regional)

1615 Phalen Dr.

651.632.5111

Featuring a peaceful lagoon and family-friendly amphitheater with sparkling Lake Phalen just a few yards beyond, this East Side park is the city's beach for hot summer days.

Pig's Eye Island Heron Rookery Scientific & Natural Area

Ramsey County Twp 28N Rng 22W Sec 14,15,22,23 (See web page for directions.)

651.259.5800

www.dnr.state.mn.us/snas /detail.html?id=sna01009

This metropolitan site, named after its famous settler, is notable for being one of the largest nesting sites for colonial waterbirds within the state. Species that nest in the rookery include great blue heron, great egret, black-crowned night-heron, double-crested cormorant, and yellow-crowned night-heron.

Rice Park (Community)

109 Fourth St. W.

651.632.5111

Surrounded by the Saint Paul Hotel, Landmark Center, Ordway, and Central Library, Rice Park features bronze statues and a beautiful fountain encircled with inviting park benches.

Samuel Morgan Regional Trail

Between Hwy 5 and Interstate 35E

www.stpaul.gov/index .aspx?NID=3698

The Samuel Morgan Regional Trail follows the Mississippi River waterfront in downtown St. Paul. It shows just how much redevelopment St. Paul has done with its riverfront area.

West Minnehaha Recreation Center

685 W. Minnehaha Ave.

651.298.5823

www.stpaul.gov/facilities.aspx? pagenum=11&RID=152&Page= detail

Facility amenities: baseball field, basketball court, child play area, craft room, game room, gym, kitchen, meeting room, softball field, and tennis courts.

Western Park (Community)

387 Marion St.

651.632.5111

This art park features a sculpture garden, including the work Democracy Speaks: standing 17 feet tall in fabricated steel, this newest installation was created by John Hock and Andrew MacGuffie.

Saint Paul Public Libraries

The Saint Paul library system provides resources for everyone, from children studying a beloved subject to adults reading their favorite newspaper on a day off from work. Offering many literary, historical, and cultural events, Saint Paul libraries also provide further learning for eager minds of the city. Each library provides a calm, safe learning environment to read, study, surf the Web, or search for information. The following is a listing of all Saint Paul's libraries, locations, and hours. All locations are handicapped-accessible. For further information visit www.stpaul.lib.mn.us.

Arlington Hills
1105 Greenbrier St.
651.793.3930

M	12 p.m.–8 p.m.
T	10 a.m.–5:30 p.m.
W	12 p.m.–8 p.m.
TH	10 a.m.–5:30 p.m.
F	10 a.m.–5:30 p.m.
SA	11 a.m.–5:30 p.m.
SU	CLOSED

Central Library
90 West Fourth St
651.266.7000

M	12 p.m.–8 p.m.
T	9 a.m.–5:30 p.m.
W	9 p.m.–5:30 p.m.
TH	9 a.m.–5:30 p.m.
F	9 a.m.–5:30 p.m.
SA	11 a.m.–5 p.m.
SU	1 p.m.–5 p.m.

© Bianca Pettis

Rondo Community Outreach Library

Dayton's Bluff
645 East Seventh St.
651.793.1699
- M   12 p.m.—8 p.m.
- T   10 a.m.—5:30 p.m.
- W   12 p.m.—8 p.m.
- TH   10 a.m.—5:30 p.m.
- F   10 a.m.—5:30 p.m.
- SA   11:30 a.m.—5 p.m.
- SU   1 p.m.—5 p.m.

Hamline Midway
1588 West Minnehaha Ave.
651.642.0293
- M   12 p.m.—8 p.m.
- T   10 a.m.—5:30 p.m.
- W   12 p.m.—8 p.m.
- TH   10 a.m.—5:30 p.m.
- F   10 a.m.—5:30 p.m.
- SA   11:30 a.m.—5 p.m.
- SU   CLOSED

Hayden Heights
1456 White Bear Ave.
651.793.3934
- M   12 p.m.—8 p.m.
- T   10 a.m.—5:30 p.m.
- W   12 p.m.—8 p.m.
- TH   10 a.m.—5:30 p.m.
- F   10 a.m.—5:30 p.m.
- SA   11:30 a.m.—5 p.m.
- SU   CLOSED

Highland Park
1794 Ford Pkwy.
651.695.3700
- M   10 a.m.—8 p.m.
- T   10 a.m.—8 p.m.
- W   10 a.m.—8 p.m.
- TH   10 a.m.—8 p.m.
- F   10 a.m.—5:30 p.m.
- SA   10 a.m.—5:30 p.m.
- SU   1 p.m.—5 p.m.

Merriam Park
1831 Marshall Ave.
651.642.0385
TTY: 651.298.4184
- M   12 p.m.—8 p.m.
- T   10 a.m.—5:30 p.m.
- W   12 p.m.—8 p.m.
- TH   10 a.m.—5:30 p.m.
- F   10 a.m.—5:30 p.m.
- SA   11:30 a.m.—5 p.m.
- SU   CLOSED

Rice Street
1011 Rice St.
651.558.2223
- M   12 p.m.—8 p.m.
- T   10 a.m.—5:30 p.m.
- W   12 p.m.—8 p.m.
- TH   10 a.m.—5:30 p.m.
- F   10 a.m.—5:30 p.m.
- SA   11:30 a.m.—5 p.m.
- SU   1 p.m.—5 p.m.

Riverview
1 East George St.
651.292.6626
- M   12 p.m.—8 p.m.
- T   10 a.m.—5:30 p.m.
- W   12 p.m.—8 p.m.
- TH   10 a.m.—5:30 p.m.
- F   10 a.m.—5:30 p.m.
- SA   11:30 a.m.—5 p.m.
- SU   CLOSED

Rondo Community Outreach

461 North Dale St.
651.266.7400
TTY: 651.266.7485

M	10 a.m.—8 p.m.
T	10 a.m.—8 p.m.
W	10 a.m.—8 p.m.
TH	10 a.m.—8 p.m.
F	10 a.m.—5:30 p.m.
SA	10 a.m.—5:30 p.m.
SU	1 p.m.—5 p.m.

St. Anthony Park

2245 Como Ave.
651.642.0411

M	12 p.m.—8 p.m.
T	10 a.m.—5:30 p.m.
W	12 p.m.—8 p.m.
TH	10 a.m.—5:30 p.m.
F	10 a.m.—5:30 p.m.
SA	11:30 a.m.—5 p.m.
SU	CLOSED

Sun Ray

2105 Wilson Ave.
651.501.6300

M	10 a.m.—8 p.m.
T	10 a.m.—8 p.m.
W	10 a.m.—8 p.m.
TH	10 a.m.—8 p.m.
F	10 a.m.—5:30 p.m.
SA	10 a.m.—5:30 p.m.
SU	1 p.m.—5 p.m.

West Seventh

265 Oneida St.
651.298.5516

M	12:30 p.m.—8 p.m.
T	11:30 a.m.—5:30 p.m.
W	10 a.m.—5:30 p.m.
TH	12:30 p.m.—8 p.m.
F	10 a.m.—5:30 p.m.
SA	CLOSED
SU	CLOSED

Courtesy Saint Paul Public Library

Songs and Stories with the Klondike Kates, Central Library

Saint Paul District Councils

The district council planning process was created more than thirty years ago to help support each of Saint Paul's unique neighborhoods. There are seventeen councils in Saint Paul. Their responsibilities include developing the community geographically, socially, and economically, and planning and sponsoring community events. It is easy and satisfying to take part in your council. Find your district below and get involved today. A map with more information is available at www.stpaul.gov/index.aspx?NID=1212.

District 1
Eastview, Conway, Battle Creek, and Highwood Hills neighborhoods
2105½ Old Hudson Rd.
55119
651.578.7600
www.district1council.org

District 2
Beaver Lake Heights, East Phalen, Frost Lake, Hayden Heights, Hazel Park, Hillcrest, Lincoln Park, Parkway/Greenbrier, Phalen Village, and Prosperity Heights neighborhoods
1365 Prosperity Ave.
55106
651.774.2220
www.district2council.org

District 3
West Side Citizens Organization
1 W. Water St., Ste. 260
55107
651.293.1708
www.wsco.org

District 4
Dayton's Bluff Community Council
798 E. Seventh St.
55106
651.772.2075
www.daytonsbluff.org

District 5
Payne-Phalen Planning Council
506 Kenny Rd., Ste. 130
55130
651.774.5234
www.paynephalen.org

District 6
North End and South Como neighborhoods
171 Front Ave.
55117
651.488.4485
www.district6stpaul.org

District 7
East Midway, Frogtown, Mt. Airy, and Capitol Heights neighborhoods
685 Minnehaha Ave. W.
55104
651.789.7480
www.frogtownmn.org

District 8
Summit-University Planning Council
627 Selby Ave.
55104
651.228.1855
www.summit-u.com

District 9
West Seventh/Fort Road Federation
974 W. Seventh St.
55102
651.298.5599
www.fortroadfederation.org

District 10
Como Park, Energy Park, and Como Campus (zoo, park, and lake) neighborhoods
1224 Lexington Pkwy. N.
55103
651.644.3889
www.district10comopark.org

District 11
Hamline Midway Coalition
1558 Minnehaha Ave. W.
55104
651.494.7682
www.hamlinemidway.org

District 12
St. Anthony Park Community Council
890 Cromwell Ave.
55114
651.649.5992
www.sapcc.org

District 13
Union Park District Council
1570 Concordia Ave., Ste. LL100
55104
651.645.6887
www.unionparkdc.org

District 14
Macalester-Groveland Community Council
320 Griggs St. S.
55105
651.695.4000
www.macgrove.org

District 15
Highland District Council
1978 Ford Pkwy.
55116
651.695.4005
www.highlanddistrictcouncil.org

District 16
Summit Hill Association
860 St. Clair Ave.
55105
651.222.1222
www.summithillassociation.org

District 17
CapitolRiver Council
101 E. Fifth St., Ste. 240
55101
651.221.0488
www.capitalrivercouncil.org

Voter Registration

Ramsey County Elections Office
90 West Plato Blvd., Suite 160
Saint Paul, MN 55107
651.266.2171

To learn about your precinct location and caucus location, view the election calendar or see a sample ballot, and for all other voting information, visit www.co.ramsey.mn.us/elections.

For online voter registration, also visit www.projectvote.org or www.rockthevote.com. Remember to vote!

League of Women Voters registering women to vote, circa 1923

Contributor Biographies

BRITT AAMODT is a lifelong suburbanite who can be seen wandering the streets of Saint Paul periodically under the guidance of local tour guide Selby the Dog.

TA-COUMBA AIKEN is a Twin Cities artist, arts administrator, educator, and community activist who focuses on public art and collaborative projects. His "rhythm paintings" on paper and canvas are loose and lively. He has participated in the creation of over 300 murals and public art sculptures, with themes ranging from local history to the artist's own style of rhythmic pattern and spirit writing. His works can be found in public and private collections, including those of the Walker Art Center, General Mills, Herbie Hancock, Taj Mahal, and Maya Angelou. www.Ta-coumbaAiken.com

LOUIS ALEMAYEHU is a writer, educator, activist, poet, father, and grandfather of African and Native American heritage. He provides workshops and consultations on racism, culture, environmental justice, and community building. His writing has appeared in national and international publications such as *The International Process Work Journal*, *DRUM*, and *The Energy Bulletin*. Alemayehu is a founding member of the seminal, award-winning poetry/jazz ensemble Ancestor Energy. In 2009, the Minnesota Spoken Word Association gave Alemayehu an Urban Griot award for thirty years of excellence as a pioneering spoken word artist. In 2012, the Process Work Institute in Portland, Oregon, certified Louis as a "World Work Elder."

Z LU ALEXANDER is a Gardener, Artist, and Healer, ZZ lives with her Dog and Cat and Houseplants, collecting Rocks and Feathers wherever she goes.

KIRK ANDERSON creates political cartoons, humorous illustration, and graphic design, now gluten-free. Molotov Comix Press, Saint Paul, Minnesota. Smell the satire. www.MolotovComics.com

POLYXENI ANGELIS was born in Athens, Greece. She holds a bachelor of arts degree in sociology from the University of Minnesota. Her work appears in the 2011 *Montreal Prize Global Poetry Anthology* and the *Burlesque Press Online Journal*. Writing is her passion, and please, don't ever call her Polly.

SERENA MIRA ASTA is an artist and writer in Lowertown. She is also a singer and a self-aware art supply addict. She loves spinning and dyeing, but is careful how often she says that out loud. www.AstaArt.com

KEN AVIDOR, the artist who created the cover to this book and whose full page art appears throughout this edition, is a cartoonist and illustrator living in a loft in Lowertown's Union Depot with his wife, Roberta Avidor (creator of the Saint Paul Almanac maps). Ken is also the custodian for and frequent contributor to the Twin Cities Urban Sketchers blog found at www.urbansketchers-twincities.blogspot.com. www.AvidorStudios.com

ROBERTA AVIDOR is the illustrator and updater of the Saint Paul Almanac maps. She works as an illustrator and lives at the Union Depot Lofts with her husband, Ken. She's a participant in the Twin Cities MetroSketchers and volunteers at Vail Place in Minneapolis running a watercolor workshop. www.AvidorStudios.com

CAROLINE BASSETT is an occasional poet (even published!) and sometime tango dancer. She directs The Wisdom Institute and teaches at Capella and Walden Universities. A transplanted Easterner, she loves the nature and culture, winter and water of the Twin Cities. She also loves and is loved by an Irreverent Insouciant.

WILLIAM BIRAWER was born in Saint Paul, received his BFA in illustration from the College of Visual Arts in the spring of 1999. William works as a freelance illustrator and caricature artist. www.WilliamBirawer.com

HARRIET BISHOP (1817–1883) came to Minnesota in 1847 and became Saint Paul's first teacher, established the first Sunday school, and was one of the founders of many social movements, such as women's suffrage. She wrote four books, both nonfiction and poetry.

DAVID BORNUS is a state employee who works in Saint Paul and lives in Shoreview. His is a true story of coming home from last year's *Saint Paul Almanac* reading. (Note: upon reaching home, he found the spider dead inside the napkin ball. Of course you wanted to know . . .)

WENDY BROWN-BÁEZ is a writer, teacher, performance poet, and installation artist. She is the author of *Ceremonies of the Spirit* and *Transparencies of Light*, and her prose and poetry have been published in numerous literary journals. She has performed her poetry nationally and in Mexico, in cafés, bars, galleries, cabarets, and community centers. Wendy is the creator of Writing Circles for Healing. She received McKnight Foundation and Minnesota State Arts Board grants to present writing workshops for at-risk youth and for nonprofits and is a member of the Minnesota Prison Writers Collective. She is the writing instructor for the after-school program at Face to Face Academy in Saint Paul, where she is kept on her toes. www.wendybrownbaez.com

HENRY L. BUSHNELL is a senior at Central High School. Unlike many teenagers nowadays, he is neither a punk nor a juvenile delinquent. He enjoys singing, acting, and helping old ladies across the street.

COLLEEN CASEY uses language and other arts to facilitate positive transformation. From Bdote and of Mdewakanton Dakota and European-American heritages, Colleen considers herself a person of crosscurrents and confluences. Through her work in community-driven educational programming, Colleen helps others build their voices. She believes we are all related.

KATE CAVETT has spent hundreds of hours listening to more than 200 individuals share their reflections on Saint Paul, careers, racism, passions, sorrows, challenges and successes. Her book, *Voices of Rondo: Oral Histories of Saint Paul's Historic Black Community*, won the 2006 Minnesota Book Award. She continues her dedication to document the stories of ordinary people with extraordinary lives.

ELENA CISNEROS is a writer and artist who grew up on the Pine Ridge Reservation. After serving as an assistant editor for *Water-Stone Review* and receiving an MFA from Hamline University, she returned to South Dakota, and writes and works in Kyle.

AMY CLARK—mother, wife, artist, teacher, writer, athlete. Student, singer, reader, caretaker of many animals. Tired most of the time, but happy.

DONTE COLLINS is an American Slam/Performance poet. Known for his spoken word poetry, he is a Minnesota spoken word finalist and the co-founder and co-director of No Projection, a group of four brothers aiming to use spoken word as an inspirational tool. Donte performs all over the Twin Cities, including at Walker Art Center, Orchestra Hall, Pillsbury House Theatre, and Penumbra Theatre. He is currently the highest-ranked youth poet in the Twin Cities and will compete in the 2013 international spoken word competition Brave New Voices. Donte is a junior at Community of Peace Academy in Saint Paul.

CAROL CONNOLLY was appointed by Mayor Chris Coleman as Saint Paul's first poet laureate. She is a longtime media columnist and curates and hosts the monthly Readings by Writers series, now in its fourteenth year, at the historic University Club of Saint Paul. Her book of poems *Payments Due* is in its fifth printing from Midwest Villages and Voices; her most recent book is *All This and More* from Nodin Press, 2009. She received the 2011 Kay Sexton Award for her dedication to literary activity in Minnesota.

MARYANN CORBETT earned a doctorate in medieval literature and linguistics from the University of Minnesota and expected to be teaching Beowulf and Chaucer and the history of English. Instead, she's spent more than thirty years working for the Minnesota Legislature in the Office of the Revisor of Statutes. Her poems, translations, essays, and reviews have been published in more than one hundred journals and several anthologies. Her two books are *Credo for the Checkout Line in Winter* (Able Muse, 2013) and *Breath Control* (David Robert Books, 2012).

LAWRENCE DANIELS has a deep love for chess, tennis, and fishing. The biggest bass he has caught was five and one-half pounds, at Como Lake! He also has a love for writing and producing short films, as well as for photography and long walks through the parks.

HOLLY DAY is a housewife and mother of two living in Minneapolis. She teaches community education needlepoint classes in Minneapolis and writing classes at The Loft. Her poetry has recently appeared in *The Worcester Review*, *Broken Pencil*, and *Slipstream*, and she is the recipient of the 2011 Sam Ragan Poetry Prize.

CAPTAIN BOB DECK is a substitute teacher in Saint Paul and a riverboat pilot for the Padelford Packet Boat Co. He writes for *Big River Magazine* and has recently self-published his towboat piloting memoir, *Between the Sticks*, as an ebook.

ELIZABETH DINGMANN was born and raised in Minnesota. She currently lives in Minneapolis with her partner and is a student in the MFA program at Hamline University. Elizabeth's work has been published in *DOGEAR*, *Studio One*, and *Among Women*. Her poetry has also been selected for the mnLIT What Light Poetry Project.

NORITA DITTBERNER-JAX was born in Frogtown and has lived in Saint Paul all of her life. She thinks the city is beautiful, with its hills and flatlands congregating around the Mississippi River. Her widely published poetry collections include *The Watch, Longing for Home,* and *What They Always Were.*

SHAUNTÉ "DR3AMCH8SR" DOUGLAS is a new spoken word artist and writer who lives in Saint Paul, and works at the Mall of America and Barnes and Noble Booksellers. She is an admitted art addict and certified shopaholic who hopes to do more work with the *Saint Paul Almanac.*

SUSAN DOWNING had being a Sidewalk Poetry winner on her bucket list. Writing has long been her hobby, from letters to the editor and doggerel poems for friends' birthdays, babies, and weddings to unfinished screenplays. She and her husband recently became empty nesters and are enjoying opportunities to travel.

TOM DUNN is an award-winning photographer specializing in business and art photography. Tom photographs on location and at his Northern Warehouse studio located in Lowertown. www.tomdunnphoto.com

D. STEPHEN ELLIOT lives in Lowertown with his wife, an artist, and daughter, a poet. They LOVE Minnesota!

HEID E. ERDRICH is author of four poetry collections, most recently *Cell Traffic: New and Selected Poems*. She is Ojibwe from the Turtle Mountain Band, and she grew up in Wahpeton, North Dakota. Heid is a longtime college professor and now an independent scholar, as well as a frequent visiting writer at educational and cultural institutions. She also curates art exhibits and runs an Ojibwe language press. A recipient of awards from The Loft Literary Center, the Archibald Bush Foundation and elsewhere, Heid has four times been nominated for the Minnesota Book Award, which she won in 2009 for her book National Monuments. She is a 2012–2013 Minnesota State Arts Board grant recipient.

TONY ERNST is a professional geek and amateur tinkerer. In his spare time, he wanders around with his camera waiting for something interesting to happen. He regularly posts photos at www.flickr.com/photos/gamelaner/.

SANDRA ERSKINE is not afraid to drink day-old coffee if her cup is small enough.

SAMANTHA ESGUERRA is an artist and aspiring illustrator currently working on her fixer-upper and living the dream in South Minneapolis. She lived in Saint Paul as a kid and remembers biking up a giant hill to get soft-serve. These days she reads constantly, grows an unruly garden, and enjoys biking to the lake to swim with her friends and dog. She loves her little brother and sister and when folks drop in for brunch.

NIMO H. FARAH uses language to express things she finds too confusing. Currently she is trying to develop her skills as an orator while blending Somali and English. She thinks herself charming and hilarious in the Somali language, often making herself laugh, but rarely does that humor translate into English. It'll be magical when she learns to fuse the two languages together seamlessly. Her poems and stories have been published in Water-Stone Review and the Saint Paul Almanac. As a storyteller she has shared her words at the Black Dog Café Lowertown Reading Jams, Equilibrium: Spoken Word at the Loft; and the Late Nite Series at Pillsbury House Theatre.

CHARLES MACOMB FLANDRAU (1871–1938) was born in Saint Paul and educated at Harvard, where he achieved his first literary success with Harvard Episodes (1897). He went on to write five more books, including the well-received travelogue Viva Mexico! (1909). He was theatre critic for the Saint Paul Pioneer Press, and also wrote for the Dispatch and Daily News, as well as contributed articles to the Saturday Evening Post.

DEBRA FRASIER, Minnesota author and illustrator, is the founder of the Alphabet Forest, the only permanent literacy activity area at state fairs in the United States.

ELI FREBERG is an aspiring author and straight A student who enjoys his work. At the age of thirteen, Eli is very busy juggling school, karate, and baseball. Besides writing, he enjoys drawing, camping, playing guitar, and hanging out with friends! An above-average kid living in Saint Paul, he strives to make a difference in his community and classroom.

MARGOT FORTUNATO GALT's book of poetry, Between the Houses (Laurel Poetry Collaborative, 2004), includes poems from more than twenty years of writing and publishing in more than sixty journals and anthologies, local and national. Her poetry and prose have received awards and grants from the Minnesota State Arts Board, the Loft, the Center for Arts Criticism, *Poets & Writers*, and others. She is also the author of the oral history memoir *Turning the Feather Around: My Life in Art* (Minnesota Historical Society Press, 1998), with Minnesota's premier Ojibwe artist, George Morrison.

MAYO GARNER was born and raised in Englewood, California, and began writing poetry at nine years of age, before moving to the Twin Cities. Tired of having emotions such as loss and grief build up inside, Mayo took to poetry as a positive outlet. Seeing his talent early, a homegirl of Mayo's asked him to promise her that he would take his writing seriously. You can say he's holding up his end of the bargain.

SAIBAL GHOSH is a digital photographer specializing in events, portraits, landscapes, architectural details, travel scenes, nature photos, and night and macro photography. He enjoys taking photos that capture everlasting moments. www.saibalghosh.com

GEORGIA A. GREELEY married into Saint Paul forty-four years ago. She has lived in the same Saint Paul house since April 11, 1971. She now has her dream job as an artist and writer and finds much inspiration from years in this capital city, which feels like a small-town neighborhood. She has an MFA from Hamline University and a B.A. from Saint Catherine's University. For more information, see her website at www.georgiaagreeley-artichokepress.com, and learn more than you might want to know.

LMNOP (LISA-MARIE GREENLY), a Saint Paul illustrator, can usually be found working on several bodies of work concurrently, often combining themes or media between them, frequently reworking an image in several forms to explore new ways to view a concept.

JAMIE HAGG is an English teacher at Gordon Parks High School and soccer coach for the Saint Paul Blackhawks. He has been a resident of Saint Paul for twenty years, after growing up "across the river." Jamie has three kids—Lili, Willy, and Dilly—and three dogs and three frogs. He'll have free time when he retires in another twenty years to do more of what he loves: writing, traveling, and playing music.

MONTE HANSON works at the Minnesota Department of Employment and Economic Development. He loves giant snowstorms, Cool Whip on anything, goat cheese, Scrabble, road trips, Lake Como, wild socks, the blues, Johnny Cash, and chocolate marshmallow ice cream with nuts.

When MARGARET HASSE was in grade school, learning poetry by heart was part of the curriculum. The first poem she chose was a short one by Emily Dickinson beginning: "I'm Nobody! Who are you?" She moved on to ballads like "The Highwayman" by Alfred Noyes with rhyme schemes that made memorization easier. *Earth's Appetite*, Margaret's fourth collection of poetry, released in 2013 by Nodin Press, relies more on image and metaphor than on rhyme.

ELDER RIVERA HERRADORA lives on the East Side of St. Paul with his wife and two baby twins.

KEVIN HERSHEY is a product of the intricate Catholic school system in Saint Paul. He writes as an activist trying to better understand the world he wishes to change.

JANE HOLLIS is a born-and-raised Saint Paulite. Having lived abroad, which she describes as "a bit interesting at times," she swears she will never leave her Saint Paul roots again, except for those brief, much-needed winter vacations. She works as a clinical psychologist—in Saint Paul, of course.

KORISSA HOWES, a Duluth-born Native American, has always had poetry and storytelling in her life. Through her culture's traditions and by using the library, she has always had a consistent relationship with poetry. Overcoming life's obstacles and surviving college in Saint Paul helped this relationship flourish.

JODY HUBER lives in the fine Saint Paul neighborhood of Merriam Park. And while she grew up in Duluth, she spent years away in Houston, Texas, and Edmonton, Alberta, before she came to her senses and returned to Minnesota. She is a freelance advertising copywriter who loves to read just about anything, with a penchant toward female fiction writers from Great Britain, India, and Russia.

KEMET EGYPT IMHOTEP was conceived in Oklahoma and born in Saint Paul. Kemet was left under the care of his great uncle and aunt through marriage. His aunt, Willia Mae Johnson, who was born on a plantation in Arkansas in 1918, was a strong believer in faith and trust in the Creator. Kemet says the school system failed him. He was in the class of 1990 at Central High School, and finished at the Area Learning Center located in the Uni-Dale mall. At present he says he is a lost troubled soul, still finding his way through the quicksand.

HILAL ISLER now drives around Saint Paul with confidence.

LOUIS JENKINS is the author of numerous books, most recently *Before You Know It: Prose Poems 1970–2005*; his book *Tin Flag: New and Selected Prose Poems* is forthcoming from Will O' the Wisp Books. He is a frequent guest on *A Prairie Home Companion*, and his poems have been published in many journals and anthologies, including *Great American Prose Poems* (Scribner, 2003). His play, *Nice Fish*, written in collaboration with renowned actor Mark Rylance, premiered at the Guthrie Theater in April 2013.

LEANN E. JOHNSON has been creating art (scratchboard illustration, relief printing, and tile design) for over fifteen years. A current resident of Minneapolis, she has illustrated for other publications, such as the *New York Times*. www.lea-way.com

RICHARD MERLIN JOHNSON JR. was born on May 20, 1972, on the Yankton Sioux Nation. His father, Richard Sr., and mother, Suzanne, met in Los Angeles, California, during the sixties. Richard Sr. was the then-director of the L. A. Indian Center and was the organizer for the Alcatraz Occupation. Richard Jr.'s life is greatly influenced by his parents' activism. He is Santee Sioux Dakota, Californian Chumash, and Chicano. Richard is an Artist, Poet, Writer, Painter, and Actor.

IBé KABA likes to write. Since he doesn't have the time or desire to follow rules, he writes free verse. He likes the word *free*, as in free to bend the rules of language any which way he wants. IBé likes to read poems out loud, especially to his children. But they don't seem to like it, at least not as much as strangers do. And speaking of strangers, they call him a spoken word poet. IBé likes this—having people listen to him read his poems. But he also wants you to read his poetry . . . for yourself. So he has a book, a chapbook, and of course has been featured on many CDs. IBé likes that you like him; however, if you visited AtlanticRock.com and spent more than fifteen minutes, he'd consider you a stalker, and probably would not want you to have his phone number.

PATSY KAHMANN is a nonfiction writer (she has witnesses to this story) who currently lives just across the river from Saint Paul. She spends hours in various Saint Paul coffeehouses writing her memoir, *House of Kahmanns*, about growing up in a family of twelve kids. Patsy is the second oldest, and her birthstone is opal, like her mother's.

SAED KAKISH's excitement at the approaching fifteenth birthday of his Cahoots Coffee Bar in the fall of 2012 soared to a more joyful level when his Moroccan Mocha won the coveted Charlie Award for Twin Cities' Outstanding Cup of Coffee. He continues to welcome all to drink coffee, sip tea, and enjoy other treats at his Selby-near-Snelling shop, including anonymous gourmet judges.

GARRISON KEILLOR is an author, humorist, host of *A Prairie Home Companion* radio show, and the proprietor of Common Good Books in Saint Paul. His first book of poetry, *O, What a Luxury: Verses Lyrical, Vulgar, Pathetic and Profound* (Grove Press) was published in fall 2013.

KATHRYN KYSAR is the author of two books of poetry, *Dark Lake* and *Pretend the World*, and she edited *Riding Shotgun: Women Write about Their Mothers*. She has received fellowships from Banfill-Locke Center for the Arts, the Minnesota State Arts Board, the National Endowment for the Humanities, and the Anderson Center for Interdisciplinary Studies. She lives with her family in Saint Paul.

ALEX KUNO is a full-time artist and illustrator living and working in Lowertown. *The Miscreants of Tiny Town*, his ongoing series of darkly satirical fairy tale paintings and mixed media sculptures, has appeared in numerous solo and group shows in galleries and private collections throughout the Twin Cities and around the country. Kuno's work has also been featured on TPT's *MNOriginal* and is currently represented by Curly Tale Fine Art in Chicago.

GLORIA BURGESS LEVIN's heart remains in Saint Paul, where she lived all her life until several years ago. Now living in Minneapolis, she makes frequent forays across the river to walk favorite streets. She is a psychoanalyst in private practice.

ABE LEVINE was born in Boston, Massachusetts, and came to the Midwest to attend Macalester College. He discovered that plaid was "in," the Twin Cities had a lot to offer, and social structures are constructed, sometimes at the expense of human and animal rights. Coming from a Chinese American family, Abe was glad to find good Asian cuisine on University Avenue. He has been inspired by his adventurous, radiant, red-haired roommate and several other quirky and radically kind people in Saint Paul.

GOZONG LOR graduated from Central Senior High School and will be attending Macalester College in the fall of 2013. She is a student by day and masked crime-fighter by night. Her greatest weakness is a good book.

CHARLES MATSON LUME is a visual artist with an MFA from the University of Wisconsin—Madison. He has received fellowships from the Bush and Jerome Foundations, and the Minnesota State Arts Board. Charles finds illumination in the poetry of Gustaf Sobin, William Bronk, and Charles Wright.

PATRICK McCUTCHAN is an artist in Lowertown whose photography focuses on people, relationships, and communities. www.PatrickMcCutchan.com

TOM McGREGOR has had a studio in Lowertown since 1990. His love for this historic area of Saint Paul and the West Side neighborhood, where he lives with his wife, artist Jerri Jo Brandt, is evident in many of his plein air paintings. An active community member, his involvement with the Saint Paul Art Crawl dates back nearly twenty years. www.mcgregorart.com

DEBORAH McLAREN is a sustainable tourism specialist with a master's in social ecology. She has written two books, *Rethinking Tourism and Ecotravel* (Kumarlan Press) and *Responsible Tourism* (Transitions Abroad), and has contributed to numerous other books, magazines, newsletters, and online media. She also occasionally teaches alternative travel writing at The Loft and at regional folk schools. Her favorite place is her back yard in Saint Paul on a summer evening, watching the stars and hanging out with family and friends by a fire.

LINDA BACK McKAY is a poet, writer, and teaching artist. She is the author of several books, including a book of poetry, *The Next Best Thing* (Nodin Press, 2011) and the nonfiction *Out of the Shadows: Stories of Adoption and Reunion* (North Star Press, 2012). She lives with the intrepid David McKay and their red-hot motorcycle just across the river from Saint Paul, and she hastens to add, they were both born and raised in Saint Paul.

ETHNA McKIERNAN is the author of three books of poems, the most recent of which is *Sky Thick with Fireflies* (Salmon Poetry, Ireland). Widely anthologized in collections as diverse as *The Notre Dame Anthology of Irish American Poetry*, *33 Minnesota Poets*, and *Beloved on This Earth*, she has twice been awarded a Minnesota State Arts Board Fellowship. She is employed by a Minneapolis nonprofit, working with the long-term homeless population.

MARIANNE McNAMARA lives in Saint Paul, where she weaves together life as a writer of poetry, a food blogger and chef de cuisine, a shutterbug, and grandmother to the amazing Nora. She began writing after she burned out as a school volunteer. Her poetry has appeared in a variety of anthologies, on sidewalks, and in a magazine.

FRANKLIN DELANO "DEL" MEATH was born in Saint Paul in 1933. After working 15 years at Lake Owasso Residence, he retired as a Ramsey County employee to work as a personal care attendant to a friend with a brain injury. Del is married and has one son and two grandchildren.

NICHOLAS "NICK" METCALF—Cetanzi (Yellow Hawk)—writes about his journey, which may be a cautionary tale or a tale of triumph. Stay tuned. He also likes to write about the complicated lives of the people and communities he loves. An enrolled member of the Rosebud Sioux Tribe, he has made the Twin Cities his home for more than eighteen years. He still believes in love and is a hopeless romantic. During the day, he is a cog in the wheel of state bureaucracy, and at night, a fantastic ever-loving parent of a teenage son, Hoksicila Cante Ma Yuha (Child of My Heart).

YUSEF MGENI is retired after having served more than forty years in leadership positions with community-based organizations serving low-income persons and communities of color as an administrator, community organizer, college instructor, policy analyst, planner, award-winning journalist, and foundation senior program officer. Mr. Mgeni has also contributed many years of service as a member of the board of directors of many local and national civic and professional organizations, as a mentor for at-risk youth, and as an external sponsor for prisoners' organizations in men's and women's correctional facilities in Minnesota. He has a forthcoming book, *The Wonder of Blackness*.

JOHN MOE is the host of *Wits*, a national public radio show based in Saint Paul. Noted for skimming "the cream off a few decades of local and national indie scenes," the show features writers, comedians, and musicians. John has brought such guests as Fred Willard, Rosanne Cash, Martha Wainwright, and Julia Sweeney to the historic Fitzgerald Theater. A widely published author as well as a reporter, he lives in Saint Paul with his family.

BOB MUSCHEWSKE is a retired management consultant who lives with his wife of four years, Leaetta Hough, in a Clarence Johnston home on Summit Avenue in Saint Paul. Both are avid photographers. Bob serves on the boards of Public Art Saint Paul and the Ramsey County Historical Society. www.370summitstpaul.com

ANNA MUSIELEWICZ is thirteen years old. She wrote this poem when she was a fifth grader at L'Etoile du Nord French Immersion School. Anna loves many kinds of art, but her favorites are drawing and playing the piano.

LISA NILLES lives in Minneapolis and works in Saint Paul. She loves to discover new places close to home.

CARTER NORMAN is a high school teacher and has been a resident of the Saint Paul area for more than twenty years. He and his wife have five energetic boys. Carter writes about Minnesota's Iron Range, where he grew up. He believes that nature has a song that can resonate through each of us in a unique, profound, and indelible way.

JAMES NUTT is an architect and artist living and drawing in Northeast Minneapolis. He is wrapping up a year-long mission to draw something every day and is never without his custom travel kit. An architect at NewStudio Architecture, he also teaches at the White Bear Center for the Arts and blogs art process and travel sketches at www.nuttdraws.blogspot.com. James has a strong belief that you should draw to remember, to record, to have fun, to get better, anything but to try making a worthy piece of art. So many people are intimidated and stopped before they start because it might not be beautiful enough.

SUSAN OLSSON, a transplant from New York, has been a special education teacher for twenty-five years. She entered college with a "talented student admissions scholarship" for her poetry, then spent thirty-seven years with writer's block. Literally and emotionally "stopped in her tracks" by sidewalk poetry, Susan decided to give it a go.

SHERONDA ORRIDGE is a longtime resident of Frogtown. She holds a doctoral degree in Holistic Life Coaching from the University of Sedona and is the owner-operator of Loving Spirit Life Coach Academy LLC. Sheronda is a mother, a community organizer, and a spoken word artist.

EMMANUEL ORTIZ is a Minneapolis-based poet and community organizer. He has published two chapbooks of poetry, *The Word Is a Machete*, and *Brown unLike Me.* He is a founding member of the Minnesota-based Latino poets' collective Palabristas: Latin@ Word Slingers.

ORA LEE O'NEAL PATTERSON has shared an active, dedicated life honored with roles such as mother, wife, aide to a mayor, chair of the human rights commission, active member of Pilgrim Baptist Church, community activist, political activist, and recipient of numerous awards. She is a respected and loved member of the community.

JENNIFER PENNINGTON works as a nonprofit consultant and sits on a number of boards including Art Shanty Projects, Sociologists of Minnesota, and Twin Cities Mobile Market. She is a cofounder of Blue Ox, an artist-designed mini golf course opening soon in Saint Paul's West Seventh neighborhood.

KAYE THOMPSON PETERS is a former print journalist who has called Saint Paul home since 1989. She is currently on leave from the Saint Paul Public Schools and taught at Central High School from 1998 until her leave this year. She is now teaching at the American Embassy School in New Delhi, India.

LISA ANN PIERCE has lived on the West Side for eighteen years. Yes, the West Side. No, not West Saint Paul. Actually, we're north of West Saint Paul and south of downtown. We're closer to the East Side than to Minneapolis. But we are west of the river. Really.

J. OTIS POWELL‽ (with interrobang) writes, "I am alternatively using punctuations in my name that express my personal journey toward wholeness while using them less in my poetry. I work as a writer, performance artist, mentor, curator, consultant, philosopher, Open Space Technology facilitator, public speaker, and arts administrator."

MARCIE RENDON, White Earth Anishinabe, is a mother, grandmother, author, playwright, poet, and sometimes performance artist. In 2010 she wrote *Native Artists: Livelihoods, Resources, Space, Gifts* with professor Ann Markusen. Her poetry has been published in numerous anthologies including: *Sing*, edited by Allison Adelle Hedge Coke, and *Traces in Blood, Bone and Stone*, edited by Kimberly Blaeser. She performed a True Ghost Story for Spirit in the House Festival in 2011, and as creator/producer of Raving Native Productions she curates community theater productions and conducts theater residencies for tribal communities.

PAIGE RIEHL's poetry has been featured in many publications, including *Meridian, South Dakota Review,* and *Nimrod,* and she won the 2012–13 Loft Mentor Series in Poetry. She loves her Victorian house in Saint Anthony Park, where she lives with her husband, son, and twenty-one-year-old cat.

STEVE ROBBINS is an illustrator and designer from Saint Paul. When he's not drawing, he's designing card games and writing an incredibly complicated internet-based "Choose Your Own Adventure." SteveRobbinsArt.com

SHELLEY ROHLF: Shelley Rohlf believes our hearts, and possibly our souls, speak to each other through the art we make. Along with painting and drawing, she loves living in Lowertown with her family and friends and exploring the Mississippi River on her bike. Find her on www.MNartists.org.

SHERRY ROBERTS, a journalist turned novelist, is the author of *Book of Mercy* and *Maud's House*. She has written essays for *USA Today* and other publications; you'll find more essays on her blog: www.sherry-roberts.com.

MARY KAY RUMMEL grew up and lived in Saint Paul for many years. She is retired from the University of Minnesota—Duluth and lives in Fridley. She teaches part time at California State University—Channel Islands. Her sixth poetry book, *What's Left Is the Singing*, was published in 2010 by Blue Light Press.

JULIA KLATT SINGER is the poet in residence at Grace Neighborhood Nursery School, and works as a visiting writer to the school through COMPAS. She is co-author of *Twelve Branches: Stories from Saint Paul* (Coffee House Press, 2003) and author of a chapbook, *In the Dreamed of Places* (Naissance Press, 2011), and a book of poetry, *A Tangled Path to Heaven* (Northstar Press, 2013). She has co-written five songs with composer Tim Tekach. When not writing, she can be found walking the dog.

CYNTHIA SCHREINER SMITH is co-owner of CyBick Creative, a video production company she owns with her husband, Bick Smith. She is most proud of their historical film *Gangsterland*, a documentary-style movie about the 1930s gangsters in Saint Paul. She has also worked at the Wabasha Street Caves since 1998, where her work as an historical tour guide complements her love of writing, history, and—of course—Saint Paul.

KAYA SOLHEID is eight years old and enjoys playing with Legos and her friend Lyra. She knows Japanese, like her mom. Her favorite color is blue and she loves to read.

TIM SPITZACK is publisher and editor of the St. Paul Publishing Company, publisher of the *St. Paul Voice, Downtown St. Paul Voice, South St. Paul Voice*, and *La Voz Latina*. He has a B.S. in journalism and sociology from the University of Wisconsin—River Falls. He is also author of *The Messenger*, released in June 2010 by OakTara.

RONALD CRAIG SPONG was born and spent his early formative years in Saint Paul before his family moved to Rochester. Visits to his mother's family in West Saint Paul kept him anchored in his hometown until college, the military, and his Waukegan, Illinois, bride lured him away from Minnesota. Returning home, they raised four children, and he worked forty years in local city and county public health agencies. Retired now with eight grandchildren, he is writing about his experiences.

MARCY STEINBERG's classmate at a school reunion once exclaimed, "You're the poet!" and recited "Haircut," which she'd remembered since fourth grade—thirty-four years ago. Marcy told this story to Saint Paul Poet Laureate Carol Connolly, who encouraged her to submit the poem to the Sidewalk Poetry contest. Marcy plans to thank that woman from elementary school for her precious gift, and she thanks Carol Connolly for her encouragement.

LISA STEINMANN is a Saint Paul–based freelance writer, editor, and laundress who specializes in sorting, soaking, and scrubbing before hanging things on the line. She loves sunny mornings spent standing in the yard watching clothing flutter in the breeze. Each sock, tee shirt, and pair of blue jeans tells a story shaped by the wearer. At the end of the afternoon, it is a pleasure to gather and fold each piece, starchy-stiff and fragrant, into her arms.

JOYCE SUTPHEN's first book, *Straight Out of View* (1995), won the Barnard New Women's Poets Prize. *Coming Back to the Body* (2000) was a finalist for a Minnesota Book Award, and *Naming the Stars* (2004) won the Minnesota Book Award in Poetry. Her poems have appeared in *Poetry*, *American Poetry Review*, *Minnesota Monthly*, *Water-Stone*, and many other journals, as well as being featured on the Writer's Almanac. In 2011 she was named the second Minnesota Poet Laureate by Governor Mark Dayton, following the tenure of Robert Bly. She grew up in St. Joseph, Minnesota, and teaches at Gustavus Adolphus in St. Peter.

BARBARA LANGER THUKRAL lives in Highland Park with her husband and their three boys. She is fiercely loyal to Gillette Children's Hospital, as well as school volunteerism. She seeks the elusive idea of sanity through her writing, running, and yoga, as well as coffee breaks with girlfriends, and wine with her sisters.

JESUS VEGA writes, "I was born and raised in Guanajuato, Mexico, and came to the United States at age five. I currently attend Gordon Parks High School and am finishing my credits from Johnson High School, so I can move on to college. I work a full time job after school to help my parents with the bills and for my own needs. I love playing sports and being outside in the summer—I'm still getting used to the crazy Minnesota winters. I love spending time with my fourteen-year-old sister and seven-year-old brother, taking them sledding, shopping, to the zoo, and Valleyfair."

CONNIE WANEK is the author of three books: *On Speaking Terms* (Copper Canyon Press, 2010), *Hartley Field* (Holy Cow! Press, 2002), and *Bonfire* (New Rivers Press, 1997). She has been chosen as a Witter Bynner Fellow of the Library of Congress by United States Poet Laureate Ted Kooser. She lives in the country outside Duluth, Minnesota, but often finds herself in a green tent somewhere in the Boundary Waters wilderness.

SARAH MARIE WASH is a mixed media artist based in Lowertown. She upcycles found objects, including furniture, to create 3-D original art pieces. Sarah also makes 2-D art using watercolor, acrylic, and oil paints. www.ErdeEcoArt.com

GREG WATSON's poetry has appeared in numerous literary journals, including *The Seattle Review*, *Poetry East*, and *Tulane Review*, and has been featured on Garrison Keillor's *Writer's Almanac*. His latest collection is *What Music Remains*, published by Nodin Press. He lives in the Mac-Groveland area of Saint Paul.

DAVID R. WEISS is the author of *To the Tune of a Welcoming God: Lyrical Reflections on Sexuality, Spirituality and the Wideness of God's Welcome* (www.davidrweiss.com). He and Margaret have a blended family of five children, five grandchildren, (usually) a pair of international high school students, and assorted animals that approximate a peaceable kingdom.

MARY VIRGINIA WINSTEAD is a Twin Cities—based writer, author of *Back to Mississippi: A Personal Journey Through the Events that Changed America in 1964* (Hyperion). She has an MFA in creative writing from the University of Minnesota and a BA in English from St. Catherine University.

LISA YANKTON, a member of the Spirit Lake Dakota, is a community organizer, educator, writer, and mother. She views the arts and creativity as stepping stones to a healthy life. Her community activities include teaching at MCTC, coordinating the Dakota Nationwide Conference, leading the Brooklyn Historical Society, and serving on *The Circle* Newspaper Ambassadors Council. During the Dakota Conflict of 1862, her grandmother fled from Minnesota to North Dakota.

JONATHAN SIAB YAWG was born in Fresno, California; he is second-generation Hmoob-American, a college student, and has lived sixteen-plus years in Saint Paul and twenty-one years total on this earth. He has been obsessed with poetry/rap, music, and other artistic expressions since the second grade, and has been living it out slowly since. It wasn't until three years ago that he fell in love with spoken word. When he writes, he tries to write from the realities that he has seen, felt, and lived. His work is not just for the Hmoob people; it is for all oppressed peoples so that we may be able to imagine and live out the meaning of true "freedom."

PATRICIA ANITA YOUNG was born in Saint Paul and now resides in Minneapolis. She is an accounting technician who enjoys writing freelance articles.

Community Editor Biographies

YUNISA ABDI loves chipotle so much that she'll love you if you buy it for her. It's just that easy. She's a book fanatic, especially when it comes to romance. She's a hopeless romantic, and she loves her family and friends.

YONIS ALI says, "This is the first time I have been a community editor. I have always enjoyed reading articles on different subjects. I became familiar with different styles of writing community stories while I was a community editor with the *Saint Paul Almanac*. I also like reading biographies and world histories. I am currently taking land surveying courses at the Saint Paul College, and I expect to graduate in the spring of 2014."

NINA HERNANDEZ BEITHON is a Chicana sister, daughter, housemate, artist, dreamer, and womyn.

NORITA DITTBERNER-JAX was born in Frogtown and has lived in Saint Paul all of her life. She thinks the city is beautiful, with its hills and flatlands congregating around the Mississippi River. Her widely published poetry collections include *The Watch, Longing for Home,* and *What They Always Were.*

SHAUNTÉ "DR3AMCH8SR" DOUGLAS is a new spoken word artist and writer who lives in Saint Paul, and works at the Mall of America and Barnes and Noble Booksellers. She is an admitted art addict and certified shopaholic who hopes to do more work with the Saint Paul Almanac.

ELIZABETH ELLIS worked for both the county government and the federal government, raised three children, and graduated college.

PAMELA R. FLETCHER serves as a writer, an editor, and an educator—all three roles, having words at their core, collaborate to make meaning of an astounding, outrageous world. She's tried to leave words, but they wouldn't give her a divorce. Although it's a contrary relationship, they make it work.

SHAQUAN FOSTER: Community editor. Board member. Assistant editor. Writer. Designer. College student. Bookseller.

Yunisa Abdi

Yonis Ali

Nina Hernandez Beithon

Norita Dittberner-Jax

Shaunté
"Dr3amCh8sr"
Douglas

Elizabeth Ellis

Pamela R.
Fletcher

Shaquan Foster

KEVIN HERSHEY is a product of the intricate Catholic school system in Saint Paul. He writes as an activist trying to better understand the world he wishes to change.

FARHA IBRAHIM writes, "I am a high school senior. I love writing and art that connect to me to the point that I'll always remember it. Life is a beautiful thing, and I love people who acknowledge that fact in writing, art, music, or any other artistic form."

KEMET EGYPT IMHOTEP was conceived in Oklahoma and born in Saint Paul. Kemet was left under the care of his great uncle and aunt through marriage. His aunt, Willia Mae Johnson, who was born on a plantation in Arkansas in 1918, was a strong believer in faith and trust in the Creator. Kemet says the school system failed him. He was in the class of 1990 at Central High School, and finished at the Area Learning Center located in the Uni-Dale mall. At present he says he is a lost troubled soul, still finding his way through the quicksand.

RICHARD MERLIN JOHNSON JR. was born on May 20, 1972, on the Yankton Sioux Nation. His father, Richard Sr., and mother, Suzanne, met in Los Angeles, California, during the '60s. Richard Sr. was the then-director of the L. A. Indian Center and was the organizer for the Alcatraz Occupation. Richard Jr.'s life is greatly influenced by his parents' activism. He is Santee Sioux Dakota, Californian Chumash, and Chicano. Richard is an Artist, Poet, Writer, Painter, and Actor.

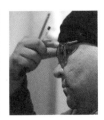

Kevin Hershey

Farha Ibrahim

Kemet Egypt
Imhotep

Richard Merlin
Johnson Jr.

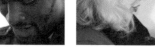

IBé Kaba   Patricia Kirkpatrick   Abe Levine   Gozong Lor

IBé KABA likes to write. Since he doesn't have the time or desire to follow rules, he writes free verse. He likes the word *free*, as in free to bend the rules of language any which way he wants. IBé likes to read poems out loud, especially to his children. But they don't seem to like it, at least not as much as strangers do. And speaking of strangers, they call him a spoken word poet. IBé likes this—having people listen to him read his poems. But he also wants you to read his poetry . . . for yourself. IBé likes that you like him; however, if you visited AtlanticRock.com and spent more than fifteen minutes, he'd consider you a stalker, and probably would not want you to have his phone number.

PATRICIA KIRKPATRICK received the first Lindquist & Vennum Poetry Prize for her book *Odessa*, published by Milkweed Editions, and awarded the 2013 Minnesota Book Award in Poetry. She has taught writing in many academic and community settings.

ABE (pronounced "uhhhh-beee") **LEVINE** was told when he was a kid that he had special genes, being of Chinese and Jewish heritage. Really he felt kind of ordinary and out of place at the same time, like many kids. Abe is now a grown-up and still finding his groove and place. Abe enjoys talking, writing, eating, dancing, rapping, bopping, teaching, and editing. You may say that he is a renaissance man, but he might say, "What?"

GOZONG LOR graduated from Central Senior High School and will be attending Macalester College in the fall of 2013. She is a student by day and masked crime-fighter by night. Her greatest weakness is a good book.

JAMILA MAME was born in Ethiopia. She loves to write poems and watch documentaries. In the future she would like to enroll at Princeton University and major in neurology.

Jamila Mame   Hafsa Mohamud   Kathryn Pulley   Simone Schneider

HAFSA MOHAMUD is someone who is always looking for meaning, whether it be the meaning of a literary piece, a picture, or life in general. She is a junior in high school and plans to be a part of next year's Almanac.

KATHRYN PULLEY has been a teacher for almost ten years and recently received her MA in English. If her life were a poem, it would be an epic: a sweeping narrative of heroic mental battles and fascinating characters, with a driving, thriving rhythm. She would be ready to write the next stanza.

SIMONE SCHNEIDER grew up in Saint Paul, aka "Saint Small." Though she loves to travel, she's always happy to return to her sweet city. Currently pursuing a master's degree in education at St. Kate's, Simone is passionate about reading, writing, learning, and teaching. As a teacher she looks forward to helping her students appreciate the joys that words can bring to their lives.

LISA STEINMANN is a Saint Paul—based freelance writer, editor, and laundress who specializes in sorting, soaking, and scrubbing before hanging things on the line. She loves sunny mornings spent standing in the yard watching clothing flutter in the breeze. Each sock, tee shirt, and pair of blue jeans tells a story shaped by the wearer. At the end of the afternoon, it is a pleasure to gather and fold each piece, starchy-stiff and fragrant, into her arms.

PARTHENIA SWYNINGAN is a candidate for a master's degree in gerontology at Bethel University in Saint Paul. Through her lengthy career in the "helping profession," she enhances, illuminates, and empowers the elderly.

Lisa Steinmann

MURIEL TATE is a mother who is always giving love mixed with counsel.

KA ZOUA VANG is a senior at Johnson High School and a community editor for the *2014 Saint Paul Almanac*. During her free time, she enjoys writing fictional pieces and poems and drawing anime cartoons.

Parthenia Swyningan

Muriel Tate

DIEGO VÁZQUEZ JR. is proud that his lineage is from people who were not afraid to cross invisible lines. They are commonly known as illegals. Yet Vázquez has never met an illegal human. This is Diego's last year serving as a community editor.

Ka Zoua Vang

Diego Vázquez Jr.

Looking for Writers

Want to see your story published in the *Saint Paul Almanac*?

The *Saint Paul Almanac* publishes authentic writing about Saint Paul. We want to read your work, whether you're an established writer or just beginning to write, and to consider it for publication.

Please send us your stories, poems, or spoken-word pieces of 650 words or less. We're happy to look at other forms, too, including song lyrics, graphic fiction, interviews, oral history, editorials, and essays.

All entries are reviewed by community editors in a blind judging process.

You may live anywhere in the world and send in your writing about Saint Paul.

WHERE AND WHEN TO SEND YOUR WRITING

December 15, 2013, is the submission deadline for the *2015 Saint Paul Almanac*. You can email your writing to stories@saintpaulalmanac.org at any time.

WRITERS' GUIDELINES

We receive hundreds of submissions every year, and we read each one carefully. Please consider the following guidelines to help you understand what the *Almanac* publishes and to give yourself the best chance to have your work accepted for publication.

MAKE IT PERSONAL

The *Almanac* is looking for expressive writing in a personal voice and from a particular point of view. Newspapers and television can give the facts. We publish writing that goes beyond the facts of what happened to why it matters. If you're describing your grandmother's house; the park where you played hockey, soccer, or basketball; or a favorite spot at the Mississippi River, show us how this person or place influenced you, your family, and/or your community. Telling a story about starting a new job, being treated unfairly, or getting stranded during a storm? Tell us what happened first, then next, then after that. Show us where it happened, who was there, what was said.

We're especially interested in writing that has a strong sense of place, whether it's your Saint Paul neighborhood, a favorite café, or Landmark Center. We also want to publish "absent narratives" and stories that may not have been told or published in other places.

BE SPECIFIC

Help readers see, hear, touch, taste, and smell the experiences you're writing about. Include particular details: name the foods at a holiday celebration; describe the tools or sound of machines; remember the color of uniforms or the kinds of birds and trees. Surprise readers or make them laugh! Write enough but not too much.

DON'T ADVERTISE

The *Almanac* is published by a nonprofit organization. We don't take advertisements, and we don't publish them in the guise of stories.

STAY WITHIN WORD COUNTS

One of the *Almanac*'s goals each year is to publish the broadest and deepest range of writing. For this reason, we limit the length of pieces, and we may further limit accepted pieces through careful copyediting. Most of our selections are between 300 and 650 words. If you want to submit a longer piece, please contact the editor by email first and describe the piece you want to submit. We will let you know if you should send the longer piece.

NEED IDEAS?

Try answering one of the following: Is Saint Paul a good place to be a teenager, learn a new language, go to college, start a business, or live without a car?

Or write a portrait of a "lost world." This lost world could be another language, school, family, or profession. It could be a place where you once lived that no longer exists or a time and place you've heard others talk about but never experienced yourself.

EDITING

Editing is standard practice in the publishing world: very little writing anywhere reaches publication without some editing. We may need to tighten or shorten what you've sent us; we may ask you to rewrite or add to it.

Community Editor
Apprenticeship Project

WANT TO BECOME A *SAINT PAUL ALMANAC* COMMUNITY EDITOR?
The next community editor project will begin in November 2013.

Community editor requirements: a love for writing and reading. Potential community editors must submit a short application including a brief essay on why they want to be an editor. Each community editor must commit to reading at least 200 selections. Small stipends are paid to community editors for their hard work. Persons age 15 or older are welcome to participate. Contact executive director Kimberly Nightingale at kimberly@stpaulalmanac.org for more information.

During the course of 20 weeks and 14 three-hour meetings, between November 2013 and February 2014, community editors/apprentice editors will:

- Learn how to gather poems and stories in their communities
- Help people they gather stories from send in their best work
- Determine collectively what goes into the *Saint Paul Almanac*, based on criteria of quality and inclusiveness
- Learn copyediting marks, tools, and resources
- Learn steps in publishing a book
- Improve their own writing and editing through workshop sessions with professional writers
- Build confidence and trust in their abilities through participating in the community editor process
- Develop relationships with professional writers that may not have occurred in other contexts

© Nigel Parry/nigelparry.net

Saint Paul Almanac
Subscription Form

SUBSCRIBE!
Three annual issues for $40
(price includes tax, shipping, and handling)

To order go to
www.saintpaulalmanac.org
Or mail to
Subscriptions
Saint Paul Almanac
275 East Fourth St., Suite 701
Saint Paul, MN 55101

If mailing, please fill out and send the info below.

- -

Begin with *2014 Saint Paul Almanac*
☐ **Check or money order enclosed**
Charge: ☐ **Visa** ☐ **MasterCard**

_____

CARD NUMBER

_____

EXPIRATION DATE

_____

SIGNATURE OF CARDHOLDER

_____

MAILING ADDRESS

_____

EMAIL

For gift orders

_____

SHIP TO NAME

_____

MAILING ADDRESS

Notes

Instead of watching TV, make TV!

If you have the **desire to produce television** to express yourself, to get your point across, to help your neighbors, or to change your community for the better, we can help!

375 Jackson St., Ste 170
Saint Paul, MN 55101

(651) 298-8908
www.spnn.org